1986 SUPPLEMENT TO

REAL ESTATE TRANSFER, FINANCE AND DEVELOPMENT

CASES AND MATERIALS

SECOND EDITION

By

Grant S. Nelson
*Enoch H. Crowder Professor of Law,
University of Missouri-Columbia*

Dale A. Whitman
*Dean and R. B. Price Professor of Law,
University of Missouri-Columbia*

AMERICAN CASEBOOK SERIES

WEST PUBLISHING CO.
ST. PAUL, MINN., 1986

COPYRIGHT © 1983 By WEST PUBLISHING CO.
COPYRIGHT © 1986 By WEST PUBLISHING CO.
50 West Kellogg Boulevard
P.O. Box 64526
St. Paul, Minnesota 55164-0526

All rights reserved
Printed in the United States of America

ISBN 0-314-96994-2

N. & W.Cs. Real Est.Fin. & Dev.2d Ed. ACB
1986 Supp.

1st Reprint—1987

Preface

The field of real estate finance and development continues to change rapidly. We've prepared this supplement to help teachers and students keep up with events that have occurred since the 1983 Supplement was published. Although we have not attempted to be exhaustive, we believe we have covered the important developments.

Users of the supplement will find three areas of particular emphasis. One is the expansion of installment land contract coverage, a mortgage substitute that is increasingly being used. The second is the treatment of due-on-sale clauses, which is now the subject of a preemptive federal statute and further federal agency regulations, although, in several jurisdictions, state law continues to be relevant. The other is bankruptcy, which continues to expand in importance to mortgage finance as the courts interpret the 1978 Bankruptcy Act. Those who work in the field today surely cannot afford to ignore the effects of bankruptcy law, if they ever could.

We have included several citations to and excerpts from the second edition of our hornbook, *Real Estate Finance Law*, which was published in late 1985.

We hope this supplement will help you in your study, and we will appreciate any suggestions and feedback which you may offer.

GRANT S. NELSON
DALE A. WHITMAN

December, 1985

Summary of Contents

	Page
PREFACE	iii
TABLE OF CASES	xi

PART I. REAL ESTATE TRANSFER

Chapter
1. Contracts for the Sale of Land 2

PART II. REAL ESTATE FINANCE

3. The Use of Mortgage Substitutes 16
4. Rights and Duties of the Parties Prior to Foreclosure: Some Problem Areas 51
5. Transfer and Discharge 66
6. Foreclosure 109
7. Some Priority Problems 188
8. Government Intervention and Private Risk-Spreading in the Mortgage Market 189

PART III. REAL ESTATE DEVELOPMENT

10. Planned Unit Developments, Condominiums and Cooperatives 200

Table of Contents

	Page
PREFACE	iii
TABLE OF CASES	xi

PART I. REAL ESTATE TRANSFER

CHAPTER 1. CONTRACTS FOR THE SALE OF LAND

Casebook Page			Supplement Page
	B.	The Statute of Frauds and Past Performance	2
28		Additional Note Material	2
	C.	Remedies and Real Estate Contracts	3
44		*Donovan v. Bachstadt*	3
		Additional Notes	9
	H.	Conditions in Contracts	10
110		Additional Note	10
		Schrader v. Benton	11

PART II. REAL ESTATE FINANCE

CHAPTER 3. THE USE OF MORTGAGE SUBSTITUTES

	A.	The Absolute Deed, The Conditional Sale, and Related Transactions	16
249		*McGill v. Biggs*	16
256		Additional Note Material	20
	B.	The Installment Land Contract	20
258		*Braunstein v. Trottier*	20
273		Additional Note Material	28
276		Additional Note Material	29
277		Additional Text	29
		Nelson and Whitman, Real Estate Finance Law	29
282		Additional Note Material	33
286		Additional Note Material	33
292–293		*Shindledecker v. Savage*	33
		Additional Notes	36
294		Additional Note	37
		Estate of Brewer v. Iota Delta Chapter, Tau Kappa Epsilon Fraternity, Inc.	39
		Estate of Brewer v. Iota Delta Chapter, Tau Kappa Epsilon Fraternity, Inc.	45
		Additional Note	49
301		Additional Note Material	49

viii   TABLE OF CONTENTS

CHAPTER 4. RIGHTS AND DUTIES OF THE PARTIES PRIOR TO FORECLOSURE: SOME PROBLEM AREAS

Casebook Page			Supplement Page
	A.	Theories of Title: Possession, Rents, and Related Considerations	51
318		*Taylor v. Brennan*	51
	B.	Receiverships	54
331		*Chase Manhattan Bank, N.A. v. Turabo Shopping Center, Inc.*	54
340		Additional Note	57
	C.	Insurance and Real Estate Taxes	57
341		*Starkman v. Sigmond*	57
346		Substitute Note	65

CHAPTER 5. TRANSFER AND DISCHARGE

	B.	Restrictions on Transfer by the Mortgagor	66
383		Nelson and Whitman, Real Estate Finance Law	66
		Section 341, Garn-St. Germain Depository Institutions Act of 1982	74
		Nelson and Whitman, Real Estate Finance Law	78
	C.	Transfer of the Mortgagee's Interest	90
408		*Hammelburger v. Foursome Inn Corp.*	90
423		*Rodgers v. Seattle-First National Bank*	98
427		Additional Note Material	102
	D.	Discharge of the Debt and Mortgage: By Payment or Otherwise	103
446		*George H. Nutman, Inc. v. Aetna Business Credit, Inc.*	103
448		Additional Note	104
460		*Thompson v. Glidden*	105
		Additional Note	108

CHAPTER 6. FORECLOSURE

	A.	The Foreclosure Amount: Problems of Acceleration	109
478		Additional Note Material	109
481		Additional Notes	109
	C.	Judicial Foreclosure	110

TABLE OF CONTENTS

Casebook Page				Supplement Page
		2.	The Omitted Party Problem	110
509			*Land Associates, Inc. v. Becker*	110
	D.		Power of Sale Foreclosure	113
		2.	Defects in the Exercise of the Power	113
522			*Cox v. Helenius*	113
		3.	Constitutional Problems With the Power of Sale	117
536			*Mennonite Board of Missions v. Adams*	117
			Additional Notes	127
538			*United States v. Ford*	128
			Additional Note	130
			Johnson v. United States Department of Agriculture	130
			Additional Notes	138
561			Additional Note	142
	E.		Disbursement of Foreclosure Sale Proceeds	142
564			Additional Notes	142
	F.		Statutory Redemption	142
575			Additional Note	142
	G.		Other Statutory Impacts on Foreclosure	143
		1.	Anti-deficiency Legislation and Related Problems	143
604			Additional Notes	143
		3.	Bankruptcy	144
612			Nelson and Whitman, Real Estate Finance Law	144
			In re Palmer River Realty, Inc.	150
623			Nelson and Whitman, Real Estate Finance Law	154
			In re Taddeo	156
			In re Glenn	161
			Additional Note	169
			Nelson and Whitman, Real Estate Finance Law	169
			In re Wheeler	177
			Additional Notes	179
			Matter of Village Properties	180
			Additional Note	187

CHAPTER 7. SOME PRIORITY PROBLEMS

	D.	Fixtures	188
660		Additional Note Material	188

CHAPTER 8. GOVERNMENT INTERVENTION AND PRIVATE RISK–SPREADING IN THE MORTGAGE MARKET

	E.	Spreading Mortgage Risk—Insurers and Guarantors	189
709		Additional Text	189
715		Additional Note Material	189
	G.	Alternative Mortgage Instruments	190

Casebook Page		Supplement Page
740	Replacement Text	190
744	Additional Note Material	192
746	Additional Text	192
748	Additional Note Material	193
748	Additional Text	193

PART III. REAL ESTATE DEVELOPMENT

CHAPTER 10. PLANNED UNIT DEVELOPMENTS, CONDOMINIUMS, AND COOPERATIVES

	B. Condominiums	200
914	Additional Note Material	200
	Hobson v. Hilltop Place Community Association	200
946	*Dutcher v. Owens*	204
	F. Managing the Project	208
951	*In re Bentley*	208

Table of Cases

The principal cases are in italic type. Cases cited or discussed are in roman type. Reference are to pages.

Allison v. Block, 143
American Federal Savings & Loan Association v. Mid-America Service Corp., 104

Bentley, In re, 208
Booth, In re, 33
Braunstein v. Trottier, 20
Brewer, Estate of v. Iota Delta Chapter, Tau Kappa Epsilon Fraternity, Inc., 39, 45, 49

Carolina Builders Corp. v. Howard-Veasey Homes, Inc., 2
Century Federal Savings and Loan Association, United States v., 142
Chase Manhattan Bank, N.A. v. Turabo Shopping Center, Inc., 54
Coleman v. Block, 143
Cox v. Helenius, 113
Curry v. Block, 143

Donovan v. Bachstadt, 3
Durrett v. Washington Nat'l Ins. Co., 142, 143, 180
Dutcher v. Owens, 204

English v. Fischer, 65
Estate of (see name of party)

Federal Deposit Insurance Corporation v. Morrison, 138, 139
Fincher v. Miles Homes of Mo., Inc., 49
First National Bank of Boston v. Larson, 102
Ford, United States v., 128
Fountain, Matter of, 179

Gamradt v. Block, 143
Giberson v. First Federal Savings and Loan Association of Waterloo, 65
Glenn, In re, 161
Graff v. Hope Bldg. Corp., 109
Gray v. Bowers, 33

Hammelburger v. Foursome Inn Corp., 90
Hamrick, United States v., 143
Hobson v. Hilltop Place Community Association, 200
Hutton v. Gliksberg, 10

In re (see name of party)

Jacoby v. Schuman, 143
Johnson v. United States Department of Agriculture, 130, 139

Karas v. Wasserman, 109
Keesee v. Fetzek, 33
Kendrick v. Davis, 49
Kosloff v. Castle, 28

Land Associates, Inc. v. Becker, 110
Landmark Land Co. v. Sprague, 102
Leonard v. Pell, 142

McGill v. Biggs, 16
Marvin v. Stemen, 33
Matter of (see name of party)
Matzke v. Block, 143
Mennonite Board of Missions v. Adams, 117, 127, 128, 138

Nutman, Inc., George H. v. Aetna Business Credit, Inc., 103

Palmer River Realty Inc., In re, 150
Peoples Bank v. McDonald, 102

Regan v. Lanze, 10
Ricker v. United States, 141
Roberts v. Morin, 37
Rodgers v. Seattle-First National Bank, 98

Schoolcraft v. Ross, 65
Schrader v. Benton, 11
Shick v. Farmers Home Administration of United States Department of Agriculture, 143

Shindledecker v. Savage, 33, 49
Slevin Container Corp. v. Provident Federal Savings & Loan Association, 104
Smith v. Fried, 20
Starkman v. Sigmond, 57, 65

Taddeo, In re, 156, 169
Tan v. California Federal Savings & Loan Association, 104
Taylor v. Brennan, 51
Thompson v. Glidden, 105, 108

United States v. _____ (see opposing party)

Village Properties, Matter of, 180, 187

Waible v. Dosberg, 57
Walker v. Benton, 10
Wheeler, In re, 177, 179

1986 SUPPLEMENT TO
REAL ESTATE TRANSFER, FINANCE AND DEVELOPMENT
CASES AND MATERIALS
SECOND EDITION

Part I

REAL ESTATE TRANSFER

Chapter 1

CONTRACTS FOR THE SALE OF LAND

B. THE STATUTE OF FRAUDS AND PART PERFORMANCE

Page 28, insert at end of Note 1:

Could a deed, delivered in fulfillment of the contract in question, constitute the writing necessary to satisfy the Statute of Frauds? Consider the following language from Carolina Builders Corp. v. Howard-Veasey Homes, Inc., 72 N.C.App. 224, 324 S.E.2d 626 (1985):

> As an executory contract for the sale of land, this agreement is subject to the statute of frauds and shall be void unless some memorandum or note sufficient to satisfy the statute be put in writing and signed by the party to be charged therewith. G.S. 22-2. Defendant here signed a deed conveying lots 50 and 51 to Veasey for valuable consideration on 12 June 1981. The deed is sufficiently definite as to the terms of the contract, the names of the vendor and vendee, and a description of the land to be conveyed to satisfy G.S. 22-2. See Smith v. Joyce, 214 N.C. 602, 604, 200 S.E. 431, 433 (1939). With the deed as a sufficient memorandum signed by defendant, the oral agreement between defendant and Veasey constitutes an enforceable contract within the provisions of G.S. 22-2. Id. As an enforceable contract for the sale of land it is subject to specific performance in equity. See 71 Am.Jur.2d *Specific Performance* Sec. 112 at 143-45 (1973).

Would it matter whether the deed itself had ever been delivered (assuming, of course, that it had been signed by the breaching vendor)?

C. REMEDIES AND REAL ESTATE CONTRACTS

Page 44, to be read following Note 4:

DONOVAN v. BACHSTADT

Supreme Court of New Jersey, 1982.
91 N.J. 434, 453 A.2d 160.

[Defendant Bachstadt contracted to sell real estate to plaintiffs Donovans for $58,900. The Donovans paid $5,890 as earnest money, and the contract provided that Bachstadt would finance $44,000 by way of a purchase money mortgage which, under current usury statutes, could not have borne an interest rate exceeding 10.5%. It developed that Bachstadt did not have and could not obtain good title to the property.]

When defendant could not obtain marketable title, the Donovans commenced this suit for compensatory and punitive damages. As previously observed the trial court granted plaintiffs' motion for summary judgment. It was indisputable that the defendant had breached the agreement. The only issue was damages. The trial court held that plaintiffs were entitled under N.J.S.A. 2A:29–1 to recovery of their costs for the title search and survey. Plaintiffs had apparently in the interim purchased a home in Middlesex County and obtained a mortgage loan bearing interest at the rate of $13\frac{1}{4}\%$ per annum. Plaintiffs sought the difference between $10\frac{1}{2}\%$ and $13\frac{1}{4}\%$ as compensatory damages, representing their loss of the benefit of the bargain. The trial court denied recovery because the contract was for the sale of the property and the financing "was only incidental to the basic concept."

The Appellate Division reversed. 181 N.J.Super. 367, 437 A.2d 728 (1981). It held that N.J.S.A. 2A:29–1 was declarative of the general common law right to recover consequential damages for breach of a contract and that the statute modified the preexisting law, which limited a realty purchaser to recovery of his deposit upon a seller's breach due to a defective title. The court concluded the statute intended that the general law of damages for breach of a contract applies and stated that the difference in interest rates could be the basis for a measure of damages depending on whether the plaintiffs "have entered into a comparable transaction for another home * * * or are likely to do so in the near future * * *." Id. at 376, 437 A.2d 728. The Appellate Division cautioned that any award of future damages should represent the true life of the mortgage and be reduced to present value. Further, the plaintiffs should be held to a duty to mitigate. Lastly, if the proofs should demonstrate that plaintiffs have not purchased and are not likely to purchase a home in the near future, their damages would be remote and speculative. The cause was remanded for a plenary hearing.

I

The initial inquiry is whether plaintiffs are entitled to compensatory damages. We had occasion recently to discuss the measure of damages available when a seller breaches an executory contract for the sale of real property. St. Pius X House of Retreats v. Diocese of Camden, 88 N.J. 571, 582–87, 443 A.2d 1052 (1982). We noted that New Jersey follows the English rule, which generally limits a buyer's recovery to the return of his deposit unless the seller wilfully refuses to convey or is guilty of fraud or deceit. The traditional formulation of the English rule has been expressed by T. Cyprian Williams, an English barrister, as follows:

> Where the breach of contract is occasioned by the vendor's inability, without his own fault, to show a good title, the purchaser is entitled to recover as damages his deposit, if any, with interest, and his expenses incurred in connection with the agreement, but not more than nominal damages for the loss of his bargain. [T.C. Williams, The Contract of Sale of Land 128 (1930)]

In *St. Pius* we found no need to reexamine the English rule, though we raised the question whether the American rule that permits a buyer to obtain benefit of the bargain damages irrespective of the nature of the reasons for the seller's default might not be more desirable.

We also referred in *St. Pius* to N.J.S.A. 2A:29–1, which provides:

> When any person shall contract to sell real estate and shall not be able to perform such contract because of a defect in the title to the real estate, the person with whom such contract was made, or his legal representatives or assigns, may, in a civil action, recover from the vendor, not only the deposit money, with interest and costs, but also the reasonable expenses of examining the title and making a survey of the property, unless the contract shall provide otherwise. This section shall not preclude the recovery by the purchaser from the vendor of any other damages to which he may be entitled.

This statute modified the common law rule to enable a buyer to recover the reasonable expenses of examining the title and making a survey of the property in addition to the deposit, unless the contract provided otherwise. The last sentence in the act as originally enacted in 1915, L.1915, c. 159, had read: "This section shall not limit the recovery where the purchaser seeks to recover for fraud and deceit." R.S. 2:45–1. In the general revision of Title 2 in 1951 the last sentence was modified to read, "This section shall not preclude the recovery by the purchaser from the vendor of any other damage to which he may be entitled by law." In *St. Pius*, we reasoned:

> We can find no legislative history explaining this change. Since the primary thrust of the revision was procedural, it is unlikely that the Legislature intended any modification in the substantive common law. Rather, it is probable that its intent was to permit recovery under Court Rules for fraud and deceit in the same action

in which the return of deposit, interest and title and survey expenses were sought * * *. We therefore conclude that N.J.S.A. 2A:29–1 has no bearing on the availability of the bargain damages. [88 N.J. at 587, 443 A.2d 1052]

Thus the common law governs the measure of damages apart from those guaranteed in the statute. There is nothing in the statute that prevents the Court from adopting the American rule and awarding loss of the benefit of the bargain damages.

We are satisfied that the American rule is preferable. The English principle developed because of the uncertainties of title due to the complexity of the rules governing title to land during the eighteenth and nineteenth centuries. Oakley, "Pecuniary Compensation for Failure to Complete a Contract for the Sale of Land," 39 Cambridge L.J. 58, 69 (1980). At that time the only evidence of title was contained in deeds which were in a phrase attributed to Lord Westbury, "difficult to read, disgusting to touch, and impossible to understand." The reason for the English principle that creates an exception to the law governing damages for breaches of executory contracts for the sale of property is no longer valid, and the exception should be eliminated. *Cessante ratione legis, cessat et ipsa lex* (the reason for a law ceasing, the law itself ceases). See Fox v. Snow, 6 N.J. 12, 14, 22–23, 76 A.2d 877 (1950) (Vanderbilt, C.J., dissenting). Indeed in England the rule has been modified by placing the burden of proof on the vendor to establish that he has done everything within his power to carry out the contract. Malhotra v. Choudhury, [1978] 3 W.L.R. 825; [1979] 1 All E.R. 186 (C.A.).

Whether titles are clear may be ascertained by record searches. See N.J.S.A. 46:21–1; Jones, "The New Jersey Recording Act—A Study of its Policy," 12 Rutgers L.Rev. 328, 329–30 (1957). Moreover, limitation periods may be applicable. See N.J.S.A. 2A:14–30; 13A N.J. Practice (Lieberman, Abstracts and Titles) § 1643 at 140 (3d ed. 1966). Thus, it is standard practice for title examiners to search the back title for 60 years and until a warranty deed is found in the chain of title. Palamarg Realty Co. v. Rehac & Piatkowski, 80 N.J. 446, 460, 404 A.2d 21 (1979). Further the parties may insert appropriate provisions in their agreements protecting them from title defects so that to a very large extent sellers may control the measure of redress.

There is no sound basis why benefit of the bargain damages should not be awarded whether the subject matter of the contract is realty or personalty. Serious losses should not be borne by the vendee of real estate to the benefit of the defaulting vendor. This is particularly so when an instalment purchase contract is involved that extends over a period of years during which the vendee makes substantial payments upon the principal, as well as extensive improvements to the property.

The innocent purchaser should be permitted to recover benefit of the bargain damages irrespective of the good or bad faith of the seller. Contract culpability depends on the breach of the contractual promise.

4 A Corbin, Contracts §§ 943–44, at 806–08 (1951). Where, as here, the seller agreed that title would be marketable, the seller's liability should depend upon his breach of that promise.

Many commentators have advocated the adoption of the American rule. 11 S. Williston, A Treatise on the Law of Contracts § 1399 at 524 (3d ed. 1968); 5 A Corbin on Contracts § 1097 at 523 (1964); D. Dobbs, Handbook on the Law of Remedies § 12.8 at 835–36 (1973); 3 American Law of Property § 11.67 at 168 (1952). English commentators have also sharply criticized the English rule and advocated permitting the buyer to recover damages for loss of profit. Oakley, supra, at 70; Sydenham, "The Anomalous Rules in Bain v. Fothergill," 41 The Conveyancer and Property Lawyer 341 (1977). Many states now follow the American rule. 5 A Corbin, supra, § 1098 at 525–35; 11 S. Williston, supra, at 524–28.

The English rule is consistent with the limitation on recovery in suits on a covenant for breach of warranty. The damages for a buyer, who has taken title and is ousted because the title is defective, are limited to the consideration paid and interest thereon. Gerbert v. Trustees, 59 N.J.L. 160, 180, 35 A. 1121 (E. & A. 1896). There appears to be no real difference between that situation and one where the vendor who does not have good title refuses to convey. In both cases the buyer loses the property because of a defect in the title. The fact that one sues for breach of a warranty covenant does not justify depriving a buyer of compensatory damages to which he is justly entitled when the seller breaches the contract of sale. Professor Corbin has suggested that any inconsistency in this respect should be resolved by awarding full compensatory damages when the action is for breach of warranty. 5 A Corbin, supra, § 1098, at 533. Moreover, an anomaly already exists, for our courts have acknowledged that a buyer may recover such damages upon a showing of the seller's bad faith. See Ganger v. Moffett, 8 N.J. 73, 83 A.2d 769 (1951).

We are satisfied that a buyer should be permitted to recover benefit of the bargain damages when the seller breaches an executory contract to convey real property. Here the defendant agreed to convey marketable title. He made that bargained-for promise and breached it and is responsible to the plaintiff for the damages occasioned thereby. The next question is how to compute those compensatory damages.

II

Judicial remedies upon breach of contract fall into three general categories: restitution, compensatory damages and performance. Separate concepts undergird each of these remedial provisions. The rationale for restitution is to return the innocent party to his status before the contract was executed. Compensatory damages are intended to recompense the injured claimant for losses due to the breach, that is, give the innocent party the benefit of the bargain. Performance is to effect a result, essentially other than in terms of monetary reparation, so that the innocent party is placed in the position of having had the contract performed. We have now adopted the American rule providing for compensatory damages upon the seller's breach of an executory contract to sell realty and we must examine the appropriate elements that should properly be included in an award.

"Compensatory damages are designed 'to put the injured party in as good a position as he would have had if performance had been rendered as promised.' 5 Corbin, Contracts § 992, p. 5 (1951)." 525 Main Street Corp. v. Eagle Roofing Co., 34 N.J. 251, 254, 168 A.2d 33 (1961); see also Giumarra v. Harrington Heights, Inc., 33 N.J.Super. 178, 196, 109 A.2d 695 (App.Div.1954), aff'd o.b., 18 N.J. 548, 114 A.2d 720 (1955); E. Farnsworth, Contracts 839 (1982). What that position is depends upon what the parties reasonably expected. It follows that the defendant is not chargeable for loss that he did not have reason to foresee as a probable result of the breach when the contract was made. Hadley v. Baxendale, 9 Exch. 341, 5 Eng. Rul. Case 502, (1854); accord Crater v. Binninger, 33 N.J.L. 513 (E. & A. 1869). The oft-quoted language in *Hadley* for this proposition is:

> Where two parties have made a contract, which one of them has broken, the damages which the other party ought to receive, in respect of such breach, should be such as may fairly be considered either arising naturally, i.e., according to the usual course of things, from such breach of contract itself, or such as may reasonably be supposed to have been in the contemplation of both parties at the time they made the contract, as the probable result of the breach of it. [5 Eng. Rul. Case at 504]

See Restatement (Second) of Contracts § 351 (1981); see also Weiss v. Revenue Building & Loan Ass'n, 116 N.J.L. 208, 210, 182 A. 891 (E. & A. 1936). Further the loss must be a reasonably certain consequence of the breach although the exact amount of the loss need not be certain. Kozlowski v. Kozlowski, 80 N.J. 378, 388, 403 A.2d 902 (1979); Tessmar v. Grosner, 23 N.J. 193, 203, 128 A.2d 467 (1957).

The specific elements to be applied in any given case of a seller's breach of an executory agreement to sell realty may vary in order to achieve the broad purposes of reparations; some items, however, will almost invariably exist. Thus the purchaser will usually be entitled to the return of the amount paid on the purchase price with interest thereon. Costs and expenses incurred in connection with the proposed acquisition, such as for the title search and survey, would fall in the same category. The traditional test is the difference between the market price of the property at the time of the breach and the contract price. Ganger v. Moffett, 8 N.J. 73, 79, 83 A.2d 769 (1951); King v. Ruckman, 24 N.J.Eq. 298 (Ch.), aff'd 24 N.J.Eq. 556 (E. & A. 1873). See cases cited in annotation, "Measure of recovery by vendee under executory contract for purchase of real property where vendor is unable to convey," 48 A.L.R. 12, 15–17 (1927). Under this standard the buyer who had taken possession before title passed would be entitled to recover for improvements he made that increased the value of the property. Sabaugh v. Schrieber, 87 Ind.App. 588, 162 N.E. 248 (1928).

The difference between market and contract price may not be suitable in all situations. Thus where a buyer had in turn contracted to sell the realty, it is reasonable to measure his damages in terms of the actual lost profit. See Bonhard v. Gindin, 104 N.J.L. 599, 142 A. 52 (E. & A. 1928) (awarding the consideration paid, search fees, taxes and assessments paid, and lost profits from a sale to a third person); see also Giumarra v. Harrington Heights, 33 N.J.Super. 178, 109 A.2d 695 (App.Div.1954) (awarding contract buyer of realty lost profits in action against contract buyer's assignee). What the proper elements of damage are depend upon the particular circumstances surrounding the transaction, especially the terms, conditions and nature of the agreement.

The plaintiffs here assert that their damages are equivalent to the difference in interest costs incurred by them in purchasing a different home at another location. This claim assumes that the financial provision of the contract concerning the purchase money mortgage that the defendant agreed to accept was independent and divisible from the purchase of the land and house. The defendant contends that he did not agree to loan these funds in connection with the purchase of some other property, but that this provision was incidental to the sale of the house. Neither position is entirely sound. This financing was an integral part of the transaction. It can be neither ignored nor viewed as an isolated element.

The relationship of the financing to the purchase of a home has changed in recent years. As interest rates rose and the availability of first mortgage funds was sharply reduced, potential homeowners, though desirous of purchasing homes, found financing difficult to obtain. The seller's acceptance of a purchase money mortgage became an important factor in effecting a sale. See Rand, "Home Resale Market: Pattern Shift," N.Y. Times, March 22, 1981, § 11, at 18, col. 3. In evaluating a contract such a financial arrangement could play an important part in determining price. The rise in interest rates, the expense of mortgage credit and the availability of funds has rendered traditional methods of financing acquisition of homes impractical. Walleser, "The Changing Complexion of Home Mortgage Financing in America," 31 Drake L.Rev. 1, 2 (1981). Favorable vendor financing could lead to increased market value. Only then might a buyer be able to purchase. Iezman, "Alternative Mortgage Instruments: Their Effect on Residential Financing," Real Est.L.J. 3, 4 (1981). The importance of a seller's purchase money mortgage to the overall agreement to convey property was recognized in King v. Ruckman, 24 N.J.Eq. 298 (Ch.), aff'd, 24 N.J.Eq. 556 (E. & A. 1873). The seller agreed to convey certain property and to accept as part of the purchase price a purchase money mortgage with 6% interest payable in five annual installments. The seller refused to convey. The buyer obtained a final decree for specific performance including the purchase money mortgage. The Chancery

Court's view of the mortgage confirmed by the Court of Errors and Appeals on review was:

> The benefit accruing to the purchaser from having time for the payment of the bulk of the principal, and of the rate agreed on for interest, is apparent. It is a material ingredient of the bargain, as much so in reality, though not in degree, as the price, and cannot be withheld from the purchaser in this case by the willful misconduct of the vendor, for the sole benefit of the vendor himself. [24 N.J.Eq. at 303]

The interest rate is not sufficiently discrete to calculate damages in terms of it alone under these circumstances.

In some circumstances interest rate differentials are an appropriate measure of damages. Where the buyer has obtained specific performance, but because of the delay has incurred higher mortgage rates, then his loss clearly should include the higher financing cost. Godwin v. Lindbert, 101 Mich.App. 754, 300 N.W.2d 514 (1981), is illustrative. The buyers lost their commitment for a mortgage with an interest rate of 8¾% when the seller refused to convey. The buyers succeeded in obtaining specific performance but were compelled to borrow funds at 11½%. They were awarded the difference reduced to present value. See also Reis v. Sparks, 547 F.2d 236 (4th Cir. 1976). Moreover, we are not unmindful of the possibility that a buyer might demonstrate that a lending institution's commitment to advance the funds initially at a certain interest rate was due to the buyer's financial condition. The particular realty might well be a secondary and incidental consideration for the loan. Therefore an interest differential occasioned by the seller's default might be a proper factor in fixing damages where the buyer shortly thereafter purchased another property financed at a higher interest rate.

This is not such a situation. The defendant's motive was to sell a house and not to lend money. In measuring the plaintiffs' loss there should be a determination of the fair market value of the property and house that could be acquired with a purchase money mortgage in the principal amount of $44,000 at an interest rate of 10½% (no appeal was taken from the judgment of reformation) for a 30-year term. The valuation should be at the time the defendant failed to comply with the judgment of specific performance. The plaintiffs would be entitled to the difference between $58,900 and that fair market value. If the fair market value was not more than the contract price, the plaintiffs would not have established any damage ascribable to the loss of the bargain. They are also entitled to their expenditures for the survey, search, and counsel fees for services rendered in preparation of the aborted closing. The plaintiffs have hitherto received the return of the deposit.

NOTES

1. The decision of the Appellate Division in the principal case is discussed in Note, 12 Seton Hall L.Rev. 916 (1982). See generally Garland, Purchaser's Interest Rate Increase; Caveat Venditor, 27 N.Y.L.Sch.L.Rev. 745 (1982).

2. The Appellate Division held that the plaintiffs could have damages for the loss of the advantageous interest rate only if they had entered into a contract for another home or were likely to do so in the near future. Does the Supreme Court also impose this requirement? Is it sensible to so require? Is the plaintiffs' financial loss nonexistent if they choose not to realize it in cash by buying another house at a higher interest rate?

3. Numerous cases in addition to those cited by the court have held that when a buyer gets specific performance, but is obliged to pay a higher interest rate from an institutional lender as a result of the delay, he or she is entitled to additional damages for the difference. See e.g., Hutton v. Gliksberg, 128 Cal.App.3d 240, 180 Cal.Rptr. 141 (1982); Walker v. Benton, 407 So.2d 305 (Fla.App.1981); Regan v. Lanze, 47 A.D.2d 378, 366 N.Y.S.2d 512 (1975). Should this reasoning be equally applicable to cases in which the plaintiff seeks loss-of-bargain damages rather than specific performance, as in the instant case?

4. Suppose the prevailing interest rates had declined rather than risen between the time of the contract and the date of breach? Should the plaintiff (whether seeking loss-of-bargain damages or specific performance) be obliged to rebate to the defendant the "windfall" present value of the reduced rates?

H. CONDITIONS IN CONTRACTS

Page 110, insert as Note 10:

10. *"Creative financing"*. Until the last few years, most home sales were financed with new mortgage loans from institutional lenders such as banks, savings and loan associations, and mortgage companies. However, the extremely high interest rates and scarcity of mortgage funds of the early 1980's caused many buyers and sellers to seek alternative or "creative" financing techniques which did not require a new loan. The variations on these methods are virtually endless, but the following list will suggest the major ways in which home sales can be financed. Many of them assume that the seller is willing to defer the receipt of all or part of his or her cash.

(1) *All cash sale*. Buyer pays all cash to seller. Buyer may have cash from savings, from gifts from relatives, or by borrowing under a new mortgage loan from an institutional lender. This has been traditionally the most common approach.

(2) *Assumption or taking subject to existing mortgage*. Buyer "takes over" the seller's existing mortgage financing and pays cash equal to the difference between the sales price of the property and the balance on the existing loan. The buyer may "take over" the loan either by signing an "assumption agreement" which makes him personally liable on the mortgage debt, or merely by "assuming" the loan without any express promise to pay it. In the latter case, he is not personally liable, but will still have a powerful economic incentive to pay the mortgage loan in order to avoid foreclosure and loss of his cash investment in the property.

(3) *Seller financing*. Buyer enters into a mortgage loan or installment contract obligation with seller for all or a large portion of the total purchase price. This is the only debt obligation involved in the transaction. The debt will bear interest and require regular installments, much as would be the case with an institutional loan. The seller treats the obligation as an

investment; this is typically feasible only if the seller has need for little or no immediate cash upon the sale of the property.

(4) *Combination of assumption/subject to and seller financing.* Buyer "takes over" the seller's existing mortgage financing, as in example (2) above, but cannot raise enough cash to pay the entire difference between the price and the loan balance. Hence, buyer gives seller a note secured by a second mortgage for part of this difference. This reduces the cash demanded of the buyer to a manageable level.

(5) *Wrap-around financing.* The transaction between buyer and seller is structured as in example (3), above. However, the seller has preexisting (usually institutional) mortgage financing on the property, and does not pay it off at the time of the transfer. Instead, the seller is required to continue making payments on the "underlying" institutional loan at the same time the buyer makes payments on the new (or "wrap-around") loan. The interest rate on the wrap-around is often higher than on the underlying loan, making a tidy profit for the seller. See generally the discussion in casebook at 1056–62. From the seller's viewpoint, one of the advantages of the wrap-around arrangement is that the seller knows immediately of any default on the preexisting first mortgage, since the payments on it are being made by him directly.

Note that any assumption, taking subject to, or wrap-around of the underlying institutional mortgage will run headlong into problems if that document contains an enforceable due-on-sale clause. Such clauses are discussed in detail in the casebook at Chapter 5, Sec. B, as augmented in this Supplement. In most cases, the clause is indeed enforceable, and if the lender chooses to enforce it in fact, the parties' contract of sale may be frustrated unless they took that possibility into account in their drafting.

In the case below, the parties contemplated a wrap-around of the existing mortgage loan, as in example (5) above, with a "three-year agreement of sale" or installment contract as the financing vehicle between the buyer and seller. However, the lender employed its due-on-sale clause as leverage for insisting that the transaction be restructured in the form of a loan assumption, as in example (2) above. The trial court ordered that the sellers complete the transaction, restructured either as in example (2) (with the sellers getting all cash for their "equity") or as in example (4) (with the sellers to be paid for their "equity" in equal installments over three years at 9% interest).

SCHRADER v. BENTON

Court of Appeals of Hawaii, 1981.
2 Hawaii App. 564, 635 P.2d 562.

BURNS, Judge.

Defendants-Appellants Charles and Elizabeth Benton (Sellers) appeal the lower court's summary judgment requiring them to specifically perform their contract to sell a condominium apartment to Plaintiff-Appellees Dean and Barbara Schrader (Buyers).

We hold that the lower court erred in granting summary judgment and we reverse.

For purposes of this opinion, we assume the following facts although, as hereinafter noted, some of them are not properly supported by the record.

On or about February 25, 1978, the Bentons, as Sellers, and Philip J. Harder, as Buyer, entered into a Deposit Receipt, Offer and Acceptance (DROA) contract.

The subject of the sale was Apartment 313, Honokowai East Condominium, Maui, Hawaii. The total price was $44,500.00, payable via $7,000.00 in cash and a $37,500.00 three-year agreement of sale at 9 percent interest per annum with payments of not less than $325.00 per month. The Buyer was entitled to pay "in full" at any time during the three years without prepayment penalty.

Although the literal language of the DROA indicates otherwise, the parties agree that the apartment was being sold free and clear of an existing $31,800.00 first mortgage in favor of Amfac Financial.

Closing was set for April 20, 1978, subject to a thirty-day extension at the discretion of the Sellers' broker.

At some point in time, the Buyer assigned his interest in the DROA to the Schraders (Buyers).

The DROA specifies that "[t]he obligations of Buyer and Seller hereunder are conditioned upon obtaining all necessary consents of third parties." Apparently the first mortgage contains a "due-on-sale" provision which requires the Sellers to obtain Amfac Financial's consent to the agreement of sale or to suffer Amfac Financial's immediate acceleration of the due date of the entire mortgage debt. Amfac Financial refused to permit an agreement of sale over its mortgage; but it was willing to consent to an assumption. The Sellers, on the other hand, refused to agree to such a change in the structure of the transaction.

On October 13, 1978, the Buyers sued for specific performance. The Sellers, in violation of Rule 8(b), Hawaii Rules of Civil Procedure (HRCP), filed an answer denying "each and every allegation in the Complaint."

Thereafter, both sides moved for summary judgment.

On May 30, 1979, the lower court granted summary judgment to the Buyers and ordered the Sellers to convey to the Buyers when the Buyers (1) pay the purchase price in cash or (2) assume the first mortgage, arrange for the Sellers to be completely released from the liability of the first mortgage by May 20, 1981, and pay the balance of the purchase price, together with interest at 9 percent per annum, in equal monthly payments amortized from actual closing to May 20, 1981, and (3) adjust "all income and ordinary expenses of the property since May 20, 1978, excluding interest paid on the first mortgage" so that the Buyers would enjoy all profits or suffer all losses since May 20, 1978.

We hold that the lower court erred in granting summary judgment for specific performance because the Buyers were required to prove the existence of a contract, Francone v. McClay, 41 Haw. 72 (1955), and they failed to do so. The record contains nothing more than a copy of the DROA as it was when it was an unaccepted offer by the Buyers.

However, in an effort to facilitate this case to its proper conclusion on remand, we will discuss the merits as if the Buyers proved that the Sellers accepted said offer.

Neither party contends that Amfac Financial's consent does not qualify as a "necessary consent" under the DROA. Consequently, under the terms of the DROA, the obligations of Buyers and Sellers are conditioned upon the obtaining of Amfac Financial's consent. In other words, no consent, no further obligation on either side.

However, "[i]t is a maxim that equity regards the substance rather than the form. The parties are not to be sacrificed to the mere letter but the intent or spirit of the transaction will, at least in equity, be the paramount consideration. Equity goes behind the form of the transaction in order to give effect to the intention of the parties * * *." Lord v. Lord, 35 Haw. 26 (1939) at 39.

Thus, "the court of equity has plenary power to mold its decrees in such form as to conserve the equities of all parties * * *." Fleming v. Napili Kai, Ltd., 50 Haw. 66, 70, 430 P.2d 316, 319 (1967), quoting Baker Sand & Gravel Co. v. Rogers P. & H. Co., 228 Ala. 612, 619, 154 So. 591, 597, 102 A.L.R. 346, 355 (1934).

Notwithstanding the literal language of the DROA, it is clear that Amfac Financial's consent is not necessary if the Buyers make full payment in cash because in that event the Sellers are required to cause the lien of the mortgage to be removed. Thus, notwithstanding Amfac Financial's refusal to consent, the Buyers should be allowed to pay in full either (1) via cash or (2) via an assumption of the mortgage together with a complete release of the Sellers from their liability thereon, effective upon closing rather than by May 20, 1981, and with payment of the balance due Sellers in cash on closing.

Here, the lower court went further and gave the Buyers a second alternative under which they could assume the mortgage at closing and wait two years until the payoff date to arrange for the Sellers to be released from the liability of the first mortgage and could pay the balance of the purchase price in equal installments from closing until the payoff date.

The issue is whether the lower court abused its discretion when it gave the Buyers the second alternative. We answer yes. The Sellers are entitled to the full benefit of the substance or essence of their bargain. See Gomez v. Pagaduan, 1 Haw.App. 70, 613 P.2d 658 (1981). Under alternative (2), the Sellers would receive less than the full benefit of the substance or essence of their bargain in at least one and possibly two or more respects.

First, as holder of an agreement of sale for the entire $37,500.00 and being solely liable for the $31,800.00 mortgage, the Sellers are in a position to know what is happening with respect to their mortgage obligation and they remain in control of it. If the Sellers hold an agreement of sale for $5,700.00 while being secondarily liable on the $31,800.00 mortgage, the Sellers may not know what is happening with respect to the mortgage and may not find out until it is too late. It may be possible to insert language into the assumption agreement to protect the Sellers but such was not required by the lower court.

Second, the DROA entitles the Sellers to receive an agreement of sale for the entire $37,500.00 balance with the Sellers remaining responsible to pay the mortgage. In alternative (2), the lower court authorized the Buyers to give the Sellers an agreement of sale for $5,700.00 and for the Buyers to assume the mortgage. If the interest rate on the mortgage is less than the interest rate on the agreement of sale, then the Sellers realize less from the lower court's alternative than it would under the DROA.

In view of the meager record, we are unable to determine whether the lower court's alternative (2) is different in any other respects.

Furthermore, the validity of the lower court's alternative (2) appears to be a moot question. The time for payment in full was scheduled to be May 20, 1981, which date has already passed. In our view, if the May 20, 1981 payment-in-full date has been extended by these legal proceedings, it has not been extended past the completion of these proceedings. Thus, if there is a contract like the one discussed herein and if the date for payment in full has passed, then the only specific performance which a court could sanction at this stage of the proceedings would be specific performance conditioned upon payment in full.

Reversed and remanded for further proceedings consistent with this opinion.

Part II

REAL ESTATE FINANCE

Chapter 3

THE USE OF MORTGAGE SUBSTITUTES

A. THE ABSOLUTE DEED, THE CONDITIONAL SALE, AND RELATED TRANSACTIONS

Page 249, add before Koenig v. Van Reken:

McGILL v. BIGGS

Appellate Court of Illinois, Third District, 1982.
105 Ill.App.3d 706, 61 Ill.Dec. 417, 434 N.E.2d 772.

SCOTT, Justice:

Plaintiff's mother, Ivory Anderson, died on October 7, 1977, leaving him as the surviving joint tenant of certain real estate located in Kankakee County, commonly known as Route 3, Box 446, Momence, Illinois. Plaintiff desired to provide her with a funeral at the Wesley Funeral Home with which his half-uncle, the defendant, was familiar and plaintiff requested defendant's assistance in raising the funds necessary which approximated $1,500.

Plaintiff asked defendant to accompany him while he attempted to borrow the money at banks in Momence, Kankakee and Chicago. Defendant accompanied plaintiff in his efforts to borrow the necessary funds for his mother's funeral but they were unsuccessful.

Plaintiff and defendant then entered into an agreement whereby in return for defendant's paying the funeral bill for plaintiff's mother (who was also the defendant's half-sister) plaintiff would deed the premises to defendant.

Plaintiff was vague as to the nature of the transaction, but testified that defendant told him he would need a quit-claim deed as "collateral." Plaintiff did not know what a quit-claim deed was but he understood the meaning of "collateral." Plaintiff testified that he didn't intend to permanently transfer the title to the property to the defendant. Plaintiff testified that he valued the property at approximately $15,000, while defendant testified he didn't know the value of the property. Defendant admitted that he knew plaintiff was upset and distressed when the transaction took place.

Plaintiff and defendant went to defendant's attorney's office where plaintiff signed a paper he thought was a contract to pay defendant $115 a month for 15 months ($1,725). A warranty deed was prepared by defendant's attorney and signed by plaintiff when he went to the lawyer's office on October 9, 1977, two days after his mother's death. The next day, defendant paid the funeral bill in the sum of $1,473.75.

Plaintiff made one payment to defendant before losing his job and generally falling on hard times by drinking heavily. No further payments were made to defendant. Plaintiff and his family made temporary use of the premises on several occasions after delivery of the deed to defendant at his lawyer's office. Defendant conceded he did not go to the house after his half-sister died. Plaintiff continued to keep the property in good repair and to pay the 1978 and 1979 taxes on the property and defendant made no attempt to pay any taxes on the property until October of 1980, when his check was returned indicating that the taxes had already been paid. In January of 1980, plaintiff had offered to pay defendant the balance of the debt but defendant refused payment. In June of 1980, defendant recorded the deed.

Defendant never used the property or interfered with plaintiff's use until June, 1980, when plaintiff discovered that defendant was attempting to list the property for rent with a real estate broker. Plaintiff contacted an attorney, discovered the warranty deed and filed the instant suit to quiet title, the issue being whether the deed was absolute with a contract back to repurchase, or whether it was intended as a mortgage to secure payment of the funeral bill.

From the trial court's ruling in plaintiff's favor (plaintiff was ordered to pay the balance due on the loan of $1,610 plus 5% per annum on $1,473.75 from January 10, 1980) that a debt relationship existed between the parties and that the warranty deed was in fact a mortgage, defendant has appealed.

We note initially that it is provided by statute that:

> "Every deed conveying real estate, which shall appear to have been intended only as a security in the nature of a mortgage, though it be an absolute conveyance in terms, shall be considered as a mortgage." Ill.Rev.Stat.1977, ch. 95, par. 55.

In order to convert a deed absolute on its face into a mortgage, the proof must be clear, satisfactory, and convincing (Burroughs v. Burroughs (1973), 11 Ill.App.3d 176, 296 N.E.2d 350), and can come from almost every conceivable fact that could legitimately aid that determination. Each case will depend upon its own special circumstances. Warner v. Gosnell (1956), 8 Ill.2d 24, 132 N.E.2d 526.

Many circumstances have been recognized or considered by Illinois courts, including the existence of an indebtedness, the close relationship of the parties, prior unsuccessful attempts for loans, the circumstances surrounding the transaction, the disparity of the situations of the parties, the lack of legal assistance, the unusual type of sale, the inadequacy of consideration, the way the consideration was paid, the retention of the written evidence of the debt, the belief that the debt remains unpaid, an agreement to repurchase, and the continued exercise of ownership privileges and responsibilities by the seller. Burroughs v. Burroughs (1971), 1 Ill.App.3d 697, 274 N.E.2d 376 * * *.

The defendant contends the trial judge erred in finding a debt relationship when neither party directly testified that plaintiff owed a debt to defendant, or that defendant would reconvey to plaintiff upon payment of such debt. However, direct evidence is not required. In fact, no particular kind of evidence is required. (Burroughs v. Burroughs (1971), 1 Ill.App.3d 697, 274 N.E.2d 376.) However, a debt relationship is essential to a mortgage.

In the case at bar, there are a number of circumstances which prove the existence of a debt relationship. Plaintiff signed the warranty deed after defendant told him that the only way to get money for the funeral would be to sign a quit claim deed for collateral. Although plaintiff thought he was signing a contract to pay off the funeral bill, defendant testified that they discussed collateral to get money for the funeral expenses, and came to the agreement that plaintiff would sell his property to the defendant for the amount of the funeral bill and then pay defendant $115 per month for 15 months to get it back. The plaintiff, however, did not intend to sell his property.

The bulk of evidence in this case is the testimony of the plaintiff and defendant. The trial judge believed they were both honest. Their testimony differs, but not substantially. They both had difficulty making responsive answers, but the answers they gave often shed light on the nature of the transaction.

A debt relationship was indicated by defendant's attempt at collection. Defendant confronted and questioned plaintiff about plaintiff's failure to make the monthly payments as he had promised. This is a reasonable action for defendant, who was concerned about plaintiff falling behind in his debt payments. It is not reasonable to expect a person obligated to reconvey to be encouraging the other party to exert their "rights."

Further support of a debt relationship comes from defendant's own characterization of the agreement to reconvey. Defendant consistently referred to the payments plaintiff could make as "my money." He spoke in terms of expectation of payment, as if the money to be paid by plaintiff was his already which was owed to him for payment of the funeral bill. This is supported further by defendant's testimony that upon payment by plaintiff, defendant would "redeem" his property back to him.

Another circumstance to consider is the value of the consideration as compared to the payback amount. The consideration was approximately $1,500 and the total payback amount after 16 months would be $1,725. These figures would be in line with a typical installment loan agreement.

In determining the issue presented in this appeal, we direct our attention to what we deem to be pertinent factors. The inadequacy of consideration has been regarded as a potent or strong circumstance tending to show that a deed was intended to operate as a mortgage and not a sale; and where consideration is grossly inadequate, a mortgage is strongly indicated. *Burroughs*, 1 Ill.App.3d at 705, 247 N.E.2d 376.

Here, the consideration was less than 10% of the value of the property.

Several factors regarding the transaction in this case are similar to the circumstances in *Burroughs*. The property was not advertised or offered for sale. The consideration was not paid to the plaintiff, but was paid to the Wesley Funeral Home for the funeral bill of plaintiff's mother. In addition, defendant did not even consider the value of the property when he purchased it, or the amount of consideration.

Plaintiff tried to borrow money for his mother's funeral in three different cities, with no mention of collateral. Defendant offered to go to his friends for help, and plaintiff ended up with defendant in the office of his attorney signing a warranty deed instead of a loan agreement. This situation is similar, but even more significant than the one noted in *Burroughs*, and should be weighed accordingly.

In Totten v. Totten (1920), 294 Ill. 70, 80, 128 N.E. 295, 299, the court stated: "The fact that the grantor in a deed absolute in form has remained in possession of the property so conveyed and controlled the property after the conveyance is evidence tending to show that the transaction, in fact, was a mortgage, as is also the payment of taxes by the grantor after the conveyance." The reason for this rule is obvious, since the grantee in an unqualified deed is entitled to immediate possession and becomes liable for payment of taxes. In the instant case the uncontradicted testimony was that plaintiff and his family made use of the premises on several occasions after the delivery of the deed, and that he kept a lock on the door. Defendant conceded he had not been in the house since his half-sister died. Plaintiff paid the 1978 and 1979 taxes and defendant made no attempt to pay taxes until October, 1980, when his check for the 1979 taxes was returned because they were already paid. It is clear he attempted to exercise none of the prerogatives of an owner until over two years after the time he claims to have become the owner and at a time when plaintiff was in default on all of the payments on the alleged contract except the first. It is of further significance that defendant failed to take another step usually associated with ownership. He did not record his deed at the time of delivery or until well beyond the time that the fifteen months had expired. This delay, while not of great significance standing alone, is a further circumstance, when considered with others, indicating a lack of intention by defendant to claim immediate ownership.

An agreement to reconvey has long been considered a significant factor in distinguishing mortgages from absolute sales. Agreements made in writing at the same time as the conveyance resolve any doubt as to the character of the conveyance in favor of a mortgage. (Illinois Trust Co. of Paris v. Bibo (1927), 328 Ill. 252, 159 N.E. 254.) However, the agreement need not be in writing. Miller v. Thomas (1853), 14 Ill. 428.

In the case at bar, the agreement to reconvey was admitted by the defendant to be a part of the deed transaction. If there is doubt as to the intent of the conveyance, it should be resolved in favor of a mortgage.

Any one of these preceding factors should be enough to find the trial court did not commit manifest error. The mass of relevant circumstances clearly and convincingly prove that the intention of the parties was to create a debt arrangement with a security. Based upon these circumstances, the trial judge was correct in finding a debt relationship existed, and that plaintiff's warranty deed to defendant was a mortgage.

For the foregoing reasons, the judgment of the circuit court of Kankakee County is affirmed.

Affirmed.

BARRY, P. J., and ALLOY, J., concur.

Page 256, add as a new paragraph to Note 4:

Additional reasons may occasionally motivate a grantee to seek to characterize an absolute deed or conditional sale as a mortgage transaction. Suppose, for example, a third party is injured on the real estate and the grantee is sued on a negligence theory in his or her status as a "landowner." Because a mortgagee normally will not be liable to third parties for unsafe conditions on mortgaged real estate unless he or she exercises dominion and control over it, a grantee in such circumstances may well be delighted to eschew ownership for the benefits of mortgagee status. See e.g., Smith v. Fried, 98 Ill.App.3d 467, 53 Ill.Dec. 845, 424 N.E.2d 636 (1981).

B. THE INSTALLMENT LAND CONTRACT

Page 258, add before Jenkins v. Wise:

BRAUNSTEIN v. TROTTIER

Court of Appeals of Oregon, 1981.
54 Or.App. 687, 635 P.2d 1379.

Before BUTTLER, P. J., and WARDEN and WARREN, JJ.

BUTTLER, Presiding Judge.

This [ejectment] action requires that we attempt to determine whether the Supreme Court has been engaged in something akin to a fan dance, or whether it really intends to tango. The issue is whether the vendor under a land sale contract, which permits, among other remedies, a declaration of forfeiture upon the vendee's default, may effectively terminate the vendee's interest in the real property and to the purchase money theretofore paid by giving reasonable notice of intention to do so, followed by a declaration of such forfeiture and by the filing of an action in ejectment to regain possession of the property. The trial court held that the plaintiff vendors could do so and entered judgment accordingly. Defendants who are vendees appeal.

Although the issue appears to be narrow, the problem of which it is a part is not. The rights, duties and interests of the parties to a land sale contract are, for the most part, creations of the courts. They have evolved piecemeal and, perhaps for that reason, not necessarily harmoniously, particularly when viewed in the overall context of security devices available to vendors of real property—mortgages, trust deeds and land sale contracts. The first two of those security devices are controlled largely by statute; the third is not. Each has it place in a vendor-financed transaction with differing rights and interests; the extent to which those differences exist, or ought to be extended, is the problem.

Usually, but not always, the vendor determines the security device for assuring payment of the purchase price. There are many reasons why a vendor would choose a land sale contract: historically, because of the variety of remedies which the contract may provide (e.g., forfeiture, strict foreclosure and specific performance), it may be more appealing; until recently, there was no requirement that the contract be recorded, so if the vendee abandoned the premises, no judicial proceeding was necessary to clear the title (but see ORS 93.635 [2]); statutory redemption rights did not apply to strict foreclosures, the vendee's only right to redeem being a matter of equity fashioned by the court in the decree; through specific performance, rather than strict foreclosure, the vendor could be entitled to a deficiency judgment.

That flexibility is not available with a mortgage or deed of trust. However, a purchaser who makes a substantial down payment might successfully demand that the balance be secured by a purchase money mortgage, which may be enforced only by foreclosure and cannot result in a deficiency judgment (ORS 88.070 [3]), and the debtor would have the

---

2. ORS 93.635 now requires land sale contracts to be recorded.

3. ORS 88.070 provides:

"When a decree is given for the foreclosure of any mortgage given to secure payment of the balance of the purchase price of real property, the decree shall provide for the sale of the real property covered by such mortgage for the satisfaction of the decree given therein, but the mortgagee shall not be entitled to a deficiency judgment on account of the mortgage or note or obligation secured by the same."

statutory right to redeem for one year. ORS 23.560(1).[4] If a deed of trust is used, the seller, as beneficiary, may proceed expeditiously by exercising the right of sale, but must deal with the buyer's right to cure the default up to five days prior to the sale, and would be limited in that event to the statutory amount of attorney fees and trustee's fees. Further, if there are questions regarding priority, he would be required to foreclose the deed of trust as a mortgage.

Because it is not this court's function to survey the entire field of law in which the problem presented falls, we will not attempt to do so here. However, as we noted at the outset, we detect some ambivalence in the Supreme Court opinions dealing with the question of non-judicial forfeiture as a contract vendor's summary remedy. As Justice Holman said in his dissent in Elsasser v. Wilcox, 286 Or. 775, 596 P.2d 974 (1979):

> "The true issue is whether the court, regardless of contractual provisions, is going to allow the remedy of immediate forfeiture. This issue has been and still is being dodged by this court under the guise of a rule that has no logical sustenance. * * *" 286 Or. at 786, 596 P.2d 974.

We also sense that the nature of a land sale contract and its place in the scheme of vendor-financed real estate transactions may have been overlooked in the piecemeal adjudication of specific disputes. For those reasons, we consider it necessary to see where we are before proceeding with the disposition of this case.

To begin with, it is worth mentioning that a land sale contract is not just a contract between two parties; it affects the land to which it relates. It is primarily a security device, and after the parties have signed the contract, the vendor, although still the legal title holder of the property, holds an encumbered title charged with the equitable interest of the vendee. Panushka v. Panushka, 221 Or. 145, 349 P.2d 450 (1960). The vendee's interest may, for example, be assigned or mortgaged, and the equitable estate may be foreclosed. Young v. Clay, 139 Or. 427, 10 P.2d 602 (1932). The vendor under the contract is said to have a vendor's lien on the property. Grider v. Turnbow, 162 Or. 622, 641, 94 P.2d 285 (1939); but see Savings Co. v. Mackenzie, 33 Or. 209, 52 P. 1046 (1898).

Basically, then, the question is: What are the rights of the vendor under that lien? The specially concurring opinion of Justice Linde and

---

4. ORS 23.560(1) provides:

"(1) The mortgagor or judgment debtor whose right and title were sold, or his heir, devisee or grantee, who has acquired by inheritance, devise, deed, sale, or by virtue of any execution or by any other means, the legal title to the property sold, may, at any time within one year after the date of sale, redeem the property; provided that a transfer of the judgment debtor's interest in the property, either before or after sale, shall preclude him from the right to redeem unless the proceeds from the sale are insufficient to satisfy the judgment, in which event the judgment debtor shall have the right to redeem at any time within 10 days after the year herein allowed for redemption, and not otherwise."

the dissenting opinion of Justice Holman in Elsasser v. Wilcox, supra, seem to say that the parties could agree that, in the event of a default by the vendee, all interest of the vendee terminates forthwith without any notice or action by the vendor, and all amounts paid by the vendee are thereby forfeited and the contract terminated by its own terms without judicial intervention or supervision. That kind of provision in a land sale contract does not sound like a remedy to enforce a lien, and we know of no cases which have sanctioned that result. (But see Sievers v. Brown, 34 Or. 454, 460, 56 P. 171 (1899), where the court, in a different context, recognized a forfeiture on breach without an express agreement, notice or declaration, apparently as a matter of law.) Rather, such a provision sounds more like an option which is irrevocable so long as the optionee makes the required payments, but terminates forthwith upon his failure to do so. An option to purchase real property, however, is not the same animal as a land sale contract, and there is no reason, from either a legal or practical standpoint, to blur the differences. Each has its useful place.

To make the point more dramatically, albeit in a different context, if the owner of real property executes and delivers a deed, absolute on its face, to another to secure a debt, with the express understanding that if the grantor pays the debt the property will be reconveyed, but that if he defaults absolute title shall vest in the grantee without further action by either party, the transaction is treated as a secured transaction, and the deed is treated as a mortgage. The grantee must enforce his rights by way of judicial foreclosure, as a result of which the grantor is entitled to the statutory redemption rights. Libel v. Pierce, 147 Or. 132, 31 P.2d 1106 (1934); but see Herrmann v. Churchill, 235 Or. 327, 385 P.2d 190 (1963). If that kind of forfeiture may not be enforced by the secured party according to the express terms of the agreement, why, then, should a forfeiture under a land sale contract be so enforced?

One might answer that question by suggesting that the difference between the two transactions is that one involves a contract and the other an instrument deemed to be a mortgage. That distinction, however, is not persuasive, because neither purports to be a mortgage, both contain contractual agreements, including the right to a forfeiture on default, and both are transactions secured by real property. It is true, however, that once an instrument is considered to be a mortgage, it is controlled by statute rather than by judicial rules. For example, the court has held that a land sale contract may be specifically enforced, rather than strictly foreclosed, if the vendor desires to obtain a deficiency judgment, and that ORS 88.070, prohibiting deficiency judgments in the foreclosure of purchase money mortgages, does not apply to land sale contracts. Renard v. Allen, 237 Or. 406, 391 P.2d 777 (1964). In that context the court has attempted to draw a clear distinction between the two types of vendor-financed transactions. However, one might wonder why the legislative policy against permitting the seller, secured by a mortgage, to collect more from the buyer than the property is worth should not apply with respect to enforcement of a land sale contract in equity.

Passing that question, ought there to be a difference between a noteholder secured by mortgage suing on the note (which may be done by a purchase money mortgagee, as well as by other mortgagees) and a vendor suing on the contract, where both are suing for the unpaid debt or price rather than foreclosing? Under the court's decisions there may be substantial differences. If the noteholder brings an action on the note and obtains a judgment, the debt is merged into the judgment, and the only lien he has is a judgment lien, the priority of which is determined by the date of the judgment; the mortgage no longer secures it, and the priority of the mortgage is lost. However, a vendor under a land sale contract may do the functional equivalent of that by a suit for specific performance: he may obtain a money judgment against the vendee, retain the vendor's lien (and, apparently, its priority) on the property, have the property sold if the judgment is not paid within the time specified and obtain a deficiency judgment if the sale proceeds do not satisfy the judgment. Renard v. Allen, supra. In other words, the vendor has the best of all worlds—*unless* the vendee (judgment debtor) is entitled to redeem under the statutory right of redemption (ORS 23.560), a question which has not been decided in Oregon. If the vendee has that right of redemption, the vendor might prefer strict foreclosure to specific performance, because, typically, the period for redemption provided in a strict foreclosure decree is substantially shorter than the one year provided by statute following execution sales.

Although the foregoing discussion is neither complete nor in-depth, it is sufficient to suggest that the courts may have turned a useful device, intended to create a vendor's lien to secure payment of the balance of the purchase price, into a security device so overweighted in favor of the vendor that it may make the land sale contract too oppressive to be a useful device.

In his specially concurring opinion in Elsasser v. Wilcox, supra, Justice Linde suggested that the questions involved are proper ones for legislative determination. However true that may be, the legislature has not acted, but has left this judicial creature to its creators. There are, of course, advantages in the legislative forum, where different interest groups may be heard and where compromises and trade-offs may be effected. An example of that process is the legislative treatment of deeds of trust: the principal trade-off there lies in permitting the secured party (beneficiary) to realize on his security by a trustee's sale, without concern for redemption rights, in exchange for giving up the right to a deficiency judgment. ORS 86.770. There appear to have been no trade-offs for the vendee under a land sale contract as the vendor's rights thereunder seem to be evolving. If there is a trade-off, it is inadvertent and lies in the pitfalls which might belay an unwary vendor simply because his rights are not as clear as they need be to permit their exercise with confidence. That kind of advantage ought not to be the bargain fixed by the courts.

That brings us back to the problem at hand—a vendor's right to declare a complete forfeiture on the vendee's default without judicial intervention. The Oregon cases have paid lip service to the existence of that right. In Nygaard et ux. v. Anderson, 229 Or. 323, 330–31, 366 P.2d 899 (1961), a strict foreclosure case, the court said:

"* * * Vendors' remedies upon default by the purchaser fall into either one of two classes; (1) remedies consistent only with the affirmance of the contract, or (2) remedies consistent only with the repudiation of the contract. If the vendor seeks to recover the installments due on the contract or brings suit for specific performance or brings suit for strict foreclosure [footnote omitted] he has elected to affirm and enforce the contract. On the other hand, if he brings an action of ejectment or takes possession of the premises under circumstances indicating an intent to deprive the purchaser of possession under the forfeiture and right of entry provision of the contract, the vendor has elected to regard the contract as no longer continuing."

In another strict foreclosure case, Zumstein v. Stockton et ux., 199 Or. 633, 264 P.2d 455 (1953), the court stated:

"* * * The option to declare a forfeiture gives to the vendor rights strictly legal in nature. It may be accomplished after reasonable notice by lawfully taking possession of the property or by bringing an action in ejectment. * * *"

At least one case recognized a forfeiture in a quiet title suit. Williams v. Barbee, 165 Or. 260, 282, 106 P.2d 1033 (1940).

Later, however, in Stinemeyer v. Wesco Farms, Inc., 260 Or. 109, 487 P.2d 65 (1971), the court stated:

"It has been our policy to encourage sellers of land to enforce their contracts in equity when the purchaser has defaulted in his performance. * * *" 260 Or. at 115–16, 487 P.2d 65.

The court's latest pronouncement is contained in Elsasser v. Wilcox, supra, in which a majority of the court recognized that a forfeiture provision in a land sale contract may be enforced summarily and without judicial intervention. However, where, as in *Elsasser* and here, the contract gives the vendor alternative remedies upon default, the declaration of forfeiture is not effective unless the vendor first gives the vendee reasonable notice and an opportunity to cure the breach prior to declaring the forfeiture. In *Elsasser*, the court refused to enforce a declaration of forfeiture, because "the [vendors] did not give [vendee] notice that a forfeiture will be effected and an opportunity to correct the default during the period given in the notice before declaring a forfeiture, * * *." 286 Or. at 782, 596 P.2d 974.

The problem with the notices given by the vendors in *Elsasser*, as we understand it, was that neither gave the vendee a specific time period within which the default could be cured. The first notice was given one week after a substantial payment was due, but was not paid; it stated that "we hereby declare this contract null and void effective this date." 286 Or. at 778, 596 P.2d 974. A subsequent notice given more than five weeks later stated the same thing, but it also advised the vendee that foreclosure proceedings may be necessary in the event vendee did not execute a quitclaim deed. There appears to have been no doubt on the part of the vendee that the axe was about to fall. After the first notice, and before the second, the vendee tendered in escrow an amount which would have been sufficient to cure the default but for instructions requiring a lot release before the money could be delivered to the vendors. A few days later, the second notice declaring a forfeiture was sent. On those facts, it is at least arguable that the vendee had both notice and was given a reasonable time, albeit the time period was not specifically stated in the notice.

The author of the majority opinion in *Elsasser*, speaking for himself only (286 Or. at 775, n.3, 596 P.2d 974), questioned whether a forfeiture provision should ever be given effect, even where the purchaser has notice and an opportunity to cure the breach.[6] At the other extreme, Justice Holman, in his dissent, expressed the view that the rule enunciated by the majority, although supported by prior decisions, made no sense. He would enforce a contract provision authorizing the summary remedy of immediate forfeiture on default without notice and opportunity to cure the default. He went on to state that the result of the court's decision would be that purchasers will no longer have the opportunity to purchase property with a small down payment, because sellers would be foolish to sell under those conditions, "when no summary method of foreclosure is available to them." 286 Or. at 787, 596 P.2d 974. That reason appears to us to be an overstatement: The question presented in *Elsasser* was whether the vendors could declare an immediate forfeiture without any judicial intervention, not whether they could strictly foreclose the contract through judicial proceedings.

In the case at bar, the parties executed a land sale contract in October, 1978, the terms of which provided for a total payment of $74,500, payable in 13 monthly installments with a final balloon payment of the entire contract balance, $64,109.84, on December 1, 1979.[8] The contract contained alternative remedies on default, but provided a ten-day grace period during which a default could be cured to avoid the consequences of the default, including a forfeiture.

Appellants did not designate the transcript of testimony as part of the record on appeal, so our review is limited. However, the facts material to the validity of the declaration of forfeiture are admitted,

---

6. The majority recognized an apparent distinction between contracts which provide only for forfeiture upon default, in which case prior decisions indicated, but did not hold, that no notice and opportunity to cure was necessary to effectuate a forfeiture, and contracts which give the vendor alternative remedies and require notice and opportunity to cure as a condition to effective forfeiture. Chief Justice Denecke, specially concurring, would apply the notice requirement to both kinds of contracts.

8. As of December 1, 1979, vendees had paid a total of $17,358.22, including interest at 10 percent, under the contract.

and the vendees do not assign error to any of the trial court's findings of fact. If forfeiture was permitted under the facts and the law, the vendees' assignments of error are either irrelevant or may receive only limited review on this record. Reeder v. Kay, 276 Or. 1111, 557 P.2d 673 (1976).

Defendant John A. Trottier (one of the vendees) was a licensed real estate salesman. Prior to the execution of the contract, he informed plaintiffs of their right to declare the contract null and void if the vendees failed to make the final payment by December 1, 1979. On several occasions after the contract was signed, the vendors made it clear that they would insist upon strict compliance with the terms of the contract requiring final payment on December 1. On November 7, 1979, vendors delivered a letter to vendees stating that they expected the contract to be paid off on or before December 1 and that they would not renew or extend the contract. On November 26, vendors' attorney wrote the vendee's attorney outlining several existing breaches of the contract and expressing his understanding that payment of the balance due under the contract would probably not be made when it was due. The letter concluded with the statement that the vendors insisted upon either prompt payment in full or restoration and delivery of the premises to the vendors.

On December 14, vendors' attorney sent another letter to the vendees explaining that under the terms of the agreement a final payment of $64,109.84 was to be paid by December 1 and that it had not been made. The letter went on to state that because the payment was over ten days past due, the vendees were in default and notified them that unless the full balance was paid by December 24, 1979, the vendors would declare the contract null and void and "effect a forfeiture on December 24, 1979." Final payment was not made by December 26, 1979, whereupon the vendors exercised their right to declare the contract null and void.

On January 14, 1980, this action for ejectment was commenced. The trial court concluded that the vendors had given reasonable notice of their intention to declare a forfeiture and were entitled to possession of the real property and that the vendees were wrongfully withholding possession from the vendors. Those conclusions are supported by findings of fact and support the judgment, if the vendors had a right to declare a forfeiture.

We conclude that the vendors did everything that was required of them under *Elsasser*[9] and, therefore, were entitled to declare the

---

9. An obvious problem with a summary declaration of forfeiture is that the reasonableness of the time given to cure the default will almost always be open to doubt until a court rules on the question after the fact in the ensuing ejectment proceeding. We are not aware of any guidelines for determining reasonableness. If foreclosure proceedings were required, that problem would not exist; the court could determine what would be a reasonable time within which the vendees must pay up or be foreclosed of any interest in the property (e.g., forfeiture). That is the function of the "equity of redemption"; it permits judicially determined flexibility to

contract null and void, which they did on December 26. Given that conclusion, the vendees' first assignment of error—that the trial court erred in refusing to give them a reasonable time to pay off the contract—misses the point. The argument assumes that this proceeding is one to foreclose the contract. It is not; it is an action at law in ejectment. Their second assignment of error is that the court erred in dismissing their counterclaim for specific performance. They concede, however, as the trial court found, that at no time prior to the vendors' declaration of forfeiture were they ready, willing and able to perform under the contract. Further, on this record, there is no evidence that the vendees could do so at the time of trial even if the contract had not been validity terminated.

In their third assignment of error, vendees contend the trial court erred in refusing to recognize their equitable defenses. As best we can determine, the argument is that the vendors refused a tender, thus excusing vendees' nonperformance. The most that can be said is that on January 18, 1980, after this action was commenced, a partial tender was made in escrow and refused by the vendors. There was no error.

Basically, the vendees contend they could have fully performed, if given more time, and that they should be entitled to the same benefits to which they would have been entitled in a strict foreclosure proceeding. If we were writing on a clean slate, we would hold that a vendor's lien under a land sale contract may be enforced only through judicial proceedings, absent a voluntary relinquishment by the vendee of whatever rights he has in the property. By requiring a judicial proceeding, the adequacy of any notice required would be subject to judicial scrutiny and, even though the vendee may end up losing the property and all he has paid in, the harshness of that result could be tempered by the court's granting a period of time during which the vendee might exercise his equity of redemption, yet still protecting the vendor's right to be paid in full or to a return of the property. However, the vendors here were entitled to rely on *Elsasser*, and we are obliged to follow it.

From what we have said, it is apparent that we have concluded that, although much of what the Supreme Court has said and done with respect to the nature of a vendor's interest under a land sale contract, particularly relating to non-judicial forfeitures, bears a resemblance to a fan dance, the court in *Elsasser* indicated it intends to tango. So we pick up that beat, although reluctantly. Whether, and how, the law is to be changed is up to that court.

The judgment of the trial court is affirmed.

Page 273, add as a new paragraph to Note 2:

Not all California appellate courts appear yet to have recognized the four vendee rights delineated above or that installment land contracts are "legally obsolete." In Kosloff v. Castle, 115 Cal.App.3d 369, 171 Cal.Rptr. 308 (1981) achieve equity under all of the circumstances, as opposed to the vendor's unilateral determination.

vendor declared a forfeiture of a contract after vendee had been in default on a final "balloon" payment for approximately a year and a half. A few months later, vendor filed an action in unlawful detainer and to quiet title. The trial court refused to permit the vendee to tender the contract balance and granted vendor his requested relief. The vendee appealed. The Court of Appeal, First District, affirmed the trial court and stated:

> Appellant urges us to complete the land sale reform initiated by Barkis v. Scott, supra, 34 Cal.2d 116, 208 P.2d 367, and ending prematurely with MacFadden v. Walker, supra, 5 Cal.3d 809, 97 Cal.Rptr. 537, 488 P.2d 1353, by today holding that the land sale contract is a mortgage under Civil Code section 2924. That section states in part that, "Every transfer of an interest in property, other than in trust, made only as a security for the performance of another act, is to be deemed a mortgage * * *" If we were to so hold, appellant would then be entitled to a right of redemption under Civil Code 2924c. One of the area's foremost commentators argues persuasively for appellant's position. (Hetland, Secured Real Estate Transactions (1974) § 2.12, pp. 59–61.)
>
> We decline to hold that the agreement in the case before us is a mortgage as defined in Civil Code section 2924. We believe that any reform in this area is more appropriately initiated by the Legislature which is in a better position to effect and coordinate comprehensive answers to the many-faceted questions that such a determination would evoke. It recently effected such an overhaul in the area of liquidated damages. (Civ.Code, §§ 1671, 1675–1681.) It specifically excepted the real estate contract from those provisions (Civ.Code, § 1681), incidentally indicating that it is not unaware of the independent existence of this type of contract.

Page 276, add as a second and third paragraph to Note 1:

Consider also Professor Durham's comments in connection with the Ohio statute that "[u]nlike defaults on land contracts not covered by [Ohio Rev.Code §§ 5313.01–10] where Ohio courts have clearly been inclined to give vendee's equitable relief, the vendee subject to statutory forfeiture may find himself faced with a judge who either feels constrained by the statute from granting equitable relief or takes comfort in the simplicity of the statute and ignores the possibility of equitable action." Durham, Forfeiture of Residential Land Contracts in Ohio: The Need for Further Reform of a Reform Statute, 16 Akron L.Rev. 397 (1983).

Page 277, insert before Nemec v. Rollo:

NELSON AND WHITMAN, REAL ESTATE FINANCE LAW *

113–117 (2nd Ed. 1985)

If the installment land contracts were governed exclusively by the law of mortgages, the vendor's remedies in the event of vendee default would be both clearly defined and relatively simple. The vendor could choose to foreclose the contract and, if less than the contract price is obtained at the foreclosure sale and anti-deficiency legislation were not a problem, seek a deficiency judgment against the vendee for that

---

* Reprinted with permission of West Publishing Co.

difference. Alternatively, if the contract imposed personal liability for the contract amount on the vendee, vendor could sue on the contract debt and attempt to collect any judgment obtained from vendee's other assets, including from the contract land.

Unfortunately, in few, if any, jurisdictions will the vendor's remedies be that unambiguous. In some jurisdictions, the installment land contract is still largely regarded as a contract and, as such, is governed primarily by contract principles. In others, courts apply an often-confusing amalgam of contract and mortgage law. This "split personality" often exists even in those states that have taken the greatest strides in treating the installment land contract as a mortgage because the courts in those jurisdictions have yet to confront the myriad issues and implications that the mortgage characterization ultimately creates.

Whatever the conceptual basis relied upon, vendors may well have a variety of non-forfeiture remedies against a defaulting vendee. While such remedies have traditionally received little attention because of pervasive emphasis on the forfeiture remedy, as the latter remedy becomes increasingly less reliable, alternatives will receive increasing attention. The following material explores the analytical underpinnings of certain non-forfeiture remedies and the practical considerations incident to their use.

Specific Performance for the Price

Under this remedy, the vendor chooses to treat the installment land contract like an earnest money contract and, consequently, tenders title to the land and seeks an order requiring the vendee to pay the remainder of the contract purchase price. While many courts will grant specific performance to the vendor under such circumstances [5] a few, like the minority of courts in the earnest money contract context [6] require the vendor to show that there is an inadequate remedy at law.[7]

However, it should be emphasized that the specific performance remedy is conceptually more problematical in the installment land contract setting than in the earnest money contract situation. This is because the latter contract typically contemplates the payment of the balance of the contract price on one closing date, whereas the installment land contract, as a financing device, is paid in installments over a long period of time. Thus, if an earnest money vendee defaults on the closing date, a suit for the full contract price seems conceptually uncomplicated. On the other hand, in the case of the installment land contract default, it is more difficult to envisage a suit for more than the installments actually in default. Consequently, it could be argued that a condition precedent to the granting of specific performance for the

---

5. See e.g., Simon Home Builders, Inc. v. Pailoor, 357 N.W.2d 383 (Minn.App. 1984); SAS Partnership v. Schafer, ___ Mont. ___, 653 P.2d 834 (1982); Glacier Campground v. Wild Rivers, Inc., 182 Mont. 389, 597 P.2d 689 (1978); Renard v. Allen, 237 Or. 406, 391 P.2d 777 (1964).

6. See Centex Homes Corp. v. Boag, 128 N.J.Super. 385, 320 A.2d 194 (1974); Suchan v. Rutherford, 90 Idaho 288, 410 P.2d 434 (1966).

7. See e.g., Williamson v. Magnusson, 336 N.W.2d 353 (N.D.1983).

balance of the contract price should be an acceleration clause allowing the vendor to declare the entire contract amount due and payable upon vendee breach. In the absence of such a clause, the vendor conceivably could be left with the undesirable option of suing only for the past due installments plus interest. In any event, it clearly is prudent for the vendor to include such an acceleration clause in such an installment contract.

Where the specific performance remedy is available, a vendor normally would use it where the vendee has assets to satisfy a judgment for the price and the land is now worth less than the contract price. In this relatively rare situation, the forfeiture remedy, assuming it is otherwise available, should be avoided because of the election of remedies rule (which we consider later in this section), which may prevent any further relief against the vendee. Specific performance, on the other hand, would entail a judgment for the full price which would be collectible by a judicial sale of all or any of the vendee's assets, including the contract real estate.[8]

Foreclosure by Sale of the Vendee's Rights

This remedy, where permitted, allows the vendor to treat the installment land contract as a mortgage and results in a judicial sale of the land. If the sale brings more than the contract price, the surplus will go to the vendee. If the sale yields less than the contract amount, a deficiency judgment against the vendee often is available. It should be noted that in those states that have opted to equate the installment land contract with the mortgage, the vendor may have little choice but to pursue the foreclosure remedy. In those states where the mortgage status of the installment land contract is less clear, courts often indicate a willingness to allow the vendor to utilize the foreclosure remedy.[10] In still other jurisdictions, however, the vendor's ability to choose the foreclosure remedy seems more doubtful in that the vendor would be seeking a mortgage remedy under a device governed to a greater extent by the law of contracts. In such situations it is advisable to include in the installment land contract itself language specifically affording the vendor the foreclosure option.

Strict Foreclosure

A number of states, including some with no tradition of foreclosing installment contracts by sale, will award strict foreclosure to a vendor.[12]

---

8. See Glacier Campground v. Wild Rivers, Inc., 182 Mont. 389, 597 P.2d 689 (1978).

10. See e.g., Ulander v. Allen, 37 Colo. App. 279, 544 P.2d 1001 (1976); Mustard v. Sugar Valley Lakes, 7 Kan.App.2d 340, 642 P.2d 111 (1981). Ryan v. Kolterman, 215 Neb. 355, 338 N.W.2d 747 (1983); Lamont v. Evjen, 29 Utah 2d 266, 508 P.2d 532 (1973). See generally, Annot., Vendor's Remedy by Foreclosure of Contract for Sale of Real Property, 77 A.L.R. 270 (1932).

12. See, e.g., Canterbury Court, Inc. v. Rosenberg, 224 Kan. 493, 582 P.2d 261 (1978); Ryan v. Kolterman, 215 Neb. 355, 338 N.W.2d 747 (1983); Swaggart v. McLean, 38 Or.App. 207, 589 P.2d 1170 (1979); Kallenbach v. Lake Publications, Inc., 30 Wis.2d 647, 142 N.W.2d 212 (1966). See generally Randolph, Updating the Oregon Installment Land Contract, 15 Wil.L.Rev. 181, 211–12 (1979); Vanneman, Strict Foreclosure of Land Contracts, 14 Minn.L. Rev. 342 (1930); Annot., supra note 10.

The effect of this remedy is much like a judicial declaration of forfeiture: the contract is cancelled and the vendor's title to the land is confirmed.[13] However, it differs from forfeiture in that the court will fix a redemption period within which the purchaser and assignees[14] of the purchaser's interest may specifically enforce the contract by tendering the balance due.[15] Only if this is not done will the contract be cancelled. Because strict foreclosure, like forfeiture, deprives the vendee of any "equity" he or she may have accumulated in the property, some courts will award it only upon a showing that the land has no value in excess of the contract balance.[16] If there is excess value, some of the courts will decree a judicial sale instead.[17]

Suit for Damages

Another remedy arguably available to the vendor is an action for damages.[18] The vendor's damages will probably be measured by the difference between the contract price and the fair market value of the land as of the date of the vendee's breach, the standard normally applied in earnest money contract settings. The pursuit of this remedy, however, is only possible where the vendee has abandoned the land. This is so because where the forfeiture remedy is necessary to regain the land the damages action will probably be barred by the election of remedies doctrine referred to earlier and next considered in this section. Moreover, the vendor faces the unenviable prospect of having to convince a court or jury that the land, as of the date of the breach, was worth less than the contract price. Obviously, if the vendee has assets to satisfy a judgment, vendor would be better off, where possible, suing for specific performance for the price or seeking to foreclose the contract as a mortgage. If the foreclosure sale yields less than the contract price, vendor can then usually obtain a deficiency judgment

---

Some courts routinely give strict foreclosure without calling it such; they simply award a "grace period" for the purchaser to pay the contract, and declare a forfeiture if he or she does not do so. See Jesz v. Geigle, 319 N.W.2d 481 (N.D.1982); Moeller v. Good Hope Farms, 35 Wn.2d 777, 215 P.2d 425 (1950) (grace period discretionary).

13. Some cases explicitly treat forfeiture and strict foreclosure as alternatives available to the vendor; see Zumstein v. Stockton, 199 Or. 633, 264 P.2d 455 (1953); Walker v. Nunnenkamp, 84 Id. 485, 373 P.2d 559 (1962).

14. See, e.g., Westfair Corp. v. Kuelz, 90 Wis.2d 631, 280 N.W.2d 364 (App.1979) (assignee of mechanics' lien or of vendee has right to redeem in strict foreclosure proceeding).

15. There is a further distinction. If the vendor declares a forfeiture, and subsequently demands or accepts payments on the contract, the court may treat his behavior as inconsistent with the forfeiture and hence as waiving it. On the other hand, acceptance of payments is entirely consistent with a vendor's demand for strict foreclosure, since until the end of the redemption period fixed by the court, the purchaser has every right to attempt to pay off the contract. See Heisel v. Cunningham, 94 Id. 461, 491 P.2d 178 (1971).

16. Ryan v. Kolterman, 215 Neb. 355, 338 N.W.2d 747 (1983); State Securities Co. v. Daringer, 206 Neb. 427, 293 N.W.2d 102 (1980).

17. Walker v. Nunnenkamp, 84 Id. 485, 373 P.2d 559 (1962); Blondell v. Beam, 243 Or. 293, 413 P.2d 397 (1966).

18. See Nemec v. Rollo, 114 Ariz. 589, 562 P.2d 1087 (App.1977).

for the deficiency.[20]

Page 282, add as a Note before the excerpt from the Mixon article:

Some state statutes ameliorate somewhat the vendor's election of remedies dilemma by authorizing, in certain limited circumstances, the award of damages to the vendor even though a contract termination election has already been made. For example, Ohio Rev.Code § 5313.10 provides that even though a judgment for cancellation of the contract has taken place, a damage award may be entered against the vendee if the latter "has paid an amount less than the fair rental value plus deterioration or destruction of the property occasioned by the vendee's use. In such case the vendor may recover the difference between the amount paid by the vendee on the contract and the fair rental value of the property plus an amount for the deterioration or destruction of the property occasioned by the vendee's use." For a recent interpretation of this provision, see Marvin v. Stemen, 68 Ohio App.2d 26, 426 N.E.2d 205 (1980). For further thoughtful analysis see Durham, Forfeiture of Residential Land Contracts in Ohio: The Need for Further Reform of a Reform Statute, 16 Akron L.R. 397 (1983).

Iowa rejects the election of remedies doctrine, but reaches the same result on the ground that it "flows from the fact that the contract between the parties has been terminated, thereby extinguishing any right to recover the unpaid purchase price". Gray v. Bowers, 332 N.W.2d 323, 325 (Iowa 1983).

Finally, the Idaho Court of Appeals has rejected the election rule entirely in the installment land contract context and has substituted for it an estoppel concept. Under this approach, "the proper inquiry should be whether the [vendee] has relied on [acts or statements by the vendor] and therefore would be unfairly prejudiced by assertion of a different inconsistent remedy. If so, the [vendor] should be bound to the remedy earlier chosen. ... Absent estoppel, he should be free to choose a different remedy." Keesee v. Fetzek, 106 Idaho 507, 681 P.2d 600 (App. 1984).

Page 286, add the following to Note 4:

For an excellent recent analysis and comparison of the impact of vendor and vendee bankruptcy, see In re Booth, 19 B.R. 53 (Bkrptcy.Utah 1982).

Page 292-293, read in connection with Note 2:

SHINDLEDECKER v. SAVAGE

Supreme Court of New Mexico, 1981.
96 N.M. 42, 627 P.2d 1241.

OPINION

PAYNE, Justice.

The plaintiff, John Shindledecker, brought suit against the defendants Savage for debts due him. He also sought to have a mortgage given him by the Savages declared superior to the claims of the other defendants and to have it foreclosed. The trial court awarded Shindledecker judgment against the Savages for the debts owed but denied all

---

20. See Glacier Campground v. Wild Rivers, Inc., 182 Mont. 389, 597 P.2d 689 (1978).

other claims. Shindledecker appeals only the trial court's refusal to recognize and foreclose his mortgage. We affirm.

The property in question was sold in 1975 by Taylor under a real estate contract to the Savages who paid $1,500 down and agreed to make monthly payments on the unpaid balance. Later, Shindledecker received from the Savages what was called a second mortgage on the property as security for several loans made to the Savages. At that time, the Savages were current in their monthly payments and all other obligations under the real estate contract. Some time after giving the "second mortgage", the Savages decided to move from the state. Although there is no evidence that they were in default on the contract, the Savages executed a document which instructed the escrow agent to release to Taylor a special warranty deed held in escrow. That deed conveyed the Savages' interest back to Taylor. Taylor, instead of creating a new escrow account with Shindledecker (the holder of the second mortgage) as buyer in place of the Savages, sold the property to the Villasenors who later conveyed the property to defendants Jacquez. From the time Taylor received the title until he sold it to the Villasenors, no payments were made on the real estate contract by Shindledecker.

Shindledecker argues that the Savages and Taylor agreed that Shindledecker could assume the real estate contract in satisfaction of the outstanding debt secured by the "second mortgage". Taylor is not a party to this lawsuit, however, and we cannot grant any relief that might be due to Shindledecker from Taylor as a result of Taylor's agreements with the Savages. We consider only the relative rights of the parties to this action.

The two issues raised on appeal are: (1) whether Shindledecker had an interest in the subject real estate which was enforceable against the Savages' equitable interest in the real estate, and (2) whether the Savages terminated or relinquished any interest they may have had in the real estate thus extinguishing any claim Shindledecker would have as against subsequent purchasers of the property.

The first issue can be alternatively stated as whether the vendee under an executory land sales contract has a mortgageable interest. The majority of courts have held that both the legal and equitable owner have mortgageable interests in the realty. Gavin v. Johnson, 131 Conn. 489, 41 A.2d 113 (1945); Sigman v. Stevens-Norton, Inc., 70 Wash.2d 915, 425 P.2d 891 (1967); see generally 55 Am.Jur.2d Mortgages § 111 (1971); Annot., 85 A.L.R. 927 (1933). Because the vendee cannot create an interest in the realty greater than his own, Campos v. Warner, 90 N.M. 63, 559 P.2d 1190 (1977), the interest acquired by the mortgagee is necessarily limited by that of the vendee. See Gavin v. Johnson, supra; Kendrick v. Davis, 75 Wash.2d 456, 452 P.2d 222 (1969). Since the mortgage is subject to the prior interest of the vendor under the sales contract, it is enforceable only if the contract is kept in force by continued performance of its terms. Sheehan v. McKinstry, 105 Or. 473, 210 P. 167 (1922).

When Shindledecker entered into the mortgage agreement with the Savages, he acquired an enforceable lien on the property subject to the prior interest of Taylor, the vendor. This interest was also limited by the amount of equity held by the Savages and was subject to continued performance under the contract. Though called a "second mortgage", the interest acquired by Shindledecker was not clothed with all the same legal rights as are generally found with second mortgages. Generally a second mortgage refers to a subsequent mortgage on a fee interest. Here the mortgage was not on a fee interest but only on the vendee's equitable interest. We follow the analysis adopted by the Washington courts in Sigman v. Stevens-Norton, Inc., supra:

> [A]ppellant [asserts] there is no substantial difference in a mortgage on purchaser's interest in a land contract and a second mortgage. There is, however, a considerable difference in that there is no lien on the fee under a mortgage on buyer's interest and forfeiture of a land contract gives the junior encumbrancer no right of redemption. * * * The term "second mortgage" means a lien right second only to a superior lien of a first mortgage on a buyer's interest in a land contract. 425 P.2d at 894.

We hold that the Savages' interest under the real estate contract was a mortgageable interest, and that Shindledecker had a valid lien on that interest.

Having held that Shindledecker did have a lien on the Savages' equitable interest in the property, we turn to the issue of whether the Savages relinquished their interest in the property and what effect it would have on the title acquired by the Jacquez. Generally, the vendor under a property sales contract can, upon default by the vendee, retake the property and retain all sums paid under the contract. Bishop v. Beecher, 67 N.M. 339, 355 P.2d 277 (1960). This right of re-entry and repossession is somewhat limited in the case, as here, where the vendee has mortgaged his equitable interest. In such a case the mortgagee cannot have his lien eclipsed by the agreement of the parties to the real estate contract to rescind it. By virtue of his mortgage, the mortgagee obtains the original purchaser's right to purchase the property for the consideration stated in the purchase contract. In other words, the mortgagee assumes the rights of the vendee under the real estate contract. As explained in First Mortgage Corporation of Stuart v. deGive, 177 So.2d 741, 746 (Fla.Dist.Ct.App.1965):

> The mortgage by a purchaser of his interest in a contract for the sale of real property merely gives the mortgagee the right to complete the purchase if the mortgagor refuses to do so, and the mortgagee takes no greater rights than the purchaser had. In other words, the mortgagee acquires a right to purchase the property for the consideration stipulated in the contract of purchase, and the enforceability of the mortgage depends upon the condition that the

contract be kept in force by the subsequent performance of its terms. Young v. Clay [139 Or. 427, 10 P.2d 602 (1932)]; Sheehan v. McKinstry [105 Or. 473, 210 P. 167 (1922)]; Nelson v. Bailey, 1959, 54 Wash.2d 161, 338 P.2d 757, 73 A.L.R.2d 1400; 59 C.J.S. Mortgages § 184.

We recognize the right in the mortgagee to assume the position of the vendee and keep the contract, and thereby his mortgage, in effect. However, even though Shindledecker had the right to assume the Savages' position under the contract, and even though there was no evidence of default by the Savages, we hold that the rights of Shindledecker must yield to the rights of the subsequent purchasers of the property.

The mortgagee of an equitable interest must protect his lien by giving notice to the vendor of his equitable interest so that he can arrange an assumption of the contract in case the vendee defaults or otherwise rescinds the contract. Recording the mortgage does not give the vendor constructive notice such as to require the vendor to notify the mortgagee of his intent to retake the property. Kendrick v. Davis, supra. Instead, the mortgagee must use one of several available contractual devices to insure that he receives both notice of a breach by the vendee and the opportunity to protect his interests.

Finally, Shindledecker argues that the powers of equity should be exercised by this Court to allow his mortgage to be enforced against the Jacquez. We do not see how the equities favor Shindledecker. The equities in this case favor the Jacquez, the innocent purchasers. Shindledecker had the opportunity to take the necessary steps to put Taylor on notice and protect against a default in the real estate contract. The Jacquez, on the other hand, had no knowledge of any agreements between the Savages, Shindledecker, and Taylor, and a title search would have revealed nothing to indicate possible defects in their title.

For the foregoing reasons the trial court's judgment is affirmed.

It is so ordered.

EASLEY, C. J., and RIORDAN, J., concur.

NOTES

1. The principal case is noted at 13 New Mex.L.Rev. 177 (1983).

2. Is the court correct in stating that "we do not see how the equities favor Shindledecker" and "a title search by [the Jacquez] would have revealed nothing to indicate possible defects in their title."? In fact, both the Taylor-Savage contract and the Savage-Shindledecker mortgage were recorded. (The editors have seen the documents.) How could the Jacquez not be deemed to have constructive notice of Shindledecker's rights? If, however, the court assumed only the Shindledecker mortgage was recorded, perhaps the court really meant that the mortgage is akin to a stray deed that is outside the chain of title because an examination of a county name-index would not have revealed it. Under this reasoning, the Jacquez could not, as a matter of law, be held to have had notice of it. See Casebook at 203–204, supra. Moreover, abstractors in New Mexico routinely maintain tract indexes and thus had the

Jacquez examined an extended abstract of title they most likely would have discovered an entry that referred to the Shindledecker mortgage, even if the Taylor-Savage contract was unrecorded.

In any event, suppose Taylor had received the requisite actual knowledge of the Shindledecker mortgage. Would the court somehow have concluded that the Jacquez lost their status as innocent purchasers with respect to the Shindledecker mortgage?

Page 294, add as Note 5:

5. To what extent should a contract vendee who "resells" his or her land on a second installment land contract be entitled to notice from the original vendor prior to a declaration of forfeiture of the first contract? Consider the following holding and language of the Montana Supreme Court in Roberts v. Morin, ___ Mont. ___, 645 P.2d 423 (1982):

On October, 12, 1977, appellants [the Robertses, vendees under the first contract] entered into a contract for the sale of the property to Warren and Kathy Iverson [vendees under the second contract]. The contract provided that the Iversons would assume the Robertses' obligations to Morin [vendor under first contract] and that upon completion of the Iversons' obligations to the Robertses, the Robertses would assign their interest in the Morin contract to the Iversons. Pursuant to this agreement an assignment of contract was drawn up to be placed in escrow and a consent to assignment was drawn and signed by Morin and placed in escrow with the assignment. Morin was aware at this time that the Robertses were selling to the Iversons on a separate contract.

Unknown to the Robertses the title company mistakenly filed the assignment of record before delivering the contract and related papers to escrow. Further, the escrow agent of the parties treated the contract as presently assigned and set up separate escrow files for the Roberts-Iverson contract and the Iverson-Morin contract. The result was that the Iversons made payments through escrow to the Robertses and payments through escrow to Morin.

Personal and financial problems beset the Iversons in 1979, resulting in their separation and falling behind on the escrow payments. The Iversons missed a payment to Morin early in 1979, but no action was taken on the part of Morin to enforce the time of the essence clause in the contract. The Iversons' last payment to Morin was on January 17, 1980. Morin sent a notice of default to the Iversons * * * after the Iversons missed their payment. Later, upon expiration of the sixty-day default period, Morin sent a notice of forfeiture to the Iversons * * * and took possession. Meanwhile, the Robertses, though having trouble with the timeliness of the payments from the Iversons, received payments until July 1980.

Morin sent no notice of default or forfeiture to the Robertses, nor did the Iversons inform the Robertses that they had defaulted on the Morin contract until July or August 1980. On August 18, 1980, the Robertses' attorney requested a statement of the balance due from Morin's attorney and offered to cure the default. This offer was rejected. On September 10, 1980, Robertses' attorney sent a written tender of payment to Morin and to her attorney, offering to pay the amount in default and related costs together with interest from the date of the last payment by Iversons to the date of tender, a total of $7,552.61 plus interest, in exchange for a deed from Morin. This offer was rejected, but the amount of the offer was not disputed.

On September 17, 1980, the Robertses commenced suit to compel Morin to accept their tender and deliver her deed, or for damages. Throughout the proceedings, Robertses have offered to pay the above-stated amount.

* * *

[The trial court entered judgment in favor of Morin and awarded her the property. The Robertses appealed.]

* * *

The first issue presented by appellants is whether they were entitled to notice prior to Morin defaulting the Iverson contract. The contract provides that notice of default be sent to the "buyer" at 1318 Defoe. Morin interpreted this to mean that notice of default had to be sent only to the address of the "buyer" named in the original contract, regardless of the assignments. The problem with this type of notice is that it fails in this situation to take into account the Robertses interest in the property.

Although there is no specific case or statute dealing directly with this situation, there is an analogy in the law that provides a sufficient rationale for notice to be given in this instance. In Chambers v. Cranston (1976), 16 Wash.App. 543, 558 P.2d 271, it was held:

> "The purchaser in an executory real estate contract has an interest which he can mortgage. Sigman v. Stevens-Norton, Inc., 70 Wash.2d 915, 425 P.2d 891 (1967); Nelson v. Bailey, 54 Wash.2d 161, 338 P.2d 757, 73 A.L.R.2d 1400 (1959). If the purchaser has mortgaged his interest, the mortgagee is entitled to notice of forfeiture if the seller knows of the mortgage, and the mortgagee has the right to tender payments to the seller necessary to protect his security, i.e., to keep the contract in effect."

558 P.2d at 273. See also, MacFadden v. Walker (1971) 5 Cal.3d 809, 97 Cal.Rptr. 537, 488 P.2d 1353.

The situation presented here and the situation presented above are not substantially dissimilar. Here, the Robertses assigned the duty of paying on the Morin contract to the Iversons but did not assign their interest to the Iversons. Further, the Iversons did not "assume" in the strict legal sense the contract of the Robertses but merely agreed, in writing, to pay Morin directly the amount that the Robertses had been initially paying according to their contract assignment. The fact that the assignment was duly recorded by the title company does not affect the intent of the parties, and it has no legal effect on the transaction itself. 66 Am.Jur.2d Records and Recording Laws, sec. 98.

The important similarity lies in the fact that here, as in *Chambers,* supra, there was a retained interest in the land. In *Chambers,* the court held that because Citizens Savings and Loan Association was the mortgagee it had "* * * the right to notice of default and to an opportunity to keep the contract in effect * * *" 558 P.2d at 274. The Robertses should have had that same opportunity. They were entitled to a notice of default because they retained an interest, similar to a mortgagee's interest, in the property, and Morin was aware of that interest.

[The supreme court then held that the Robertses should be permitted to redeem by paying to Morin the amount due on the first contract.]

Suppose the Iversons now have the money to redeem the second contract. Since they were provided with notice of forfeiture of the first contract, has their interest in the second contract automatically been wiped out? To what extent are the issues discussed in Note 3 supra relevant?

Suppose that the second contract had never been executed, but that instead the Iversons had simply paid the Robertses for their "equity" in one lump sum cash payment and that the latter had assigned all of their rights in the first contract to the Iversons. Would Morin have been required to provide notice to the Robertses under such circumstances?

Page 294, insert prior to Cascade Security Bank v. Butler:

ESTATE OF BREWER v. IOTA DELTA CHAPTER, TAU KAPPA EPSILON FRATERNITY, INC.

Court of Appeals of Oregon, 1984.
69 Or.App. 82, 686 P.2d 393.

Before BUTTLER, P.J., and WARREN and ROSSMAN, JJ.

BUTTLER, Presiding Judge.

Plaintiff brought this action to quiet title to real property consisting of a house and lot which plaintiff's decedent previously had sold on a land sale contract to defendant Iota Delta Chapter, Tau Kappa Epsilon Fraternity, Inc. (Chapter). Defendant TKE House Fund, Inc. (House Fund) counterclaimed, contending that, as the holder of an equitable mortgage on the vendee's interest in the property, it is entitled either to judicial foreclosure of that lien or to specific performance of the land sale contract between plaintiff's decedent and Chapter. The trial court granted plaintiff's motion for summary judgment and denied defendant House Fund's similar motion. House Fund appeals from the resulting final judgment quieting title in plaintiff.

The essential facts are not in dispute. On April 28, 1965, Gail and Mildred Brewer, husband and wife sold the property in question by land sale contract to Eleanor Johnson and Lydia Nissen. After acquiring Johnson's interest, Nissen assigned her vendee's interest to defendant Chapter on June 5, 1972, at which time the unpaid contract balance was $12,196.55. To make the down payment, the Chapter obtained a loan of $9,200 from House Fund. A condition of the loan was that House Fund be given a mortgage on the vendee's interest in the contract. On July 11, 1972, House Fund recorded in the deed records of Jackson County an installment promissory note, dated May 15, 1972, in the amount of $9,200 with interest at 6 percent per annum, to which was attached a legal description of the property. The parties agree that House Fund acquired an equitable mortgage on the vendee's interest by virtue of that documentation and recording.

In April, 1973, Gail Brewer (Mildred Brewer had died earlier) and defendant Chapter entered into an agreement amending their contract to provide that Brewer would loan $3,000 to the Chapter, thereby increasing the unpaid contract balance to $15,563.05. That agreement expressly recognized the interest of House Fund by providing that

$2,000 of the loan proceeds would be paid to House Fund "in partial payment of a second mortgage loan on the property * * *."

During 1974, the Chapter was unable to pay its debts including the contract payments, and in August or September of that year its advisor, Terry Adams, delivered the keys to Brewer and stated that the Chapter would be unable to continue purchasing the property. At that time, Adams gave Brewer the name, address, and telephone number of the person at House Fund with whom Brewer should speak regarding the House Fund's interest in the premises. Brewer took possession of the property and, without contacting House Fund, resold the premises to third-party defendants Krebs on October 1, 1974. On February 19, 1976, Krebs sold the property to third-party defendant Lenchner, who assigned his interest in the contract to third-party defendant Crowley on October 8, 1979.

By letter of September 29, 1975 after Brewer's sale to Krebs, Brewer's attorney, Lombard, notified House Fund of the Chapter's default and asserted that House Fund had no further interest in the property. He also informed House Fund that he was filing a suit for strict foreclosure and requested that House Fund execute a bargain and sale deed relinquishing its interest. That suit was filed in September, 1975; however, it was dismissed without prejudice in December, 1976.

The attorney for House Fund, Leagre, responded to Lombard's letter on November 14, 1975, stating that he was reviewing the law regarding the bargain and sale deed. On January 7, 1976, Leagre asserted the validity of House Fund's equitable lien, and Lombard agreed to provide authority to the contrary. More than a year later, on August 25, 1977, Lombard sent Leagre a legal memorandum outlining Brewer's position, with a letter stating that he was filing a new action to quiet title, which he did on that date. Leagre, in turn, submitted a memorandum to Lombard in October, 1977, and proposed a settlement whereby House Fund would relinquish its interest in the property for $9,200, an amount less than that owing under House Fund's loan to Chapter. That offer was rejected the next month, at which time Lombard requested that House Fund obtain local counsel and appear in the pending quiet title action. House Fund did retain local counsel, who obtained an extension of time within which to appear while the parties negotiated. In February and April, 1978, House Fund made other settlement offers of $9,500 and $9,650 and stated that it would seek specific performance of the Chapter's contract if no settlement was reached. On December 27, 1978, the court dismissed without prejudice the quiet title proceeding for want of prosecution. The present action was filed in March, 1980.

Although the trial court concluded that a vendee, by voluntary relinquishment of its interest to the vendor, may not terminate a mortgagee's interest when the vendor has knowledge of that interest, it found that defendant House Fund had neglected, for an unreasonable and unexplained length of time, to assert its claim of an equitable lien,

which resulted in prejudice to plaintiff. The court thus held that House Fund's claim was barred by laches. Plaintiff concedes that the trial court erred in raising and deciding that issue, which was not raised or affirmatively pled by either party as required by ORCP 19 B.
* * *

The underlying issue is whether the rights of a holder of an equitable lien on the vendee's interest in real property are extinguished when, without more, the vendee has abandoned its interest in the property and the vendor has actual knowledge of the lienholder's interest. As we noted in Braunstein v. Trottier, 54 Or.App. 687, 689, 635 P.2d 1379 (1981), rev. den. 292 Or. 568, 644 P.2d 1129 (1982), because the rights, duties and interests of parties to a land sale contract are, for the most part, creations of the courts, they have evolved piecemeal and not always harmoniously. The same may be said of cases in which the rights, duties and interests of an equitable lienholder have been discussed. However, to the extent that House Fund claims that it is entitled to judicial foreclosure of its equitable mortgage against the property, that claim may be disposed of summarily. If anything is clear from the cases, it is that the holder of an equitable mortgage on a vendee's interest under a land sale contract has no lien on the property. Sanders v. Ulrich, 250 Or. 414, 443 P.2d 231 (1968); State Hwy. Comm. v. Demarest, 263 Or. 590, 503 P.2d 682 (1972). As a matter of law, plaintiff is entitled to prevail on that claim.

There remains, however, the question whether House Fund is entitled to assert any claims under the land sale contract even though the vendee, its assignor, may not, because the vendee abandoned the property and its contract rights. There are no Oregon cases in point, and the cases dealing with equitable mortgages contain language that appears to create cross-currents. Although all of the cases recognize that an assignment of a vendee's interest given to secure a debt creates an equitable mortgage or lien on the interest assigned in favor of the assignee, it is not clear whether that lien survives after the vendee unilaterally has extinguished its interest. There is no doubt that a vendee's abandonment of the property extinguishes *its* interest in it, Hull v. Clemens et al., 200 Or. 533, 267 P.2d 225 (1954), or that a vendee who abandons the property is not entitled to notice of default and a defined opportunity to cure before a forfeiture may be effected. Morgan v. Baunach, 68 Or.App. 496, 684 P.2d 589 (June 6, 1984).

It is also clear that, as a general proposition, the holder of an equitable mortgage acquires no greater interest than that of the vendee-mortgagor. *Young v. Clay,* 139 Or. 427, 10 P.2d 602 (1932). In that case, the court stated that it subscribed to the doctrine set forth in 41 C.J. 478, which it quoted:

"'A mortgage given by one holding land under an executory contract for the purchase covers his interest, whatever it may be, at the date of the mortgage, giving the mortgagee the right to complete the purchase if his mortgagor refuses to do so; and *the mortgagee* *cannot be ousted of his rights by a rescission of the contract of sale by the original parties to it.* But the mortgagee will take no other or greater rights than the vendee had, that is he will acquire simply a right to purchase the property for the consideration stipulated in the contract of purchase, or to require a conveyance of the estate from the vendor according to the terms of the agreement, on completing the payment of the purchase price. * * *

"'It is a general rule that, where a mortgage contains full covenants of warranty, a title acquired by the mortgagor after its execution inures to the benefit of the mortgagee and is bound by the mortgage lien.'" 139 Or. at 432, 10 P.2d 602. (Emphasis supplied.)

Although the emphasized language is *dictum*, taking it at face value it indicates that the court has accepted the proposition that the equitable mortgagee's interest is no less than that of the vendee and, therefore, that the mortgagee may not be deprived of his rights by the unilateral act of the vendee. Stated differently, even though the vendee's rights have been terminated, either voluntarily or by the vendor pursuant to the contract, the vendee's mortgagee continues to have rights under the contract sufficient to protect its security interest, which the vendor may not ignore. Cases in other jurisdictions have adopted that rule. See Fincher v. Miles Homes of Mo., Inc., 549 S.W.2d 848 (Mo. 1977); Shindledecker v. Savage, 96 N.M. 42, 627 P.2d 1241 (1981). The facts in *Fincher* are similar to those here. In 1967, the Finchers entered in to a land sale contract by which they agreed to sell the Staceys a vacant lot for $1,200 to be paid in installments; the deed was to be delivered on payment of the total purchase price. The contract was not recorded. The Staceys purchased materials for construction of a house on the lot and gave Miles Homes a recorded deed of trust to secure the price. Because the Staceys defaulted in the payments due under the contract, the Finchers terminated their rights, which was evidenced by their acknowledgement of termination on the bottom of the contract of sale. The Finchers acknowledged that they knew of Miles Homes' lien on the property, and a month after the Staceys had relinquished their rights, the Finchers wrote Miles Homes that they had made a deal with the Staceys and that they would like to talk to Miles Homes to "get this worked out if possible." The letter said nothing about an unpaid balance on the lot or terminating the Staceys' interest for default or foreclosing any rights of Miles Homes. The Finchers later instituted a suit to quiet title claiming that the surrender of the Staceys' rights had the effect of terminating Miles Homes' rights as well.

The court concluded that Miles Homes' lien rights had not been terminated, because the Finchers had an obligation to notify it of the delinquency that existed and of their intention to forfeit the Staceys' rights under the contract. For that reason the court remanded the case for resolution on equitable principles, stating that Miles Homes was entitled to have its deed of trust foreclosed but also that the plaintiffs should have the option of paying the balance due on the deed of trust.

Because the question presented was one of first impression in that jurisdiction, the court reviewed a number of cases from other jurisdictions, including *Young v. Clay,* supra.

Although the language used in *Young v. Clay,* supra and relied on in *Fincher* is expansive, other Oregon cases contain language that may be viewed as more restrictive. In Sheehan v. McKinstry, 105 Or. 473, 210 P. 627 (1922), a vendor brought a suit for strict foreclosure of the vendee's interest under a contract. The vendee had executed a mortgage in favor of a bank, which was joined as a defendant. In granting strict foreclosure, the court stated:

> "By defendant's partial compliance with and performance of the terms of the contract an equitable interest or estate in the land had become vested in the defendant and this equitable interest or estate was subject to mortgage by him, *but the enforceability of such mortgage, as a lien against the land, depended upon the condition that the contract be kept in force by the subsequent performance of its terms.*" 105 Or. at 485, 210 P. 627. (Emphasis supplied.)

Although plaintiff appears to rely on the emphasized language as requiring that the contract be kept in force by the vendee in order to preserve the equitable lien or, perhaps, that in order for that lien to be effective the vendee must pay off the contract and obtain legal title, we do not view it so broadly. We understand the language to say that, as a general proposition, the contract must be performed by the vendee or the equitable mortgagee in order for the equitable lien to remain viable, and that, in order for the lienholder to have a lien on the *property,* the contract must be fully executed. The court specifically provided in its disposition that either defendant could redeem the property by paying the balance owing within four months. The equitable mortgagee was protected, notwithstanding the vendee's and the mortgagee's default or the vendee's failure to redeem, so long as the mortgagee redeemed.

Although the cited Oregon authorities do not resolve the issue presented here, we believe that their rationale in recognizing the protectable interest of a mortgagee of a contract vendee's interest leads to the conclusion that House Fund's equitable mortgage could not be extinguished by the mutual cancellation of the contract by the vendor and vendee, or by the unilateral act of abandonment by the vendee, when the vendor had notice (here actual, as well as constructive) of the interest of the equitable mortgagee. Although the vendee may surrender his interest, the equitable mortgagee is entitled, if need be, to step into his shoes and, therefore, is entitled, generally, to the vendee's rights under the contract if he is willing to perform the vendee's obligations thereunder. Under the land sale contract, the vendor had a choice of remedies, including a declaration of forfeiture. In order to effect a forfeiture plaintiff would have been obligated, but for Chapter's abandonment, to give notice to Chapter of its default and to give it a reasonable time within which to pay the balance due. Elsasser v. Wilcox, 286 Or. 775, 596 P.2d 974 (1979); *Braunstein v. Trottier,* supra.

Whether that or some other notice should have been given House Fund remains to be decided.

As indicated above, the reported cases tend to equate the rights of a mortgagee of a vendee's interest with those of the vendee. However, they have done so in contexts different from that presented here—two parties, the vendor with a vendor's lien to secure the purchase price and the equitable mortgagee with a lien to secure payment of a loan. Theoretically, neither party has a right to more than repayment of the amount secured by his respective lien. Yet, in many cases one of them will receive more than is due him, regardless of how we balance their respective rights. If we were dealing with first and second mortgages in a foreclosure, the first mortgagee would be entitled to be paid first from the proceeds derived from an execution sale, the second mortgagee would then be entitled to payment and the balance, if any, would be payable to the mortgagor. Those rules would be applicable if the court in a strict foreclosure action were to order that the property be sold by sheriff's sale, as a matter of equity, or when the vendor seeks specific performance of the contract, Renard v. Allen, 237 Or. 406, 391 P.2d 777 (1964), and might be applicable in a foreclosure of a lien on the vendee's interest, which *Young v. Clay,* supra, appears to hold may be done. However, an attempt to apply them when, as here, the vendee has voluntarily forfeited its interest in the property and the contract would not work. But see *Fincher v. Miles Homes of Mo., Inc.,* supra.

We write on a clean slate and, in doing so, attempt to evaluate the equities of the two parties in an effort to determine what the rights, as between them, should be in this situation. If the equitable lienholder were not in the picture, the vendor could declare a forfeiture of the vendee's interest, accept a voluntary cancellation of the contract or reacquire the property by strict foreclosure. In any such case, the vendor may receive more than the amount owed under the contract. We see no reason why those traditional remedies, at least in concept, should be thrown askew by circumstances over which the vendor has no control, particularly when the party who has intervened in the vendor-vendee relationship has simply loaned money to the vendee and has accepted a lien on the vendee's interest to secure repayment. The lienholder's only valid interest is in being repaid the loan according to its terms and, so long as the traditional rights of the vendor do not cut off that right, they should remain intact. Accordingly, we conclude that, under the circumstances of this case, plaintiff (vendor) was obligated to notify House Fund of Chapter's default and abandonment of the contract and, at his option, either to tender the amount owing to House Fund in return for a satisfaction of its lien, or to advise House Fund of the balance owing under the contract and demand payment within a specified reasonable time, absent which House Fund's interest would be forfeited.

Because plaintiff did not give such notice and opportunity, or make such tender to House Fund, the forfeiture was ineffective as to it. Accordingly, plaintiff may obtain a decree quieting title in it if it tenders the full balance, with interest, owing to House Fund on its lien, or it may seek strict foreclosure, the counterpart of which in this case is House Fund's right to specific performance of the contract, assuming that it is ready, willing and able to pay the contract balance. It has alleged that it is, but because plaintiff's motion for summary judgment was made and granted on the theory that House Fund was barred as a matter of law from asserting its interest, that question was not before the trial court and is not before us. The trial court erred in granting plaintiff's motion for summary judgment.

Reversed and remanded.

ESTATE OF BREWER v. IOTA DELTA CHAPTER, TAU KAPPA EPSILON FRATERNITY, INC.

Supreme Court of Oregon, En Banc, 1984.
298 Or. 383, 692 P.2d 597.

JONES, Justice.

* * *

The Court of Appeals found that Chapter's interest was voluntarily relinquished or abandoned, but held that because Brewer had knowledge of the equitable mortgage House Fund's interest was not extinguished by Chapter's abandonment. The Court of Appeals also held that Brewer must either pay off the equitable mortgage to obtain clear title or allow House Fund to purchase the property for the balance of the contract.

It is established law in Oregon that a vendee's interest may be extinguished by abandonment. In Hull v. Clemens, 200 Or. 533, 267 P.2d 225 (1954), we addressed the issue of abandonment by a vendee of his interest. In *Hull*, the vendee purchased real property for $9,000. A down payment of $1,500 was made and two annual installments of $810 were paid. Because of some serious financial setbacks, the vendee told the vendor that he wished to be released from the contract, and that it was his intention to give up the land and release his interest back to the vendor. He then vacated the property. The vendor resumed possession and resold the property to another. The court discussed the concept of abandonment:

"* * *

'* * * The interest of the vendee is equitable merely, and whatever puts an end to the equitable interest—as notice, an agreement of the parties, a surrender, an abandonment—places the vendor where he was before the contract was made.'

"* * *

'No mode of terminating an equitable interest can be more perfect than a voluntary relinquishment, by the vendee, of all rights under the contract, and a voluntary surrender of the possession to the vendor. The finding of the court shows that this took place in relation to the premises in question, and that the surrender was accepted by the vendor.'" 200 Or. at 545–47, 267 P.2d 225, quoting Jennisons v. Leonard, 88 U.S. 302, 309–10, 21 Wall. 302, 309–10, 22 L.Ed. 539 (1874).

We concluded that under the facts of that case the vendee's manifest intent to abandon, coupled with actual acts of abandonment, extinguished any right of the vendee in the real property. We stated:

> "In the case at bar, the Hulls' title—an unperfected equitable title—was inchoate when they quit the property. Therefore, it was subject to abandonment. * * * Abandonment has the novel phase that it is entirely unilateral—it requires action by only the possessor of the title, right or equity which it is proposed to abandon. Rights and equities are never abandoned in favor of anyone. Therefore, Clemens' attitude was immaterial." 200 Or. at 549–51, 269 P.2d 225.

Chapter, an assignee, has no greater rights than the vendee, its assignor. In Oregon a vendee holds only an equitable interest in the land subject to the land sale contract. The vendee's interest can be mortgaged, Sheehan v. McKinstry, 105 Or. 473, 485, 210 P. 167 (1922), but the mortgagee of a vendee's interest does not have a lien on the real property. State Hwy. Comm. v. Demarest, 263 Or. 590, 609, 503 P.2d 682 (1972); Sanders v. Ulrich, 250 Or. 414, 416, 443 P.2d 231 (1968).

The relationship between vendor, vendee and the mortgagee of the vendee's interest has been previously addressed by this court. At issue is what impact a vendee's abandonment has on a mortgagee of a vendee's interest.

In *Sheehan v. McKinstry,* supra, Sheehan had sold real property to McKinstry who later mortgaged his vendee's interest to a bank. In a suit for strict foreclosure the court recognized that the vendee could mortgage his interest, but the mortgage would only be enforceable if the underlying contract was kept in force. We held that, upon termination of the contract, the mortgage would cease to be enforceable against the vendor and the property would be free and clear of any claims of the mortgagee. 105 Or. at 485–86, 210 P. 167.

In Merchant Land Co. v. Barbour, 65 Or. 235, 130 P. 976, 132 P. 710 (1913), the vendee, Graham, assigned one-half of his interest in a land sale contract to Barbour. Later, the vendee quitclaimed the entire property back to the vendor. The vendor brought suit to quiet title as to Barbour's claim of a mortgage interest in the real property. We discussed the relationship of the vendor, vendee and assignee of the vendee's interest as follows:

> "It will be observed that the writing executed by Graham November 8, 1890, and delivered to the defendant does not purport to be a conveyance of any interest in any land, neither does it convey the impression of having been agreed to by Merchant or of establish-

ing any privity of contract between him and the defendant. At best, that instrument can be construed only as attempting to define contractual relations between Graham and Barbour. * * *

"The pleading does not show any privity of estate or of contract with the plaintiff. * * * [Barbour's] grievance, if any, must be adjusted with the man with whom he contracted. His psuedo title cannot rise above its source, R.A. Graham. The latter divested himself of his estate by the deed already mentioned, and with it fell the pretensions of ownership in which the defendant may have indulged. * * *

"* * *

"* * * Barbour, having no contract with Merchant has no claim upon him. Barbour has not agreed with Merchant to purchase nor to pay $90,000. Therefore, Merchant had no one to deal with other than Graham; and on March 20, 1894, when Graham quitclaimed to Merchant, he waived the demand provided for in the fifth paragraph of the contract, and terminated and surrendered it. Consequently Barbour could not object unless before that time he had tendered the purchase price of the land. * * *" 65 Or. at 240–42, 130 P. 976.

In *Sanders v. Ulrich*, supra, the vendees assigned as security a partial interest in their contract with the vendor. The vendees defaulted on the land sale contract. In a suit for strict foreclosure a decree was entered allowing the vendees 60 days to pay the balance of the contract or be foreclosed of all their rights. The vendor accepted a quitclaim deed from the vendees and entered into possession. The assignee of the partial interest then claimed that her lien on the land was superior to the vendor's interest.

We held that the assignment of a partial interest as security was a mortgage against the vendees' interest, but that, as to the vendor, the assignee was not a mortgagee. The court observed:

"* * * [T]he [vendor] was not a party to the assignment, had no knowledge of the making of the loan by Mrs. Curtis to the purchasers until long after that transaction, and no knowledge of the execution of the assignment other than constructive notice of it when the instrument was recorded, more than a year after the contract of sale was entered into, and received no money from Mrs. Curtis. As to the plaintiff, Mrs. Curtis was not a mortgagee, but she stood in the shoes of the purchasers and her rights could rise no higher than theirs. * * * The plaintiff was under no obligation to Mrs. Curtis and the latter could demand nothing of the plaintiff except a deed upon tendering the purchase price of the land. * * * Her only claim, however, is that she has a lien on the property and that claim is without any support in law or the facts. If the purchasers are indebted to her, it is to them that she must look for satisfaction." 250 Or. at 416, 443 P.2d 231.

In *State Hwy. Comm. v. Demarest,* supra, a vendee assigned his interest in a purchase contract to secure a note. We held that the assignment created an equitable mortgage on the vendee's interest but did not create a mortgage lien on the real property. We stated:

> "The assignment by Malone to Hay was for the purpose of securing the Malone note and created an equitable mortgage as between Malone and Hay on the Malones' equitable title in the property being purchased. However, as to the vendor Demarest, the assignment by Malone does not give Hay as the assignee a mortgage lien on the property.
>
> "* * *
>
> "It is true that in *Sanders* the vendor did not know about the assignment of the purchase contract by the purchaser-assignor to the assignee, and in the instant case the trial court found that Demarest did know of the assignment. Assuming that finding to be true, we do not believe it changes the result.
>
> "Hay's rights under the assignment could not be greater than Malone's. * * *" 263 Or. at 609–10, 503 P.2d 682 (citations omitted).

The above cases consistently demonstrate that a unilateral act by the vendee can operate to cut off the rights of a party claiming through the vendee. In particular, *Sanders v. Ulrich,* supra, and *State Hwy. Comm. v. Demarest,* supra, demonstrate that abandonment by the vendee extinguishes the equitable mortgagee's interest, and that knowledge of the mortgagee's interest is irrelevant to the outcome.

There is no dispute that House Fund acquired an equitable mortgage on the Chapter's vendee's interest by virtue of the recording of the note with a legal description attached. We also agree that Chapter abandoned its interest.

Before Chapter abandoned the contract, House Fund, as an equitable mortgagee, had the right to step in to ensure that the underlying contract remained in force. The time limit for the exercise of this right is discussed in *Sheehan v. McKinstry,* supra, as follows:

> "By defendant's partial compliance with and performance of the terms of the contract an equitable interest or estate in the land had become vested in the defendant and this equitable interest or estate was subject to mortgage by him, *but the enforceability of such mortgage, as a lien against the land, depended upon the condition that the contract be kept in force by the subsequent performance of its terms.*" 105 Or. at 485, 210 P. 167 (emphasis supplied).

Once the contract was abandoned by Chapter, the contract was no longer in force and House Fund lost any rights in the property. There was no contractual relationship between Brewer and House Fund. Knowledge alone did not create such a relationship. It was up to House Fund to protect its own interest. The vendor had no duty to protect the mortgagee's interest. When House Fund chose not to take the proper legal steps necessary to protect its interest before the contract was abandoned, any interest House Fund had was extinguished as a matter of law when Chapter abandoned its vendee interest.

The Court of Appeals is reversed. The trial court is affirmed for the reasons set forth in this opinion.

NOTE

Which of the two Oregon decisions makes the more serious attempt to analyze and reconcile the difficult issues inherent in the relationship between the vendor and the vendee's mortgagee? Which opinion makes more sense? It is perhaps ironic that while the *Kendrick* and *Shindledicker* courts are forced to confront the difficult decision of whether recording by the mortgagee should constitute constructive notice to the vendor, the Oregon Supreme Court avoids the issue altogether by holding that the vendor's knowledge of the mortgagee is simply irrelevant. To what extent will the Oregon approach, to use the language of the *Fincher* court, "open the door to connivance for the purpose of eliminating the rights of the [vendee's mortgagee]"?

Suppose the main financing device in *Brewer* had been a mortgage instead of an installment land contract. Could a first mortgagee take a deed in lieu of foreclosure and, in so doing, wipe out the interest of a junior lienor? See Nelson and Whitman, Real Estate Finance Law §§ 6.18–6.19 (2nd Ed. 1985). Is the Oregon Supreme Court affording the delivery of the keys greater preclusive effect than a deed in lieu?

Will Oregon lenders hereafter be willing to make loans on the security of a vendee's interest? Should the lender simply refuse to lend money unless the vendor agrees to notify it of a potential contract termination and afford it the opportunity to protect its interest? If such an approach is impractical, should the vendee be required to make the contract payments to the mortgagee so that the latter can pay the vendor and thus prevent the contract from going into default? Or will the mortgagee simply be required to make regular inquiries of the vendor as to the status of the contract?

Page 301, add the following to Note 2:

Consider the following commentary in this regard:

The *Freeborn* approach has been followed by several other courts.[11] The court's basic thrust, which is to analogize installment contracts to notes secured by mortgages, is a trend ... we applaud. Under this analysis, the case is correct in part and wrong in part. It is now becoming clear that Article 9 of the UCC is applicable to the perfection of security interests in mortgage notes. On this point *Freeborn* is right. True, the method of perfection for notes, which is the transfer of possession to the secured party, is probably inapplicable to installment contracts, since they are evidently not "instruments" as the UCC employs the term.[14] Hence, an installment

---

11. Southwest National Bank v. Southworth, 22 B.R. 376 (Bkrtcy.Kan.1982) (both realty and Code filing necessary); In re Shuster, 47 B.R. 920 (D.Minn.1985) (Code filing necessary, no decision as to realty filing); S.O.A.W. Enterprises v. Castle Rock Industrial Bank, 32 B.R. 279 (Bkrtcy. Tex.1983) (Code filing sufficient); In re Equitable Development Corp., 20 U.C.C.Rep. Serv. 1349 (S.D.Fla. 1976) (Code filing sufficient).

14. See U.C.C. § 9–105(g), defining an "instrument" as a paper "of a type which is in the ordinary course of business transferred by delivery with any necessary in-

contract is correctly understood to be a "general intangible" in the Code's parlance, and a security interest in it must be perfected by the filing of a financing statement.[15]

But it is with respect to the real property interest that *Freeborn's* attempt to assimilate installment contracts to mortgages breaks down. It is well recognized that an assignment of a mortgage note will carry the mortgage with it automatically, and the cases are increasingly taking the view that, even when the transfer is for security purposes, the mortgage will attach to the note when it is delivered into the hands of the pledgee, and will be regarded as perfected irrespective of whether any assignment was recorded in the real estate records. *Freeborn* displays no awareness of these cases, and instead insists on treatment of the realty interest as a separate species which must be perfected (by recording) in its own right.

Surely this is a waste of effort. Separation of the real estate interest from the payment stream may be conceptually possible, but it is meaningless in practical terms. If one holds the realty interest but has no right to the payments, his interest has no value. He obviously cannot sue for damages, specific performance, or any other money remedy. He cannot declare a forfeiture, for the reason that there is no debt owed to him. His "rights" are as empty and useless as those of a mortgagee when someone else holds the note; they are nugatory.

Why, then, put the pledgee of the vendor's interest at risk of losing his security in the land if he does not record in the real estate records? Certainly one recording—in the financing statement files—is sufficient, once practitioners and the public know that they must search there. No policy is served by forcing everyone to use both belt and suspenders. The court, we suggest, should simply have carried the mortgage law analogy to its logical conclusion and held the Code filing sufficient for complete perfection. The only objection to this view is that it is contrary to long-established habits in many areas; but once the law is clarified, those habits can readily be changed.

Nelson and Whitman, Real Estate Finance Law § 3.37 (2nd Ed. 1985).*

---

dorsement or assignment." Customs vary from one area of the nation to another, but it would be difficult to say that there is a broad custom of transferring or pledging installment contracts by delivery of the original contract document. Perfection of a security interest in an "instrument" can be accomplished only by delivery; see U.C.C. § 9–304(1).

15. U.C.C. § 9–106. A security interest in a "general intangible" can be perfected only by filing a financing statement; see U.C.C. § 9–304, Comment 1. See cases cited at note 11 supra.

* Reprinted with permission of West Publishing Co.

Chapter 4

RIGHTS AND DUTIES OF THE PARTIES PRIOR TO FORECLOSURE: SOME PROBLEM AREAS

A. THEORIES OF TITLE: POSSESSION, RENTS, AND RELATED CONSIDERATIONS

Page 318, add at bottom of page:

TAYLOR v. BRENNAN

Supreme Court of Texas, 1981.
621 S.W.2d 592.

McGEE, Justice.

This is a suit for damages for waste of security involving the interpretation of an assignment of rentals instrument executed in connection with the purchase of realty. The trial court rendered judgment against the purchaser for waste of security and failure to refund security deposits, plus attorneys' fees. The court of civil appeals affirmed. 605 S.W.2d 657. We reverse that part of the judgment of the court of civil appeals which awarded damages against Taylor for waste of security. We affirm the remainder of the judgment of the court of civil appeals.

In January, 1974, T. C. Brennan, Jr., sold the Sagewood Apartments, located in Houston, to James S. Taylor, Jr. The conveyance was made subject to a first lien deed of trust and an assignment of rentals in favor of First Continental Mortgage Company. Taylor also executed a promissory note, a second lien deed of trust, an assignment of rentals, a U.C.C. security agreement and an assignment of lessor's interest in leases, all in favor of Brennan. The deed of trust and general warranty deed contained a promise by Taylor to make all payments and perform all obligations pursuant to the first lien note and the first lien in favor of First Continental. However, the parties expressly agreed that Taylor would not assume any personal liability on the obligation to First Continental.

In the latter part of September, 1974, First Continental notified Brennan that Taylor had defaulted on the August and September first lien payments. Taylor was current on all second lien payments to Brennan. Taylor collected rents from tenants for August and September but did not apply them to discharge the delinquency on the first lien. Brennan responded by foreclosing on his second lien and regaining possession of the property. The first lien was not foreclosed. Once in possession, Brennan collected $4,082.64 in rents, but was forced to pay First Continental, the first lienholder, $19,976.32 for the payments due on the first lien.

Brennan sued Taylor for damages for waste of security. He alleged that the various security agreements assigned the rents from the Sagewood Apartments, and the rents were to used specifically for payment of the first lien and second lien mortgage notes. Consequently, while he was in default, Taylor's failure to apply the rents he collected to discharge the first lien payments constituted waste of security. The trial court filed findings of fact and conclusions of law. One of those conclusions of law reads as follows:

> "(3) That the Assignment of Rents (Plaintiff's Exhibit No. 8) *pledged* the rents from the tenants' leases in the Sagewood Apartments as *security* against the debts between defendant Taylor and plaintiff." (Emphasis added).

The trial court awarded Brennan damages of $19,976.32 for waste. In affirming the trial court, the court of civil appeals held that the first assignment of rentals instrument, which Taylor took the property subject to, was an absolute assignment to the first lienholder, which upon default, gave rise to a cause of action for waste of security.

Texas follows the lien theory of mortgages. Under this theory the mortgagee is not the owner of the property and is not entitled to its possession, rentals or profits. Thus, it has become a common practice to include in the deed of trust, or in a separate instrument, terms assigning to the mortgagee the mortgagor's interest in all rents falling due after the date of the mortgage as additional security for payment of the mortgage debt.

The Texas cases addressing rentals assigned as security have followed the common law rule that an assignment of rentals does not become operative until the mortgagee obtains possession of the property, or impounds the rents, or secures the appointment of a receiver, or takes some other similar action. Simon v. State Mutual Life Assur. Co., 126 S.W.2d 682 (Tex.Civ.App.—Dallas 1939, writ ref'd); McGeorge v. Henrie, 94 S.W.2d 761 (Tex.Civ.App.—Texarkana 1936, no writ).

Most jurisdictions are in accord. 59 C.J.S. Mortgages § 316 n. 71 at 411.

On the other hand, an absolute assignment of rentals operates to transfer the right to rentals automatically upon the happening of a specified condition, such as default. Kinnison v. Guaranty Liquidating Corporation, 18 Cal.2d 256, 115 P.2d 450, 453 (Cal.1941). The absolute assignment does not create a security interest but instead passes title to the rents. In Re Ventura—Louise Properties, 490 F.2d 1141 (9th Cir. 1974).

Courts have been reluctant to construe assignment of rentals clauses to operate as absolute assignments. The public policy embracing the rule was articulated by Justice Augustus Hand in Prudential Insurance Company of America v. Liberdar Holding Corp., 74 F.2d 50 (2d Cir. 1934):

"It seems unlikely that mere words of assignment of future rents can entitle a mortgagee to claim rentals which have been collected by a mortgagor and mingled with its other property. Sound policy as well as every probable intention should prevent a mortgagee from interfering with the mortgagor's possession until the mortgagee takes steps to get the rentals within his control. To hold otherwise would be to impose unworkable restrictions upon industry in cases where mortgagors have been led to suppose that they might rightfully apply the rentals to their own business."

It has also been felt that to construe the clause as an absolute assignment of rents would impose no duty upon the mortgagee to collect rents, and gives the mortgagor no assurance that the mortgagee would collect them and apply them to the debt. Osborne, G., Mortgages (2d ed. 1970) § 150 at 252.

The question before us is whether the assignment of rentals operated as an absolute assignment to Brennan so as to transfer rents automatically upon default, or a pledge to secure a debt which must be activated by some affirmative act by Brennan.

The deed, deed of trust, and assignment of rentals were executed contemporaneously on January 11, 1974, and therefore the intent of the parties is to be ascertained by construing those instruments together. Mazzola v. Lucia, 109 S.W.2d 273 (Tex.Civ.App.—Beaumont 1937, writ ref'd); Stubblefield v. Cooper, 37 S.W.2d 818 (Tex.Civ.App.—Amarillo 1930, writ dism'd w.o.j.). Accordingly, we must determine from a reading of the documents whether the parties intended the assignment of rentals to be absolute or merely a pledge. When an assignment of rentals is given as "further" or "additional" security, there is a strong indication the parties intended a pledge, Simon v. State Mutual Life Assur. Co., supra, while an absolute assignment of rentals is not security, but is a *pro tanto* payment of the obligation. Malsman v. Brandler, 230 Cal.App.2d 922, 41 Cal.Rptr. 438 (1964).

The granting clause of the assignment of rentals contains the following language:

> NOW, THEREFORE, in order *further to secure* the payment of the indebtedness of the Borrower to the Lender, * * * the said Borrower does hereby sell, assign, transfer and set over unto the Lender all of the rents, issues and profits of the aforesaid mortgaged premises." (Emphasis added).

Additionally, the assignment permits the lender at its option upon default to enter upon the premises and collect the rents accrued but unpaid, and those rents thereafter accruing and becoming payable. The deed of trust gives the lender (mortgagee) a similar right of entry and power of collection.

The foregoing language and provisions manifest an intention by the parties to create a pledge of rentals. The assignment of rentals not only states that it is "further" security for the debt, but also contemplates that the mortgagee, upon default, will be required to take some type of affirmative action pursuant to its right of entry. These facts are entirely consistent with a pledge. Our construction of the documents is further reinforced by the conclusion of law filed by the trial court. As a result, Brennan could not recover the rents collected by Taylor before Brennan took any action to foreclose the second lien.

Taylor breached an obligation to Brennan by failing to make the August and September first lien payments. Taylor's obligations to Brennan were defined by the documents attendant to the second lien mortgage. The court of civil appeals, however, construed the assignment of rentals attendant to the first lien mortgage. Since Taylor took the property "subject to" that mortgage, it was improper for the court to determine his rights with respect to Brennan by construing documents to which he was not a party and upon which he had no personal liability. In any event, as the assignment of rentals was given as further and additional security to the first lien mortgagee, it was a mere pledge and not an absolute assignment.

We reverse that part of the judgment of the court of civil appeals which awarded damages against Taylor for waste of security. We affirm the remainder of the judgment of the court of civil appeals.

WALLACE, J., not sitting.

B. RECEIVERSHIPS

Page 331, insert before Note 1:

CHASE MANHATTAN BANK, N.A. v. TURABO SHOPPING CENTER, INC.

United States Court of Appeals, First Circuit, 1982.
683 F.2d 25.

Before COFFIN, Chief Judge, PHILLIPS, Senior Circuit Judge, BOWNES, Circuit Judge.

BOWNES, Circuit Judge.

Turabo Shopping Center, Inc. (Turabo) appeals an order of the district court appointing a receiver to manage, operate, and control a shopping center owned and run by Turabo during the pendency of a mortgage foreclosure action on the center brought by Turabo's creditor and mortgagee, The Chase Manhattan Bank, N.A. (Chase). This is an appealable interlocutory order, 28 U.S.C. § 1292(a)(2).

Turabo owns and operates the shopping center, the Plaza del Carmen Shopping Center, in Caguas, Puerto Rico. In the mid-1970's, Turabo obtained interim construction financing from Chase in order to build the center and mortgaged the shopping center to Chase. Chase loaned Turabo a total of $6,799,800, all of which, according to Chase, is still owing. The amount of interest now owing is disputed, Chase claiming that it just over $3,000,000 and Turabo contending that it is closer to $2,300,000. Turabo was expected to obtain permanent financing elsewhere and to pay off Chase, but that has not come to pass. Under the terms of the mortgage agreement, Chase is now to be repaid by the assignment of rents due Turabo from tenants in the shopping center, and Chase has received some—but, Chase claims, not all—of the rents to which it is entitled. Adrian Perez-Agudo, president of Turabo, and Maria Eugenia Gonzalez de Perez are guarantors of Turabo's loan and codefendants in this foreclosure action, although only Turabo has appealed the order.

In April, 1981, Chase filed suit to foreclose on the mortgage and, approximately a month later, moved for the appointment of a receiver. After a hearing, the district court granted the motion and appointed a still-unnamed receiver with wide powers to supervise operation of the shopping center. The district court based its order on alternative grounds: first, that the twenty-first clause of the mortgage agreement entitled Chase to have a receiver appointed, and, second, that even in the absence of that clause, equity favored the appointment.

We turn first to the equitable justification for the award. Most federal court decisions dealing with the appointment of a receiver pendente lite appear to apply federal law without discussion. See Democratic Central Comm. v. D.C. Transit System, Inc., 459 F.2d 1178, 1181 (D.C.Cir.1972); Tanzer v. Huffines, 408 F.2d 42, 43 (3d Cir. 1969); Garden Homes, Inc. v. United States, 200 F.2d 299, 301 (1st Cir. 1952); CFTC v. Comvest Trading Corp., 481 F.Supp. 438, 441 (D.Mass.1979); United States v. Mansion House Center North Redevelopment Co., 419 F.Supp. 85, 87 (E.D.Mo.1976); Bookout v. Atlas Financial Corp., 395 F.Supp. 1338, 1341–42 (N.D.Ga.1974), aff'd per curiam sub nom. Bookout v. First Nat'l Mortgage & Discount Co., 514 F.2d 757 (5th Cir. 1975); Haase v. Chapman, 308 F.Supp. 399, 406 (E.D.Mo.1969). But see In re Armstrong Glass Co., 502 F.2d 159, 163–64 (6th Cir. 1974) (applying Tennessee law). We need go no further because appellant agrees that the appointment of receivers in federal court is controlled by federal law. Appellant's Brief at 11.

The law governing the appointment of receivers in federal courts has not been reduced to a convenient formula. We have observed that

> to warrant the appointment of a receiver to manage and operate [mortgaged property pending foreclosure], as well as only to collect [its] rents and profits, there must be at the least a "sufficient showing" of something more than the inadequacy of the security and the doubtful financial standing of the debtor.

Garden Homes, Inc. v. United States, 200 F.2d at 301. We did not determine what that "something more" was, but other courts have looked to such factors as

> fraudulent conduct on the part of the defendant; imminent danger that property would be lost, concealed, injured, diminished in value, or squandered; the inadequacy of the available legal remedies; the probability that harm to plaintiff by denial of the appointment would be greater than the injury to the parties opposing appointment; and the plaintiff's probable success in the action and the possibility of irreparable injury to his interests in the property.

CFTC v. Comvest Trading Corp., 481 F.Supp. at 441 (footnotes (citing cases) omitted). Also relevant are the probability that appointment of a receiver will protect the interests of the party seeking appointment and the nature of the receiver's duties. Id. The district court's ruling on a motion for appointment of a receiver will be reversed only if the court abused its discretion. Tanzer v. Huffines, 408 F.2d at 43; View Crest Garden Apartments, Inc. v. United States, 281 F.2d 844, 849 (9th Cir.), cert. denied, 364 U.S. 902, 81 S.Ct. 235, 5 L.Ed.2d 195 (1960); Garden Homes, Inc. v. United States, 200 F.2d at 302.

We believe that the district court was well within its discretion in appointing a receiver; indeed, the evidence compelled such an order. In addition to the fact that the value of the shopping center is probably inadequate to cover amounts still owed to Chase by Turabo, three pieces of essentially uncontradicted evidence showed unfair and arguably fraudulent dealing on Turabo's apart and the likelihood of continuing injury to Chase's interest in the shopping center. First, Turabo's general laxity in rent collection from shopping center tenants was especially marked in its treatment of three tenant companies run by the sister of Perez-Agudo, Turabo's president. Those companies paid no rent for a considerable period of time.[1] Second, Turabo, not having paid its lawyer and agent for obtaining tenants, allowed the lawyer to set up a restaurant[2] in the shopping center without charging rent and without signing a rental contract. The admitted reason for the absence of a contract was to prevent Chase from making a claim to rental payments from the restaurant. Finally, Perez-Agudo withheld approxi-

---

[1]. The district court was within its discretion in concluding that Chase had not agreed to forbear collection of some rents because of flood damage to the three tenants.

[2]. This lawyer, Ema Sara Portela, acted through a number of corporate entities, but the district court did not treat them as distinct, and Turabo has not argued to the contrary.

mately $100,000 in rent assigned to Chase in order, among other purposes, to retain attorneys to defend Turabo in the mortgage foreclosure action and to obtain an appraisal of the shopping center to be used in the foreclosure litigation.

Because we uphold the appointment of the receiver on equitable grounds, we have no occasion to consider the effect of the twenty-first clause of the mortgage agreement.[3]

The order of the district court is affirmed.

Page 340, add as Note 8:

8. Suppose a junior mortgagee obtains the appointment of a receiver. Must rents collected by that receiver be utilized to reduce senior mortgage debt? Consider the language of the court in Waible v. Dosberg, 83 A.D.2d 983, 443 N.Y.S.2d 621 (1981):

> "A receiver appointed at the instance of one mortgagee acts on behalf of that mortgagee and not generally on behalf of all lienholders. Sullivan v. Rosson, 223 N.Y. 217, 119 N.E. 404; Collins v. Wallens, 143 Misc. 329, 256 N.Y.S. 453. Therefore the senior mortgagee must either obtain the appointment of his own receiver or an extension of the junior receivership before rents may be collected for his benefit. Sullivan v. Rosson, supra; Kroehle v. Ravitch, 148 A.D. 54, 132 N.Y.S. 1056."

Is this a defensible policy? See Nelson and Whitman, Real Estate Finance Law § 4.43 (2nd Ed.1985).

C. INSURANCE AND REAL ESTATE TAXES

Page 341, delete Schoolcraft v. Ross and substitute the following case:

STARKMAN v. SIGMOND

Superior Court of New Jersey, 1982.
184 N.J.Super. 600, 446 A.2d 1249.

DEIGHAN, J. S. C.

The question to be resolved herein is whether plaintiff mortgagors are entitled to the proceeds of a fire insurance policy (which insures the interest of both the mortgagors and the mortgagees) to rebuild the residence or must the proceeds be applied in reduction of the mortgage where the value of the vacant land exceeds the balance due on the mortgage which has been kept current. Research has revealed no New Jersey case which addresses this problem of payment of the fire insurance proceeds where the security is not impaired and the mortgage is not in default. It is held that under the facts of this case the mortgagors are entitled to the proceeds to rebuild the residence.

---

3. Chief Judge Coffin, while concurring in this opinion, would prefer to place primary emphasis on this clause, its validity never having been put in issue below. The court's recitation of the equitable grounds, in his view, makes crystal clear that whether or not such a contract clause is sufficient, without more, to justify appointment of a receiver, the "more" exists here in abundance.

Plaintiff mortgagors Tami Starkman and Dora Birnbaum executed a purchase money mortgage to defendant mortgagees Robert Sigmond and Barbara Sigmond, his wife, in the amount of $60,000. A fire loss occurred on the mortgaged premises; mortgagees demand that the insurance proceeds be applied to the outstanding mortgage balance. Plaintiff mortgagors seek the proceeds of the fire insurance to rebuild the residence. The essential facts are not in dispute and both parties move for summary judgment.

After the complaint was filed and before filing an answer, defendant mortgagees moved for summary judgment. At the time the motion was heard the insurance company, Prudential Property and Casualty Insurance (Prudential), was not a party to the action. The court determined it should have the benefit of Prudential's position on its obligation under the insurance policy, and on August 23, 1981 denied defendants' motion. Thereafter, plaintiffs filed an amended complaint against Prudential; defendants Sigmond filed an answer and crossclaim against Prudential. Prudential filed its answer, including a third-party complaint against plaintiffs' husbands, Morris Starkman and Simon Birnbaum, asserting they were the real parties in interest.

Subsequently, Prudential agreed to issue a $135,000 check in settlement of all claims made under the insurance policy. After application by plaintiffs, the court on December 21, 1981, by consent of the parties, ordered Prudential to issue the $135,000 in two drafts: one in the sum of $60,000 payable to both mortgagees and mortgagors and the other in the sum of $75,000 payable to plaintiff mortgagors only. Thereafter, plaintiffs, defendants Sigmond and Prudential entered into a consent order to invest the $60,000 pending a determination by the court of the rights of the parties. Prudential required a release from the Sigmonds before it would issue the $60,000 check. On February 16, 1982 the court entered another consent order which provided that payment of the $60,000 would be in a nature of an interpleader. The Sigmonds were to execute the release and assert any claims against the fund which may have been asserted against Prudential.

On January 6, 1981 plaintiffs purchased a house and lot located at 112 South Sacramento Avenue, Ventnor, New Jersey from defendants for $150,000. Defendants took back a purchase money mortgage in the sum of $60,000 with interest at the rate of 10% payable in monthly amortization installments of $525. The mortgage is for a 30-year term but has a "balloon" at the end which requires full payment to be made on January 6, 1986, i.e., the entire mortgage is payable within five years. The mortgage also required the mortgagors to maintain hazard insurance on the premises for the benefit of the mortgagees. Prudential issued the insurance policy to plaintiffs as the "insureds"; defendants are listed as mortgagees on the face of the insurance policy. The loss payable clause to the mortgagee appears in the body of the policy and provides:

Loss, if any, under this policy, shall be payable to the mortgagee * *, named on the first page of this policy, as interest may appear * *, and this insurance as to the interest of the mortgagee * * *, shall not be invalidated by any act or neglect of the mortgagor * * *.

This clause is known as a "union mortgage clause" because it insulates the mortgagee from policy defenses which may be available against the mortgagor. 5A Appleman, Insurance Law and Practice, § 3401 at 282 (1970). The union mortgage clause is to be distinguished from an "open loss payable clause." Under an open loss clause the policy merely identifies who is to collect the proceeds. Ibid. "In the open form, the indemnity of the mortgagee is subject to the risk of every act and neglect of the mortgagor which would avoid the original policy in the mortgagor's hands." 5A Appleman, op. cit., § 3401 at 293.[1]

On February 23, 1981 the house was substantially destroyed by fire. On November 17, 1981 plaintiffs received notification from the building inspector of Ventnor to demolish the dwelling because the fire damage amounted to total destruction creating a dangerous situation—the walls could collapse and youngsters were playing on the rotting floors. Plaintiffs submitted a certification from a real estate appraiser evaluating the vacant land at approximately $71,500, an amount which is at least $10,000 in excess of the outstanding balance on the mortgage. Plaintiffs have kept the monthly mortgage payments current.

Plaintiffs argue that since the mortgage is not in default and the security is not impaired, defendants cannot insist on applying the proceeds of the insurance to pay off the mortgage debt. Plaintiffs place primary reliance on the terms and conditions for acceleration in the mortgage and note. Plaintiffs observe that the provisions of the note and mortgage were negotiated[2] and these documents are silent as to acceleration in the event of fire. They contend that if defendants use the proceeds to satisfy the mortgage debt, they will be deprived of the loan from defendants and defendants are currently getting what they bargained for, i.e, continuous monthly payments over a period of time.

In contrast, defendants rely on the terms of the insurance policy. They argue that the policy is an independent agreement between the insurer and the mortgagees and that their rights cannot be affected by any acts of the mortgagors in rebuilding. Defendants claim their rights under the insurance policy became vested at the time of the fire and no subsequent act of the mortgagor can defeat their right to the proceeds. Defendants suggest that payment of the $60,000 to plaintiffs will result in a windfall to plaintiffs.[3] Defendants maintain that plaintiffs will

---

1. For a short discussion of the two clauses, see 495 Corp. v. N. J. Ins. Underwriting Ass'n, 173 N.J.Super. 114, 117, n.2, 413 A.2d 630 (App.Div.1980).

2. Various provisions of the note were deleted pursuant to the negotiations.

3. $135,000 (insurance proceeds)
   + 71,500 (value of lot) =
   ―――――
   206,500
   150,000 (purchase price) =
   ―――――
   $ 56,500 (profit).

have realized $56,000 profit within a few months. While defendants acknowledge that part of the proceeds of the insurance represent a loss of contents by plaintiffs, they suggest that the contents claim would not in any way approximate $56,000.

The standard mortgage clause creates an independent contract of insurance, for the separate benefit of the mortgagee, engrafted upon the main contract of insurance contained in the policy itself. 495 Corp. v. N. J. Ins. Underwriting Ass'n, supra, 173 N.J.Super. at 123, 413 A.2d 630, citing Reed v. Firemen's Ins. Co., 81 N.J.L. 523, 526, 80 A. 462 (E. & A. 1910); 5A Appleman, op. cit., § 3401 at 292. An independent agreement exists between the mortgagee and the insurer. Employers' Fire Ins. Co. v. Ritter, 112 N.J.Eq. 418, 420, 164 A. 426 (Ch.1933). There are two beneficiaries of the insurance policy, the owner and the mortgagee, each with distinct and dissimilar rights. Id. at 421, 164 A. 426.

One line of cases and commentators state as a general rule that the mortgagee can recover the insurance proceeds regardless of the value of the remaining security once a fire loss occurs. E.g., Walter v. Marine Office of America, 537 F.2d 89, 97–99 (5 Cir. 1976) (applying Louisiana law); Savarese v. Ohio Farmer's Ins. Co., 260 N.Y. 45, 53, 182 N.E. 665, 667, (Ct.App.1932); 5A Appleman, op. cit., § 3405 at 320; 29 N.J. Practice (Cunningham & Tischler, Law of Mortgages), § 164 at 756 (1975). The rationale of these cases results from a singular approach which focuses solely on the insurance policy. The policy is categorized as an independent contract [4] between the insurer and the mortgagee. Once a fire loss occurs, the mortgagee's right to the insurance proceeds vests. Any future act of the mortgagor which restores the property to its pre-fire condition is deemed irrelevant since the mortgagee is entitled to immediate payment after the fire.

Defendants Sigmond urge that the following section of the insurance policy requires direct payment to the mortgagee:

4. Mortgage Clause

Loss, if any, under this policy, shall be payable to the mortgagee (or trustee) named on the first page of this policy, as interest may appear, under all present or future mortgages upon the property

---

4. See discussion of union mortgage clause, supra. One court has concluded that such a clause creates an *independent cause* of action by the mortgagee as a third-party beneficiary of the insurance policy, *not an independent contract*:

The fact that practically a limitless benefit is conferred by the standard clause [union clause] upon the mortgagee makes it none the less a benefit, and, however limitless a benefit may be, it can never reach the dignity of a contract. [Walker v. Queen Ins. Co., 136 S.C. 144, 160–163, 134 S.E. 263, 269 (1926), cited in 2 Williston, Contracts (3 ed. Jaeger 1959), § 401A at 1086, n.6].

herein described, in which the aforesaid may have an interest as mortgagee (or trustee), *in order of precedence of said mortgage* * *. [Emphasis supplied]

The foregoing clause does not establish that losses are to be paid to the mortgagees, but rather sets the order of priority for payment if there is more than one mortgagee. The clause negatives proportionate payment by the insurer as between the mortgagees in the event that the mortgage claims exceed the amount to be paid by the insurance company or in the event both mortgagees make a claim for the proceeds of insurance.

Other courts and commentators adopt the opposite rule of law and allow the mortgagor to recover the insurance proceeds in order to rebuild the damaged property. E.g., Schoolcraft v. Ross, 81 Cal.App.3d 75, 146 Cal.Rptr. 57 (D.Ct.App.1978); Fergus v. Wilmarth, 117 Ill. 542, 7 N.E. 508 (Sup.Ct.1886); Cottman Co. v. Continental Trust Co., 169 Md. 595, 182 A. 551 (Ct.App.1936); Osborne, Nelson & Whitman, Real Estate Finance Law (3d ed. 1979), § 4.15 at 150, 46 C.J.S.d, Insurance, § 1147 at 29 (under authority of a covenant to repair).

Various analytical approaches allow courts to reach this result. Some courts conclude that the purpose of the insurance is to maintain the security for the mortgage debt—if the property is restored, the security has not been impaired. Therefore, the purpose of the insurance has been fulfilled as to the mortgagee's interest and the mortgagor recovers the proceeds. Cottman v. Continental Trust Co., supra.

Osborne, Nelson and Whitman, in their treatise Real Estate Finance Law (3d ed. 1979), § 4.15 at 150, comment:

> At least in the absence of mortgage provisions to the contrary, it would seem that in the modern standard mortgage policy context where the mortgage is not in default, the mortgagor normally should be able, where rebuilding is practical, to insist upon the application of the insurance proceeds to rebuild the premises. To be sure, to permit the mortgagor to defeat the mortgagee's right to recovery by rebuilding may force the mortgagee to litigate the extent and sufficiency of repairs. On the other hand, it is almost always the mortgagor who is paying the premiums on the casualty insurance policy. Moreover, while permitting the mortgagee to utilize the insurance proceeds to pay the mortgage debt presumably benefits the mortgagor by rendering the property free from the mortgage lien to the extent of the loss, in many cases the mortgagor probably cannot afford to rebuild or is unable to obtain new mortgage financing for that purpose. Thus, on balance, it would seem more equitable in most cases to permit the mortgagor to rebuild and have the insurance applied to that purpose.

There is precedent for this view. One leading case is Cottman Co. v. Continental Trust Co., supra. There, plaintiff mortgaged its tugboats to secure a debenture with defendants as trustee (mortgagee). Pursuant to the requirements of the mortgage, insurance was taken out to protect the interest of the trustee (mortgagee). Thereafter, several of the tugs were damaged and repaired at plaintiff's expense. The insurer paid the claim of the trustee, who refused to reimburse plaintiff. Plaintiff sued the trustee for the proceeds of the insurance. In reversing a judgment for defendant trustee and holding that plaintiff mortgagor was entitled to the proceeds of the insurance, the Maryland Court of Appeals stated:

> Few cases, apparently, have reached appellate courts where the use of the insurance money for the repair and restoration of the security has been combatted by the recipient mortgagee. In such cases the argument is made that by virtue of the replacement or restoration, the creditor is left in the same position as he was before the loss, and therefore has no ground of complaint. It cannot be denied that if the restoration of the security, at the expense of the debtor, to the value it had before the loss or damage, leaves the parties in statu quo, then the retention of the insurance money by the creditor, mortgagee, or trustee, as additional security, would put the holder in a better position than he had originally bargained for. The theory of insurance, however, does not contemplate a resulting profit to the insured, or his mortgagee or other creditor. The interest of the mortgagee is to maintain the equilibrium of debt and security; and if, by the application of the insurance money to the upkeep of the security, that parity would be continued, it is not inequitable to require the payee of the fund to transfer the same to the debtor for that purpose, upon properly safeguarding its application to that end. [169 Md. at 601–02, 182 A. at 554]

In Schoolcraft v. Ross, supra, the deed of trust (mortgage) specifically gave the beneficiary (mortgagee) an option to use the insurance proceeds to rebuild or to apply in reduction of the mortgage debt. The mortgagee, relying on the option clause, elected to apply the proceeds to the debt despite the mortgagor's request to use the proceeds for rebuilding. The mortgagor could not afford to continue to pay the mortgage and also pay rent for an apartment, and thus defaulted in payment on the mortgage. In an action by the mortgagor for damages the California court held:

> [T]he right of a beneficiary (e.g., mortgagee) to apply insurance proceeds to the balance of a note secured by a deed of trust must be performed in good faith and with fair dealing and that to the extent the security was not impaired the beneficiary *must* permit those proceeds to be used for the cost of rebuilding. [81 Cal.App.3d at 77, 146 Cal.Rptr. at 58; emphasis supplied]

Since there was no evidence of the impairment of the security, the court held the mortgagee had no right to the funds. The court, even in face of the mortgagee's option, observed:

> Forcing the buyer to pay off in advance would result in a buyer losing certain property rights contemplated by the parties, *among them the benefit of a long term loan which permits the buyer to*

spread the purchase price of the property over a long time. [81 Cal.App.3d at 81, 146 Cal.Rptr. at 60; emphasis supplied]

The court found no evidence of impairment of the security and concluded "To the extent the security was not impaired, [mortgagee] had no right to the funds." Ibid.

Cottman and *Savarese*, both supra, demonstrate a general principle that hazard insurance is to protect the mortgagee's interest if the security for the debt is impaired. Absent an impairment, the mortgagee has no right to insist on payment from the insurer. The proceeds are to be paid to the insured mortgagor to effect the repair. New Jersey has recognized impairment of security as a rationale for recovery by mortgagees in other situations. "[T]he theory of recovery by a mortgagee is indemnity against an impairment of the mortgaged property * * *." 495 Corp. v. N. J. Ins. Underwriting Ass'n, supra, 173 N.J.Super. at 118, 413 A.2d 630 (foreclosure). A similar principle of impairment of security of mortgage has been applied to condemnation proceedings. In Transportation Comm'rs v. Kastner, 179 N.J.Super. 613, 433 A.2d 448 (Law Div.1981), a part of the mortgaged property was taken by condemnation. The mortgage made no provision for payment of the condemnation award in the event of a partial taking. In holding that the mortgagees were not entitled to have the condemnation award paid the court stated:

> [A] lienholder cannot enforce his lien against the condemnation award unless the remaining property is of insufficient value to satisfy his lien. [at 615, 433 A.2d 448]

If the proceeds are paid to the mortgagees in the present case, mortgagors will be damaged to the extent that they will lose the benefit of a long-term loan which was bargained for. The court takes judicial notice of the current prevailing high interest rates and the general scarcity of mortgage money, particularly for construction mortgages. If plaintiffs were forced to obtain a mortgage in the open market, it certainly would be greatly to their disadvantage and at a much higher interest rate than that to which plaintiffs and defendants Sigmond had bargained for. If construction mortgage financing were not available, plaintiffs could not even rebuild their home.

Moreover, there is evidence that the parties did not intend to accelerate the debt in case of fire. Under the insurance policy the insurer has the option to repair, rebuild or replace the property destroyed or damaged within a reasonable time and on giving notice of its intention to do so within 30 days after the receipt of the proof of loss. The dissent in Savarese v. Ohio Farmer's Ins. Co., supra, focused on the insurer's policy option to repair the property or to pay the loss as evidence of the purpose of the policy to maintain the security.

> [T]his clause [option to repair] in the agreement furnishes some indication that the purpose of the policy and the provision therein contained [to pay the mortgagee] *was to protect the mortgagees interest in the property* only if such damage was not repaired. [260

N.Y. at 60, 182 N.E. at 670 (Lehman, J. dissenting); emphasis supplied]

If the insurer had elected to exercise that option, both mortgagees and mortgagors would be bound. See 5A Appleman, op. cit., § 3405 at 317. This provision, coupled with the covenant to repair in the mortgage, indicates that the purpose of the insurance was to protect the mortgagees' interest if the security was impaired. As a further indication of this intent the parties specifically deleted a provision in the note which would have permitted acceleration in the event of a breach of the covenant to repair. A similar provision in the mortgage was not deleted. Where acceleration provisions of a note and mortgage are in an irreconcilable conflict the note will prevail. See 55 Am.Jur.2d, Mortgages, § 176 at 304.

While a covenant to repair and a covenant to rebuild are not identical, the deletion of acceleration for breach of the covenant to repair in the note is indicative of the parties intent. The mortgagees in the present case are attempting to accelerate the debt indirectly by demanding payment of the proceeds, a right which by negotiation they specifically gave up.

Lastly, defendant mortgagees are not prejudiced by permitting rebuilding of the residence and have sustained no damages. Property insurance is a contract of indemnity. 29 N.J.Practice, op. cit., § 164 at 737. The mortgagee collects the proceeds to compensate for its loss.

> It is an elementary principle of insurance law that fire insurance * * * is a contract of personal indemnity, not one from which a profit is to be realized * * * [T]he right to recover must be commensurate with the loss *actually* sustained. [Glens Falls Ins. Co. v. Sterling, 219 Md. 217, 222, 148 A.2d 453, 456 (Ct.App.1959); emphasis in original]

Since the vacant land remains as full security for the mortgage debt, it is difficult to identify any loss sustained by the mortgagee. This case differs from others in that, at the time the right to proceeds vested, unlike the *Savarese*, supra, rationale, the vacant land fully secured the debt. Cases which permit the mortgagee to recover refuse to take a hindsight view if the property has been restored by the trial date; the courts concentrate on the impairment of the security on the date of the fire. There has never been in this case impairment for purposes of the mortgagees interest.

> The court looks to the substance of the whole transaction *rather than to seek a metaphysical hypothesis upon which to justify a loss that is no loss.* [Ramsdell v. Ins. Co. of N. Amer., 197 Wis. 136, 139, 221 N.W. 654, 655 (Sup.Ct.1928); emphasis supplied]

The court finds that mortgagees have suffered no damage as a result of the fire, and until the building is commenced they have the security of the $60,000 fund which is in escrow. They have no loss for which indemnification is required nor have they been prejudiced. * * *

Page 346, delete Note 1 and substitute the following as Note 1:

1. Notwithstanding the *Starkman* holding, in the absence of mortgage language to the contrary, many cases give the mortgagee the option of applying the insurance proceeds to the mortgage debt or rebuilding the mortgaged premises. Moreover, this right of the mortgagee is normally not conditioned on a finding that rebuilding will jeopardize the mortgage security. See Nelson and Whitman, Real Estate Finance Law § 4.15 (2nd Ed. 1985). Finally, it should be stressed that the *Schoolcraft* approach is hardly universal. While the latter decision endorsed the use of insurance proceeds to rebuild in the face of specific mortgage language giving the mortgagee the option of compelling prepayment of the mortgage debt, other courts seem to interpret much less precise language in a more pro-mortgagee fashion. See e.g., Giberson v. First Federal Savings and Loan Association of Waterloo, 329 N.W.2d 9 (Iowa 1983) (where clause allowed proceeds to be used for rebuilding "when authorized by the [mortgagee]," court refused to give summary judgment for mortgagors who sought the funds for rebuilding with mortgagee's consent). Other courts simply reject the *Schoolcraft* approach. See e.g., English v. Fischer, 660 S.W.2d 521 (Tex. 1983) (the "novel" approach of "good faith and fair dealing" inapplicable where the mortgage language affords the mortgagee the prepayment option).

Chapter 5

TRANSFER AND DISCHARGE

B. RESTRICTIONS ON TRANSFER BY THE MORTGAGOR

Page 383, delete pages 383–400 and insert the following:

NELSON AND WHITMAN, REAL ESTATE FINANCE LAW*

316–332 (2nd Ed. 1985)

The Due-On Clauses—Introduction

The law of real property usually develops in an evolutionary fashion. Change is often measured in terms of decades and centuries rather than in months and years. Yet economic turmoil can accelerate this process. Just as the Great Depression of the 1930s spurred the enactment of mortgage moratoria and antideficiency legislation, so too has the inflationary economic climate of the 1970s and early 1980s engendered new mortgage law.

The major focus of this latter period has been on the due-on-sale clause, a mortgage provision that affords the mortgagee the right to accelerate the mortgage debt and to foreclose if the mortgaged real estate is transferred without the mortgagee's consent.[2] While the clause is sometimes used to protect mortgagees against transfers that endanger mortgage security or increase the risk of default, its major

---

* Reprinted with permission of West Publishing Co.

2. A typical due-on-sale clause provides: "If all or any part of the Property or an interest therein is sold or transferred by Borrower without Lender's prior written consent, * * * Lender may, at Lender's option, declare all the sums secured by this mortgage to be due and payable." Federal National Mortgage Association/Federal Home Loan Mortgage Corporation Mortgage, Clause 17 (one to four family) [hereinafter cited as FNMA/FHLMC Mortgage].

purpose is to enable mortgagees to recall lower-than-market interest rate loans during periods of rising interest rates. Because its use in this context pits lenders against borrowers and real estate buyers, the clause has become a major economic, political, and legal issue. It has been confronted and evaluated by most state supreme courts, many legislatures, certain federal regulatory agencies, the United States Supreme Court, and ultimately Congress. It has also been the subject of a great deal of scholarly commentary.[9]

Given recent economic conditions, this close scrutiny is hardly surprising. Due to high interest rates and the limited availability of home financing, large numbers of potential home buyers have been excluded from the housing market. For many purchasers, the assumption of an existing lower-than-market interest mortgage has represented one of the few practical financing alternatives. The financial climate has also made it much more difficult for owners to sell. Many sellers have been forced either to reduce significantly the price of their properties to enable buyers to qualify for institutional high-interest financing, or to suffer an effective price reduction by financing part of the purchase price themselves at lower-than-market interest rates. Thus, for those sellers with lower-than-market interest rate mortgages

9. See Gorinson & Manishin, Garn-St. Germain: A Harbinger of Change, 40 Wash. & Lee L.Rev. 1313 (1983); Nelson & Whitman, Congressional Preemption of Mortgage Due-on-Sale Law: An Analysis of the Garn-St. Germain Act, 35 Hast.L.J. 241 (1983); Comment, Section 341 of the Garn-St. Germain Depository Institutions Act of 1982: An End to the Due-on-Sale Controversy?, 14 Tol.L.Rev. 1427 (1983); Note, The Due-On-Sale Controversy: Beneficial Effects of the Garn-St. Germain Depository Institution Act of 1982, 1984 Duke L.J. 121 (1984); Ashley, Use of "Due-on" Clauses to Gain Collateral Benefits: A Common Sense Defense, 10 Tulsa L.J. 590 (1975); Bonanno, Due on Sale and Prepayment Clauses in Real Estate Financing in California in Times of Fluctuating Interest Rates—Legal Issues and Alternatives, 6 U.S.F.L.Rev. 267 (1972); Hetland, Real Property and Real Property Security: The Well-Being of the Law, 53 Calif.L.Rev. 151 (1965); Maxwell, The Due-On-Sale Clause: Restraints on Abenation and Adhesion Theory in California, 28 U.C.L.A.L.Rev. 197 (1982); Segreti, The Borrower as Servant of the Lender: Enforcement of Mortgage Due-on-Sale Clauses, 51 U.Cin.L.Rev. 779 (1982); Volkmer, The Application of the Restraints on Alienation Doctrine to Real Property Security Interests, 58 Iowa L.Rev. 747 (1973); Comment, The Future of the Due-On-Sale Clause in Alabama, 33 Ala.L.Rev. 83 (1981); Comment, Mortgages—A Catalogue and Critique on the Role of Equity in the Enforcement of Modern-Day "Due-on-Sale" Clauses, 26 Ark.L.Rev. 485 (1973); Comment, Applying the Brakes to Accelera Clauses: Controlling Their Misuse in Real Property Secured Transactions, 9 Cal.W.L. Rev. 514 (1973); Comment, Beyond Tucker v. Lassen: The Future of the Due-on-Sale Clause in California, 27 Hastings L.J. 475 (1975); Comment, South Dakota's Approach to the Due-on-Sale Clause: An Analysis of Automatic Enforcement, 27 S.D.L.Rev. 261 (1982); Comment, Judicial Treatment of the Due-on-Sale Clause: The Case for Adopting Standards of Reasonableness and Unconscionability, 27 Stan.L. Rev. 1109 (1975); Note, Property—The Demise of the Due-on-Sale Clause, 64 Calif.L. Rev. 573 (1976); Note Mortgages—Due-on-Sale Clause: Restraint on Alienation—Enforceability, 28 Case W.Res.L.Rev. 493 (1978); Note, Due on Sale and Due on Encumbrance Clauses in California, 7 Loy. L.A.L.Rev. 306 (1974); Note, Deeds of Trust—Restraints Against Alienation—Due-on Clause is an Unreasonable Restraint on Alienation Absent a Showing of Protection of Mortgagee's Legitimate Interests, 47 Miss.L.J. 331 (1976); Note, Mortgages—Use of Due on Sale Clause by a Lender is Not a Restraint on Alienation in North Carolina, 55 N.C.L.Rev. 310 (1977); Note, The Due-on-Sale Clause: Enforcement Standards, 60 Neb.L.Rev. 594 (1981); Note, Due-on-Sale Clauses: Separating Social Interests From Individual Interests, 35 Vand.L.Rev. 357 (1982).

on their properties, assumability of the mortgage may be the key to obtaining a higher asking price for the property.

On the other hand, the economic stake of institutional lenders in upholding due-on-sale clauses is also great. During the past several years many institutional lenders, especially savings and loan associations, have experienced severe economic difficulty. Because they hold portfolios that include large numbers of fixed rate, lower-yielding mortgage loans, they have been hard pressed to pay the higher short-term rates demanded by depositors. Many savings and loan associations and similar institutions have failed, and others remain in precarious financial positions. Because the due-on-sale clause provides one means of eliminating lower-interest mortgage loans from institutional portfolios, and does so without resort to expensive federal "bailout" or other subsidy schemes, its enforceability has been deemed important for the economic health of the thrift industry.

* * *

Due-on-Encumbrance Restrictions

Mortgages may restrict mortgagor transfers by means other than a due-on-sale clause. For example, a mortgage may contain a clause authorizing the mortgagee to accelerate the debt if the mortgagor "further encumbers" the mortgaged real estate. Such language is usually referred to as a "due-on-encumbrance" provision. While due-on-encumbrance language is often included as part of a due-on-sale clause, it is not uncommon for a mortgage to contain a separate due-on-encumbrance clause. Unlike the due-on-sale situation, in which the mortgagee's desire to increase the interest rate predominates, due-on-encumbrance language is utilized mainly to protect against impairment of mortgage security by a debtor who incurs a junior mortgage debt and thus reduces his or her economic stake in the mortgaged real estate. However, the due-on-encumbrance clause probably is used much less frequently than its due-on-sale counterpart.

Increased-Interest-on-Transfer Clauses

Another provision closely related to the due-on-sale clause authorizes the mortgagee to increase or adjust the mortgage interest rate in the event of a transfer by the mortgagor. We refer to this as an "increased-interest-on-transfer" clause. This type of clause fulfills the same economic function as the due-on-sale clause in that it enables the mortgagee to use a transfer by the mortgagor as the basis for increasing the interest yield on the mortgage. However, unlike a due-on-sale clause, it does not confer on the mortgagee an absolute right to accelerate the mortgage debt upon a transfer; hence it gives no direct protection against transfer to an uncreditworthy buyer. Only if the transferee fails to pay the increased mortgage payments will there be grounds for declaration of a default and acceleration of the debt.

Installment Land Contract Prohibitions on Transfer

Transfer restrictions may also appear in installment land contracts, which are probably the most commonly used mortgage substitute.

Known in many areas of the country as a "contract for deed" or "long term land contract," the installment land contract performs the same economic function as a purchase-money mortgage: it provides seller financing of all or part of the unpaid real estate purchase price. Vendors often find the installment land contract attractive because of its forfeiture clause—language specifying that "time is of the essence" and that upon vendee default in payment or other contract obligations the vendor has the option to terminate the contract, retake possession of the premises, and retain all prior payments as liquidated damages. However, in many jurisdictions legislatures and courts have placed restrictions on the forfeiture remedy, especially when the vendee has acquired substantial equity in the property. Other jurisdictions have gone so far as to treat the installment land contract as a mortgage, thus affording the vendee the traditional substantive and procedural rights of a mortgagor, including the right to a public sale after a judicial foreclosure proceeding.

Installment land contracts frequently include a provision that prohibits assignment by the vendee without the vendor's permission. Violation of such a provision constitutes a default and might result in vendor termination of the contract and loss of the purchaser's equity. In this respect the provision differs from a due-on-sale clause, under which an unapproved transfer will at most trigger an acceleration of the mortgage debt and, if the accelerated debt is unpaid, a public foreclosure sale of the mortgaged real estate.

Events Triggering Acceleration

A common question is what kind of event will trigger acceleration of a debt under a due-on-sale or other transfer restriction clause. While some early clauses used a "sale" alone as a triggering event, most of the recent forms employ broader language, often modeled after the mortgage form specified by use by lenders who sell mortgages to the Federal National Mortgage Association (FNMA) and the Federal Home Loan Mortgage Corporation (FHLMC). This language refers to a transfer of any part of the property or any interest in it. Under such language, in principle at least, even a short-term lease or a grant of an easement or other limited interest in the land would suffice to trigger the lender's right to accelerate.

Perhaps the most significant question is whether a sale by installment land contract permits acceleration. The answer depends on the exact wording of the clause in question, but under broad language like that of the FNMA/FHLMC clause the courts have nearly uniformly permitted acceleration.

* * *

Due-On Clauses—Pre-Garn-St. Germain Act State Judicial and Legislative Response

Due-on-Sale Clauses

Due-on-sale clauses have come under judicial attack as unreasonable restraints on alienation. Traditionally, a direct restraint on alienation has been viewed by many courts as invalid per se unless the restraint falls within certain limited exceptions. Under a minority approach, a direct restraint is void unless the policy underlying its purpose outweighs the degree of restraint imposed on the property interest. Indirect restraints, on the other hand are generally deemed valid if they are reasonable. An indirect restraint is one that arises "when an attempt is made to accomplish some purpose other than the restraint on alienability, but with the incidental result that ... [it] would restrain practical alienability."[5] Thus, a mortgage that provides for forfeiture of the mortgaged real estate to the mortgagee upon an impermissible transfer probably constitutes a direct restraint. To the extent that the mortgagee is able to enforce, through specific performance or injunctive relief, a mortgagor's promise not to convey without the mortgagee's consent, a promissory and presumably direct restraint exists.

* * *

The vast majority of courts has been unconcerned about classifying the clause into traditional "restraint" categories. No court has held that a due-on-sale clause is per se unlawful as a restraint on alienation. Indeed, some courts have suggested that it is not a restraint on alienation at all. While many courts probably view the clause as an indirect restraint on alienation, all courts recognize that there are circumstances in which enforcement of the clause is reasonable and thus permissible. Some courts, however, are more sympathetic to enforcement than others, and two broad judicial approaches to the clause have emerged.

Under the predominant judicial approach, the clause is deemed per se reasonable unless the borrower can show that the lender engaged in unconscionable conduct.[14] The courts employing this approach have recognized the desirability of protecting the mortgagee from the vagaries of the interest rate market. The mortgagee need not establish

---

5. L. Simes & A. Smith, The Law of Future Interests § 1112, at 5 (2d ed. 1956).

14. See, e.g., Tierce v. APS Co., 382 So.2d 485, 487 (Ala.1979); Income Realty & Mortgage Inc. v. Columbia Savings & Loan Association, 661 P.2d 257, 265 (Colo.1983); Olean v. Treglia, 190 Conn. 756, 765, 463 A.2d 242, 248 (1983); Baker v. Loves Park Savings & Loan Association, 61 Ill.2d 119, 125, 333 N.E.2d 1, 5 (1975); Martin v. Peoples Mutual Savings & Loan Association, 319 N.W.2d 220, 228–29 (Iowa 1982); Dunham v. Ware Savings Bank, 384 Mass. 63, 68, 423 N.E.2d 998, 1001 (Mass.1981); Occidental Savings & Loan Association v. Venco Partnership, 206 Neb. 469, 482, 293 N.W.2d 843, 848 (1980); First National Bank of Vicksburg v. Caruthers, 443 So.2d 861 (Miss.1984) (overruling Sanders v. Hicks, 317 So.2d 61 (Miss.1975)); Stenger v. Great Southern Savings and Loan Association, 677 S.W.2d 376 (Mo.App.1984); First Commercial Title Insurance Co. v. Holmes, 92 Nev. 363, 365, 550 P.2d 1271, 1272 (1976); Mills v. Nashua Federal Savings & Loan Association, 121 N.H. 722, 725, 433 A.2d 1312, 1315–16 (1981); Crockett v. First Federal Savings & Loan Association, 289 N.C. 620, 630–31, 224 S.E.2d 580, 587 (1976); Gunther v. White, 489 S.W.2d 529, 530 (Tenn.1973); Sonny Arnold, Inc. v. Sentry Savings Association, 633 S.W.2d 811, 815 (Tex.1982); Slusky v. Coley, 668 S.W.2d 930 (Tex.Civ.App.1984); United Virginia Bank v. Best, 223 Va. 112, 114–15, 286 S.E.2d 221, 223 (1982), certiorari denied 459 U.S. 879, 103 S.Ct. 175, 74 L.Ed.2d 144 (1982); Magney v. Lincoln Mutual Savings Bank, 34 Wn.App. 45, 659 P.2d 537, 541 (1983).

that a proposed transfer would impair security; the validity of the due-on-sale clause is not normally judged by the facts of an individual case. Under one variant of this approach, such facts are relevant only to the extent that the mortgagor attempts to meet the burden of proving that enforcement is unconscionable or inequitable in his or her case. An increase in the market interest rate is not usually thought sufficient to meet this burden, and due-on-sale clauses in such jurisdictions are usually enforced.

Under the minority approach, enforcement of due-on-sale clauses must be reasonable in individual cases, necessitating a case-by-case determination.[19] Under this approach, the mortgagee's desire to increase interest rates is not considered a sufficient reason to justify the clause. The mortgagee has the burden to establish reasonableness, and normally must establish that the transfer would result in security impairment or an increased risk of default. As a practical matter, lenders have rarely sought due-on-sale enforcement in jurisdictions that follow this approach.

Some of the courts that apply the majority approach display a concern that the borrower be fairly warned that the clause can be employed to exact a higher interest rate upon transfer, and insist that language explicitly stating that possibility be included in the documents. There may well be a valid need for such a warning; the FNMA/FHLMC clause, for example, is extraordinarily technical and difficult for a lay reader to follow, and its implication that a higher interest rate may result from a transfer is oblique at best. One court has been even more punctilious, requiring that the clause be inserted in the promissory note and not merely in the mortgage.

As noted above, majority or "automatic enforcement" jurisdictions often state that due-on-sale clauses are unenforceable when the mortgagor can establish that enforcement would be "unconscionable" or "inequitable." While it is difficult to articulate precisely when enforcement will be so categorized, it is probable that most courts will be unwilling to enforce the clauses in "non-substantive" or "non-sale" transfers. For example, one court has indicated that enforcement should be denied in

---

19. See, e.g., Baltimore Life Insurance Co. v. Harn, 15 Ariz.App. 78, 81, 486 P.2d 190, 193 (1971); Tucker v. Pulaski Federal Savings & Loan Association, 252 Ark. 849, 855, 481 S.W.2d 725, 728 (1972); Abrego v. United Peoples Federal Savings and Loan Association, 281 Ark. 308, 664 S.W.2d 858 (1984); Wellenkamp v. Bank of America, 21 Cal.3d 943, 953, 148 Cal.Rptr. 379, 385–86, 582 P.2d 970, 976–77 (1978); Nichols v. Ann Arbor Federal Savings & Loan Association, 73 Mich.App. 163, 168, 173, 250 N.W.2d 804, 808 (1977) (does not decide if a rate increase would have been reasonable if the clause had mentioned rate increases); State ex rel. Bingaman v. Valley Savings & Loan Association, 97 N.M. 8, 12, 636 P.2d 279, 283 (1981) (judicial extension of statute to loans made before statute's effective date); Consolidated Capital Properties, II, Inc. v. National Bank of North America, 420 So.2d 618, 622 (Fla.App.1982); Magney v. Lincoln Mutual Savings Bank, 34 Wn. App. 45, 659 P.2d 537, 541 (1983). Cf. O'Boskey v. First Federal Savings & Loan Association of Boise, 106 Idaho 339, 678 P.2d 1112 (1984) (impairment of security must be shown where due-on-sale clause title referred to protecting security); North Point Patio Offices Venture v. United Benefit Life Insurance Co., 672 S.W.2d 35 (Tex. App.1984), error refused n.r.e. (use of due-on-sale clause to "coerce" transfer fee deemed unreasonable).

situations such as transfers to a spouse who becomes a co-owner, transfers to a spouse incidental to a marriage dissolution proceeding or settlement, and transfers to an inter vivos trust of which the mortgagor is a beneficiary. This principle is recognized in the FNMA/FHLMC form due-on-sale clause, which specifically exempts transfers "by devise, descent or by operation of law upon the death of a joint tenant."

* * *

No-Transfer Provisions in Installment Land Contracts

While there was some early support for enforcement of "no-transfer" provisions in installment land contracts, contemporary courts are much less sympathetic. This attitude is reflected in two ways. First, "no-transfer" language is often construed narrowly against the vendor. Second, in contrast to the majority approach to due-on-sale clause enforcement, courts often eschew an "automatic enforcement" approach; the "no-transfer" language is enforced only when it is established that the transfer will impair the vendor's security. Moreover, even when a vendor demonstrates such an impairment, it is likely that a court will avoid the imposition of forfeiture by permitting the transferee to pay off the contract balance, or by ordering that the real estate be foreclosed by public sale.

State Legislation

Several states have imposed legislative limitations on due-on-sale clauses.[38] While the details of these statutes vary considerably, they commonly prohibit due-on-sale enforcement in residential mortgages unless the mortgagee can establish that a transfer would impair mortgage security. Most of the statutes permit the mortgagee to condition transfer of the property upon payment of a limited "assumption fee" or upon an increase in the mortgage interest rate by a modest amount, usually no more than one percent. Some of the statutes impose similar restrictions on increased-interest-on-transfer provisions. In addition, at least one state, Iowa, confers generous post-foreclosure redemption rights when real estate is foreclosed incident to enforcement of a due-on-sale clause.[42]

38. See Ariz.Rev.Stat. § 33–806.01; Colo.Rev.Stat. 38–30–165; O.C.G.A. § 44–14–5; Iowa Code Ann. § 535.8; N.M.Stat. Ann.1981, §§ 48–7–11 to –14; Minn.Stat. Ann. § 47.20; Utah Code Ann.1981, §§ 57–15–1 to –10.

42. See Iowa Code Ann. § 535.8(2)(e). While normally an Iowa mortgagor has only a one year post-sale redemption right, id. § 628.3, when foreclosure of a mortgage on real property results from the enforcement of a due-on-sale clause, the mortgagor may redeem the real property at any time within three years from the day of sale, id. § 535.8(2)(e). In the meantime, the mortgagor is entitled to possession of the property and for the first thirty months after the sale, the right of redemption is exclusive. Id. The time for redemption by creditors is extended to thirty-three months in any case in which the mortgagor's period for redemption is extended. Id. This statute represents a significant burden on lenders.

This type of redemption should not be confused with "equitable redemption," available in every state, which allows the mortgagor and junior lienors to pay off a mortgage in default at any time until a valid foreclosure sale has occurred.

A few other states legislatively prohibit due-on-sale enforcement in "non-substantive" and certain non-sale transfers. In California, for example, acceleration is prohibited in residential mortgages when there is a transfer to a spouse resulting from the death of the mortgagor, to a spouse who becomes a co-owner, to a spouse incident to a marriage dissolution, or to an inter vivos trust of which the mortgagor is a beneficiary. In addition, some statutes deny enforcement of due-on-encumbrance clauses in a variety of residential housing settings.

Due-on Clauses—Pre-Garn-St. Germain Act Federal Regulation

In 1976 the Federal Home Loan Bank Board (the Board), the federal agency that regulates federally-chartered and federally-insured savings and loan associations, became concerned about the increasing controversy over whether federally-chartered associations had the authority to enforce due-on-sale clauses. The Board issued a regulation effective July 31, 1976 (the 1976 Regulation) which provided that a federal association

> continues to have the power to include * * * a provision in its loan instrument whereby the association may, at its option, declare immediately due and payable sums secured by the association's security instrument if all or any part of the real property securing the loan is sold or transferred by the borrower without the association's prior written consent.[1]

Except as provided in paragraph (g) of the regulation, the Board authorized federal associations to exercise the due-on-sale option and provided that all rights and remedies of the association and borrower "shall be exclusively governed by the terms of the loan contract." Paragraph (g) prohibited due-on-sale enforcement in certain "nonsubstantive" transfers of mortgagor-occupied homes resulting from junior liens, purchase-money security interests in household appliances, transfers by devise, descent, or operation of law upon the death of a joint tenant, and leaseholds for less than three years with no option to purchase. In the preamble to the 1976 Regulation the Board also expressed its intent that the due-on-sale practices of federal associations be governed exclusively by federal law, and emphasized that federal associations "shall not be bound by or subject to any conflicting state law which imposes different * * * due-on-sale requirements."[4]

A similar regulation was promulgated in 1978 by the National Credit Union Administration (NCUA) to apply to due-on-sale clauses in federal credit union mortgages. The NCUA regulation went beyond the 1976 Board Regulation by specifically requiring federal credit unions to utilize due-on-sale clauses as well as preempting state restrictions on due-on-sale clause enforcement.

While lower federal courts concluded that the 1976 Board Regulation foreclosed the application of state due-on-sale law to federal associ-

---

1. 12 C.F.R. § 545.8–3(f) (1983).   4. 41 Fed.Reg. 18,286, 18,287.

ations, a few state courts reached contrary results. Ultimately, this conflict was resolved by the United States Supreme Court in Fidelity First Federal Savings & Loan Association v. de la Cuesta,[9] a case that addressed the effect of the 1976 Regulation on California law. California generally limited due-on-sale enforcement to situations in which impairment of mortgage security was established. In *de la Cuesta*, the Supreme Court held that: 1) the Board intended to preempt state law; 2) the 1976 Regulation in fact conflicted with California law, despite the fact that it merely authorized, and did not require, federal associations to utilize due-on-sale clauses; 3) the Board acted within its statutory authority under section 5(a) of the Home Owner's Loan Act, which authorized the Board to promulgate rules for the operation and regulation of federal associations; and 4) although the 1976 Regulation's merits might be debatable, it was a reasonable, and therefore a valid, exercise of the Board's authority.

The *de la Cuesta* Court did not address the enforceability of due-on-sale clauses included in the mortgage loans made by federal associations before the effective date of the 1976 Board Regulation. The Board had issued an earlier regulation that one federal court held sufficient to preempt contrary state due-on-sale law as to pre-1976 Regulation loans. Also, the 1976 Regulation specified that a federal association "continues" to have the power to include due-on-sale clauses in their mortgages. Although this language may have represented bureaucratic timidity in dealing with the retroactivity issue, it can be argued that it signified the Board's view that it had already preempted state law before 1976. The Supreme Court in *de la Cuesta*, however, expressly avoided reaching the retroactivity question. While *de la Cuesta* confirmed the validity of the Board's response to the needs of federally-chartered savings associations with respect to due-on-sale clauses, it did nothing for other types of lenders. Therefore, these lenders sought a uniform national solution: congressional preemption of state laws restricting the enforcement of due-on-sale clauses.

SECTION 341, GARN–ST. GERMAIN DEPOSITORY INSTITUTIONS ACT OF 1982,

96 Stat. 1505, 12 U.S.C.A. § 1701j–3
as amended, November 30, 1983, 97 Stat. 1237.

DUE–ON–SALE CLAUSES

Sec. 1701j–3. Preemption of due-on-sale prohibitions

(a) Definitions

For the purpose of this section—

(1) the term "due-on-sale clause" means a contract provision which authorizes a lender, at its option, to declare due and payable

---

9. 458 U.S. 141, 102 S.Ct. 3014, 73 L.Ed.2d 664 (1982).

sums secured by the lender's security instrument if all or any part of the property, or an interest therein, securing the real property loan is sold or transferred without the lender's prior written consent;

(2) the term "lender" means a person or government agency making a real property loan or any assignee or transferee, in whole or in part, of such a person or agency;

(3) the term "real property loan" means a loan, mortgage, advance, or credit sale secured by a lien on real property, the stock allocated to a dwelling unit in a cooperative housing corporation, or a residential manufactured home, whether real or personal property; and

(4) the term "residential manufactured home" means a manufactured home as defined in section 603(6) of the National Manufactured Home Construction and Safety Standards Act of 1974 [42 U.S.C.A. § 5402(6)] which is used as a residence; and

(5) the term "State" means any State of the United States, the District of Columbia, the Commonwealth of Puerto Rico, the Virgin Islands, Guam, the Northern Mariana Islands, American Samoa, and the Trust Territory of the Pacific Islands.

(b) Loan contract and terms governing execution or enforcement of due-on-sale options and rights and remedies of lenders and borrowers; assumptions of loan rates

(1) Notwithstanding any provision of the constitution or laws (including the judicial decisions) of any State to the contrary, a lender may, subject to subsection (c) of this section, enter into or enforce a contract containing a due-on-sale clause with respect to a real property loan.

(2) Except as otherwise provided in subsection (d) of this section, the exercise by the lender of its option pursuant to such a clause shall be exclusively governed by the terms of the loan contract, and all rights and remedies of the lender and the borrower shall be fixed and governed by the contract.

(3) In the exercise of its option under a due-on-sale clause, a lender is encouraged to permit an assumption of a real property loan at the existing contract rate or at a rate which is at or below the average between the contract and market rates, and nothing in this section shall be interpreted to prohibit any such assumption.

(c) State prohibitions applicable for prescribed period; subsection (b) provisions applicable upon expiration of such period; nonFederal and Federal loans subject to State and Federal regulation or subsection (b) provisions when authorized by State laws or Federal regulations

(1) In the case of a contract involving a real property loan which was made or assumed, including a transfer of the liened property

subject to the real property loan, during the period beginning on the date a State adopted a constitutional provision or statute prohibiting the exercise of due-on-sale clauses, or the date on which the highest court of such State has rendered a decision (or if the highest court has not so decided, the date on which the next highest appellate court has rendered a decision resulting in a final judgment if such decision applies State-wide) prohibiting such exercise, and ending on October 15, 1982, the provisions of subsection (b) of this section shall apply only in the case of a transfer which occurs on or after the expiration of 3 years after October 15, 1982, except that—

(A) a State, by a State law enacted by the State legislature prior to the close of such 3-year period, with respect to real property loans originated in the State by lenders other than national banks, Federal savings and loan associations, Federal savings banks, and Federal credit unions, may otherwise regulate such contracts, in which case subsection (b) of this section shall apply only if such State law so provides; and

(B) the Comptroller of the Currency with respect to real property loans originated by national banks or the National Credit Union Administration Board with respect to real property loans originated by Federal credit unions may, by regulation prescribed prior to the close of such period, otherwise regulate such contracts, in which case subsection (b) of this section shall apply only if such regulation so provides.

(2)(A) For any contract to which subsection (b) of this section does not apply pursuant to this subsection, a lender may require any successor or transferee of the borrower to meet customary credit standards applied to loans secured by similar property, and the lender may declare the loan due and payable pursuant to the terms of the contract upon transfer to any successor or transferee of the borrower who fails to meet such customary credit standards.

(B) A lender may not exercise its option pursuant to a due-on-sale clause in the case of a transfer of a real property loan which is subject to this subsection where the transfer occurred prior to October 15, 1982.

(C) This subsection does not apply to a loan which was originated by a Federal savings and loan association or Federal savings bank.

(d) Exemption of specified transfers or dispositions

With respect to a real property loan secured by a lien on residential real property containing less than five dwelling units, including a lien on the stock allocated to a dwelling unit in a cooperative housing corporation, or on a residential manufactured home, a lender may not exercise its option pursuant to a due-on-sale clause upon—

(1) the creation of a lien or other encumbrance subordinate to the lender's security instrument which does not relate to a transfer of rights of occupancy in the property;

(2) the creation of a purchase money security interest for household appliances;

(3) a transfer by devise, descent, or operation of law on the death of a joint tenant or tenant by the entirety;

(4) the granting of a leasehold interest of three years or less not containing an option to purchase;

(5) a transfer to a relative resulting from the death of a borrower;

(6) a transfer where the spouse or children of the borrower become an owner of the property;

(7) a transfer resulting from a decree of a dissolution of marriage, legal separation agreement, or from an incidental property settlement agreement, by which the spouse of the borrower becomes an owner of the property;

(8) a transfer into an inter vivos trust in which the borrower is and remains a beneficiary and which does not relate to a transfer of rights of occupancy in the property; or

(9) any other transfer or disposition described in regulations prescribed by the Federal Home Loan Bank Board.

(e) Rules, regulations, and interpretations; future income bearing loans subject to due-on-sale options

(1) The Federal Home Loan Bank Board, in consultation with the Comptroller of the Currency and the National Credit Union Administration Board, is authorized to issue rules and regulations and to publish interpretations governing the implementation of this section.

(2) Notwithstanding the provisions of subsection (d) of this section, the rules and regulations prescribed under this section may permit a lender to exercise its option pursuant to a due-on-sale clause with respect to a real property loan and any related agreement pursuant to which a borrower obtains the right to receive future income.

(f) Effective date for enforcement of Corporation owned loans with due-on-sale options

The Federal Home Loan Mortgage Corporation (hereinafter referred to as the "Corporation") shall not, prior to July 1, 1983, implement the change in its policy announced on July 2, 1982, with respect to enforcement of due-on-sale clauses in real property loans which are owned in whole or in part by the Corporation.

(g) Balloon payments

Federal Home Loan Bank Board regulations restricting the use of a balloon payment shall not apply to a loan, mortgage, advance, or credit sale to which this section applies.

NELSON AND WHITMAN, REAL ESTATE FINANCE LAW *

(332–354 2nd Ed. 1985)

The Garn-St. Germain Act

The enactment of section 341 of the Garn-St. Germain Depository Institutions Act of 1982 (Act) signaled the dawn of a new era for due-on-sale clause enforcement. The Act broadly preempts state laws that restrict the enforcement of due-on-sale clauses, thereby making such clauses generally enforceable.

Yet Congress responded to effective lobbying by the real estate brokerage industry and related interests by softening the impact of the Act in most states that previously restricted due-on-sale enforcement. To accomplish this, Congress created complex exceptions to the preemption based on so-called "window periods," and conferred authority on states with window periods to enact legislation to avoid the impact of the Act on certain mortgage loans. In so doing, Congress created a host of important and difficult interpretation problems. Congress delegated to the Board the authority to issue regulations interpreting the Act, and in April, 1983, the Board issued a final regulation entitled "Preemption of State Due-on-Sale Laws" (Regulation). The following material analyzes the more important provisions of the Act and Regulation, their scope, and the complex problems of interpretation they have engendered.

Lenders Covered

The Act covers any "person or government agency making a real property loan." According to the Regulation, the foregoing definition includes,

> without limitation, individuals, Federal associations, state-chartered savings and loan associations, national banks, state-chartered banks and state-chartered mutual savings banks, Federal credit unions, state-chartered credit unions, mortgage banks, insurance companies and finance companies which make real property loans, manufactured-home retailers who extend credit, agencies of the Federal government, [and] any lender approved by the Secretary of Housing and Urban Development for participation in any mortgage insurance program under the National Housing Act.[8]

The Board emphasized that the foregoing list is "intended to be representative and not exclusive."[9] Consequently, every mortgagee, whether a natural person, business entity, or government agency, is covered by the Act.

---

* Reprinted with permission of West Publishing Co.

8. 48 Fed.Reg. 21,561 (codified at 12 CFR 591.2(g)).

9. 48 Fed.Reg. 21,555 (definitions section of the Regulation).

* * *

Loans Covered

The Act covers every "loan, mortgage, advance, or credit sale secured by a lien on real property, the stock allocated to a dwelling unit in a cooperative housing corporation, or a residential manufactured home, whether real or personal property." Although the Act makes no reference to mortgages on leasehold interests, the Regulation provides that a loan is secured by a lien on real property if it is made on the "security of any instrument * * * which makes * * * a leasehold or subleasehold * * * specific security for payment of the obligation secured by the instrument."[17]

* * *

Types of Mortgage Transfer Restrictions Covered

The Act preempts state law only with respect to due-on-sale clauses that "authoriz[e] a lender, at its option, to declare due and payable sums secured by the lender's security instrument if all or any part of the property, or an interest therein, securing the real property loan is sold or transferred without the lender's prior written consent." The Regulation adopts this statutory definition virtually unchanged.

Presumably the Act is inapplicable to an increased-interest-on-transfer clause because that type of clause confers on the lender only the right to modify or increase the interest rate upon a sale or transfer and not the "option to declare [the debt] due and payable." Consequently, every state is probably free to make increased-interest-on-transfer provisions unenforceable. This result is bizarre, for such clauses have an economic effect similar to that of the due-on-sale clauses. Nevertheless, the practical effect of excluding increased-interest-on-transfer provisions from the scope of the Act is unlikely to be substantial. Mortgagees can simply include due-on-sale language in any mortgages executed after the Act's effective date. As to pre-Act loans, few state courts are likely to exercise their freedom. In states that follow an automatic enforcement approach to the due-on-sale clause, courts are unlikely to restrict enforcement of an increased-interest-on-transfer provision, as it is the less burdensome of the two clauses. Even in states that impose substantial restrictions on due-on-sale clause enforcement, courts that have addressed the issue have been less hostile toward enforcement of increased-interest-on-transfer clauses. Courts in these latter states are thus not likely to take advantage of this "loophole" in the Act's preemptive effect.

One could draft mortgage language that would fall outside the Act's definition of a due-on-sale clause. For example, a provision for *automatic* acceleration upon transfer seems to be outside the definition, which speaks of the lender's "option" to accelerate. Similarly, a clause that merely makes an unapproved transfer by the mortgagor a default, but says nothing about acceleration, may fall outside the Act. How-

---

17. 48 Fed.Reg. 21,561 (codified at 12 CFR 591.2(h)).

ever, this argument is weakened if the mortgage or note also contains a standard acceleration-for-default clause that the courts could read together with the no-transfer clause to find the equivalent of a due-on-sale clause. These illustrations should have little practical importance, since in post-Act mortgages well-advised lenders will simply refrain from using such uncommon and idiosyncratic language. An occasional pre-Act document may raise this sort of problem, but the number of documents with such non-standard clauses is small. In any event, only clauses in states that restrict due-on-sale enforcement potentially pose a problem. In overall economic terms, then, the Act's narrow definition of a due-on-sale clause is likely to be of little importance.

Coverage of Installment Land Contracts

While the Act itself does not specifically mention installment land contracts, its preemption does apply to any "loan, mortgage, advance, or credit sale secured by a lien on real property." Does an installment contract vendor retain a "lien on real property," as well as legal title? The Regulation answers affirmatively,[32] and is probably correct. While a few courts have had conceptual difficulty with the notion that one can have legal title to land and a lien on it simultaneously, there is substantial authority that the installment land contract vendor retains a "vendor's lien" for the unpaid purchase price. Moreover, courts are increasingly equating installment land contracts with mortgages, and requiring foreclosure as the vendor's primary remedy. In such cases the vendor is surely foreclosing a "lien." Finally, while the analytical underpinnings for their decisions are not always clear, numerous courts routinely afford the vendor the option to foreclose an installment land contract as a mortgage. This practice constitutes a persuasive argument that the contract vendor is also a "lienor."

The conclusion that the Act's preemption applies to installment land contracts does not mean that a violation of a contract prohibition on transfer will necessarily result in a forfeiture of the vendee's interest. When no-transfer provisions are upheld, it is likely that foreclosure of the contract will instead be ordered, and then only after the vendee has been afforded the opportunity to pay off the contract balance. The Act does not appear to change this. Literally, it only validates "due-on-sale" clauses—those that authorize the acceleration of the debt when the real estate is transferred without the lender's consent. A prohibition on transfer that purports to go beyond simple acceleration, and defines the remedies (such as forfeiture) to be imposed on the vendee, is unaffected by the Act and is thus still subject to pre-Act state law. It is highly improbable that a state court would enforce forfeiture, with its harsh consequences, simply because a transfer was made without the vendor's consent. A more likely judicial response would be to permit

---

32. 48 Fed.Reg. 21,561 (codified at 12 CFR 591.2(h)) (" 'loan secured by a lien on real property' means a loan on the security on any instrument (whether a mortgage, deed of trust, or *land contract*) which makes the interest in real property (whether in fee or on a leasehold or subleasehold) specific security for the payment of the obligation secured by the instrument") (emphasis added).

forfeiture vs foreclosure

foreclosure of the contract as a mortgage. Such an approach would not be inconsistent with the policy inherent in the Act.

Time of Transfer

The Act applies to all mortgage *loans*, whether consummated before or after October 15, 1982, the effective date of the Act. However, a *transfer* is covered only if it is made after the Act's effective date. Although the Act itself does not state this, this conclusion is supported by the well-settled rule that a statute had only prospective effect unless Congress evinces a clear intent that it have retroactive effect. Congress indicated no such intent regarding the Act. Note, however, that federally-chartered savings and loan associations have the authority to enforce due-on-sale clauses as to many pre-Act transfers by virtue of the 1976 Regulation upheld in the *de la Cuesta* case. The Act itself recognizes this authority.

The application of the Act can be illustrated as follows. Suppose that on March 1, 1982, MR transferred mortgaged real estate located in State X to Grantee in violation of a due-on-sale clause contained in the mortgage executed in 1980. During early 1983, ME (a state-chartered lender) accelerated the debt and commenced judicial foreclosure proceedings. Because the transfer took place before October 15, 1982, the Act is inapplicable and the State X court is free to apply state law to such pre-Act transfers.

While the Act is inapplicable to pre-Act transfers, it is retroactive in the sense that it governs mortgage loans executed prior to the Act's effective date. Thus, if in the previous example the property had been mortgaged in 1980, but the transfer had taken place on December 20, 1982, the Act would have applied, and the due-on-sale clause would have been enforceable.

* * *

Transfers in Which Due-on-Sale Enforcement is Prohibited

The Act expressly enumerates several types of transfers that may not be used as the basis for due-on-sale acceleration. The list is similar, but not identical, to the analogous provisions of the FNMA/FHLMC mortgage form and the 1976 FHLBB regulations. It includes:

(1) the creation of a lien or other encumbrance subordinate to the lender's security instrument which does not relate to a transfer of rights of occupancy in the property;

(2) the creation of a purchase money security interest for household appliances;

(3) a transfer by devise, descent, or operation of law on the death of a joint tenant or tenant by the entirety;

(4) the granting of a leasehold interest of three years or less not containing an option to purchase;

(5) a transfer to a relative resulting from the death of a borrower;

(6) a transfer where the spouse or children of the borrower become an owner of the property;

(7) a transfer resulting from a decree of a dissolution of marriage, legal separation agreement, or from an incidental property settlement agreement, by which the spouse of the borrower becomes an owner of the property;

(8) a transfer into an inter vivos trust in which the borrower is and remains a beneficiary and which does not relate to a transfer of rights of occupancy in the property; or

(9) any other transfer or disposition described in regulations prescribed by the Federal Home Loan Bank Board.

When a transfer of one of these types is involved, the Act is preemptive: acceleration under a due-on-sale clause is prohibited even if permitted by state law. However, the above transfers are insulated from acceleration only if the mortgaged real estate contains "less than five dwelling units." The latter language was added to the Act on November 30, 1983. In its original form, the Act contained no such qualification. Thus prior to the amendment, there was substantial concern that the above exceptions would prevent due-on-sale enforcement in a variety of purely commercial and non-residential settings. For example, in item (1) above, the Act prohibits due-on-sale enforcement upon the creation of a junior lien if no transfer of occupancy is involved. Suppose a first mortgage on a shopping center contains a prohibition on further encumbrances without the mortgagee's consent. If the mortgagor borrows money for a non-business purpose and gives the lender a junior mortgage on the center, the Act appears to prohibit acceleration. This is true even if the first mortgagee can establish that the junior lien will increase the risk of mortgagor default or will impair the security of its mortgage. This result doubtless came as an unpleasant surprise to countless mortgage lenders who had relied on the due-on-encumbrance concept in a variety of commercial lending contexts.

The Board had sought to avoid such a result by limiting the application of the statutory list to mortgage loans made "on the security of a home occupied * * * by the borrower."[55] Even though such a limitation was absent from the Act itself, the Board argued in its preamble to the Regulation that "this approach is most consistent with the Congressional purpose of restricting due-on-sale exercise to protect consumers."[56] While it is true that courts sometimes defer to an interpretation of a statute by the agency charged with its administration, there is also a strong tradition that the "plain meaning" of an unambiguous statute should be respected. In short, there was substantial doubt as to the validity of the Board's attempt to limit the impact of the Act's exceptions. In any event, because of the 1983 amendment

55. 48 Fed.Reg. 21,562 (codified at 12 CFR 591.5(b)).

56. Id. at 21,559.

The Exemption for Window Period Loans

As a result of pressure from the real estate brokerage industry and a desire to protect the reasonable expectations of borrowers who believed that they had acquired "assumable" loans for purposes of future resale, Congress provided partial relief from the Act's preemption. Thus, in some states the Act's effect is deferred and state law continues to govern enforcement of certain due-on-sale clauses. This was accomplished through creation of "window periods," which give rise to the postponement of the Act's preemptions. The concept of window periods is complex, and is not clearly defined in the Act or susceptible to easy explanation. On the other hand, as the following material indicates, the problems created by the window period are relatively short-lived.

A state may be a window period state if it restricted enforcement of due-on-sale clauses before the Act. The window period in such a state began when the state first restricted enforcement of due-on-sale clauses, and ended when the state ended such restrictions, or upon passage of the Act. Certain loans in a state that had a window period remained assumable for three years if they would have been assumable under state law prior to the passage of the Act. This three-year deferral period began on October 15, 1982 (the effective date of the Act), and lasted until October 15, 1985. Only states that "prohibited the exercise of due-on-sale clauses" before the effective date of the Act qualify for window period treatment and the three year extension. To qualify, a state must have prohibited exercise of the due-on-sale clause by a statute, its constitution, or a decision of its highest court (or if no such decision, a decision by the state's next highest appellate court whose decisions apply statewide).

However, not all loans in states qualifying for window period treatment were assumable for this three year period. Only loans that were "made or assumed" between the date of the state's prohibition of enforcement of the due-on-sale clause and October 15, 1982, are governed by state law and thus remained assumable. The Regulation defines "assumed" to include transfers under which a grantee takes "subject to" the mortgage but does not agree to be personally liable for the mortgage debt.

The window period concept can be best understood through factual examples. Suppose State X enacted a statute on July 1, 1979, limiting due-on-sale enforcement in mortgages on single family dwellings to situations in which the mortgagee can establish impairment of mortgage security. MR purchased his house on September 1, 1981, and simultaneously executed a mortgage on it that contained a due-on-sale clause. If MR sold his house on April 1, 1984, to Grantee, the mortgage was assumable by Grantee unless the mortgagee could establish that the transfer impaired mortgage security. This would also be true if

MR had assumed an existing mortgage on September 1, 1981, rather than obtaining a new loan, since the assumption would have occurred after July 1, 1979, the effective date of the state statute. Finally, the transferees of Grantee, if any, were able to assume the mortgage so long as the transfer took place prior to October 15, 1985, and the mortgagee was not able to establish that such a transfer would impair mortgage security.

Although the Board was requested to identify the states that qualify for window period treatment, it declined to do so on the ground that Congress intended window period determinations to be left to "state interpretation and state judicial decision." Only states that have "prohibited the exercise of due-on-sale clauses" qualify for window period treatment. This language is susceptible to several possible interpretations. If it is taken to refer to total and absolute prohibitions, no window periods would be created anywhere, as no state bars the enforcement of due-on-sale clauses under all circumstances. Such a reading would mean that no post-Act transfers would be exempt from the Act's preemption, even though the transfers took place in a state that substantially restricts due-on-sale enforcement. This result would obviously be contrary to congressional intent. In reliance on language in the Senate Committee Report, the Regulation takes a more moderate view, providing that a state qualifies for window period treatment when it has "adopted a law * * * prohibiting the *unrestricted* exercise of due-on-sale clauses upon *outright transfers* of property."[87]

---

[87]. 48 Fed.Reg. 21,562 (to be codified at 12 CFR 591.2(p)(2)(i)–(ii)) (emphasis added). The Board expressly refused to identify specific window period states. See id. at 21,555. However, the two major federally-sponsored purchasers of mortgage loans on the secondary market have attempted to identify such states. The FNMA listed Arizona, California, Colorado, Georgia, Iowa, Michigan, Minnesota, New Mexico, Utah, and Washington as "window period" states. See FNMA Press Release, Feb. 22, 1983. See Perry v. Island Savings and Loan Association, 101 Wn.2d 795, 684 P.2d 1281 (1984) (Washington has window period for loans by non-federally chartered lender from August 19, 1976 to October 15, 1982).

The FHLMC designated the same states as having window periods. The only variation is the date of commencement of the Arizona period, with the FNMA listing of Mar. 13, 1978 (the date of Patton v. First Federal Savings & Loan Association, 118 Ariz. 473, 578 P.2d 152 (1978)), and the FHLMC listing of July 8, 1971 (the date of Baltimore Life Insurance Co. v. Harn, 15 Ariz.App. 78, 486 P.2d 190 (1971)). See Freddie Mac Issues Guidelines for Due-on-Sale Enforcement, 11 Hous. & Dev.Rep. (BNA) 26 (1983). In Scappaticci v. Southwest Savings & Loan Association, 135 Ariz. 456, 662 P.2d 131 (1983), the Arizona Supreme Court resolved the issue by using *Harn* for deeds of trust as well as mortgages.

The Comptroller of the Currency has issued a regulation that includes a state-by-state list of window periods. See 48 Fed. Reg. 21,561–63. This list agrees with that of the FHLMC, except that it adds Arkansas.

Several states not listed by FNMA or FHLMC may have window periods. The Arkansas Supreme Court adopted a rule requiring lenders to show impairment of security in Tucker v. Pulaski Federal Savings & Loan Association, 252 Ark. 849, 481 S.W.2d 725 (1972). Subsequent cases have held that *Tucker*'s restrictions on due-on-sale clause enforcement have been preempted by federal regulation as to savings and loan associations. See First Federal Savings & Loan Association v. Myrick, 533 F.Supp. 1041, 1045–46 (W.D.Ark.1982); Schulte v. Benton Savings & Loan Association, 279 Ark. 275, 651 S.W.2d 71 (1983); Independence Federal Savings & Loan Association v. Davis, 278 Ark. 387, 646 S.W.2d 336 (1983). However, *Tucker* still

Sec. B RESTRICTIONS ON TRANSFER 85

* * *

State Extension of Window Period Protection

If a state has a window period, it was permitted, prior to October 15, 1985, to enact legislation "otherwise regulat[ing]" window period loans originated by lenders other than certain federally-chartered institutions. Thus, the legislature in such a state conceivably could insulate window period loans from the Act's preemption indefinitely. While this means that such a state could effectively extend preexisting state law with regard to some loans, it had to recognize the power of mortgagees to use due-on-sale clauses as a tool to ensure that proposed transferees meet customary credit standards. Thus, in no circumstances could a state absolutely prohibit enforcement of the clause. Since virtually all state judicial decisions and statutes have recognized the validity of the clause for the limited purpose of insuring the credit worthiness of proposed transferees, the Act is not likely to present a serious conflict with state law in this respect. Finally, it should be emphasized that states without window periods could not restrict enforcement of due-on-sale clauses.

The exact nature of this authority to "otherwise regulate" certain window period loans is not clear. Suppose that in 1980 the Supreme Court of State X held that a due-on-sale clause could not be enforced with respect to loans on single family dwellings unless the mortgagee could establish that the transfer would impair security or create an increased risk of default. State X thus has a window period for mortgage loans that were made or assumed on such dwellings after the 1980 judicial decision. A mortgagor or his transferee was free to transfer, subject only to state law restrictions, until October 15, 1985.

Suppose further that during 1984 State X enacted legislation with a clear intent to insulate such window period loans from the Act's preemption. Assume that the legislation extended this protection to pre-Act mortgage loans on duplexes made or assumed after the 1980 judicial decision. The time extension is valid, but according to the preamble to the Regulation, the duplex provision is invalid because a

appears to be good Arkansas law except for federal and state savings associations, and it is unclear why Arkansas was omitted from the FNMA and FHLMC lists.

California has a complex window period situation. See Nelson and Whitman, Congressional Preemption of Mortgage Due-on-Sale Law: An Analysis of the Garn-St. Germain Act, 35 Hast.L.J. 241, 275–286 (1983).

The Florida district courts of appeals have consistently required a showing of impairment of security for due-on-sale enforcement. See Consolidated Capital Properties, II, Inc. v. National Bank of North America, 420 So.2d 618, 622–23 (Fla.App. 1982), petition for review dismissed 429 So.2d 7 (1983); Woodcrest Apartments, Limited v. IPA Realty Partners, 397 So.2d 364, 366 (Fla.App.1981); First Federal Savings & Loan Association v. Lockwood, 385 So.2d 156, 159–60 (Fla.App.1980); see also Turner, Due-on-Sale Clause: Forcing the Issue, 56 Fla.B.J. 360 (1982). There is Florida Court of Appeal authority that Florida is a window period state. See First Federal Savings & Loan Association v. Siegel, 456 So.2d 579, 581 (Fla.App.1984). Florida may have been omitted from the FNMA and FHLMC lists on the supposition that the decisions of the Florida Courts of Appeals are not decisions which apply Statewide, whatever that phrase from the Act may mean. See 12 U.S.C.A. § 1701j–3(c)(1), see also Nelson and Whitman supra at 291–294.

state could not "expand the type of loan to which the window period applies." This seems a justifiable restriction on state legislative action. If, as was noted earlier, a state legislature cannot expand the type of loan protected from the Act's preemption during the 1982–1985 grace period, it surely should be unable to do so for the life of the loan.

The Board's interpretation on this point is entirely reasonable. Unfortunately, the drafting of the relevant portion of the Act was extremely inept. While the Act provides that state legislatures "may otherwise regulate such contracts," it is unclear whether "such contracts" refers to all real property loans except those originated by federally-chartered lenders, or only to window period loans. The latter construction is more consistent with the Act's overall objective of protecting reasonable reliance, and the Board's view should be upheld.

On the other hand, it appears that legislatures in window period states had the power to modify the *content* of existing state law so long as they did not attempt to extend it to non-window period loans. In the example above, the legislature could have theoretically affected due-on-sale enforcement for window period loans by adopting specific credit standards, either more or less severe than those in the hypothetical 1980 judicial decision, which a prospective grantee would then be required to meet. As we noted, however, the legislature could not take away the power of lenders to apply "customary credit standards." In light of this limitation, the practical ability of legislatures to change credit standards, was unidirectional: they could only impose standards stiffer than "customary" standards.

Special Rules Under the Act for Certain Federally-Chartered Lenders

As noted earlier, federally-chartered savings and loan associations had the pre-Act power to enforce due-on-sale clauses by virtue of the 1976 Bank Board regulation upheld in *de la Cuesta*. The Act, with minor modifications, simply continued that power. Moreover, while prior to the Act some doubt existed as to the enforceability of due-on-sale clauses in pre-1976 regulation mortgage loans, the Act's preemption definitely applies to such clauses, which are now clearly enforceable. Neither the window period concept nor a window period state's ability to "otherwise regulate" window period loans is applicable to such federal associations. Thus, so far as any post-Act transfer is concerned, federal associations are entirely free of state due-on-sale law.

With respect to national banks and federal credit unions, window period loans originated by these lenders were subject to state law until October 15, 1985, unless the Comptroller of the Currency (Comptroller) or the National Credit Union Administration (NCUA) acted prior to that date otherwise to regulate these loans. Thus, the Comptroller or the NCUA had the power to either extend or contract the time period in which these loans were subject to state law. The NCUA acted, effective November 18, 1982, to render immediately enforceable due-on-sale clauses in transfers made on or after that date.[14] In effect, the NCUA's rules preempted state law, regardless of the reasonable expectations of the consumers in states that would otherwise have had assumable window period loans.

The Comptroller's rule, effective December 8, 1983, was similar to the NCUA rule but more lenient to owners of one to four family homes who obtained or assumed loans during a window period. Until April 15, 1984, such loans could be assumed to the extent allowed by state law, except that the lender could increase the interest rate to a "blended" level that was the average of the original contract rate and the current average contract interest rate on existing homes, as published by the Board. For other types of loans, the full federal preemption was effective immediately.[15]

* * *

Release of The Original Mortgagor Under the Act

When a mortgagee waives its right to accelerate under a due-on-sale clause (typically after a higher interest rate or "assumption fee" is agreed upon) and the transferee assumes (rather than merely takes "subject to") the existing mortgage, the Regulation requires that the mortgagee release the original mortgagor from personal liability on the mortgage debt. For several years this requirement has been part of Board regulations applicable to federally-chartered savings and loan associations. The mortgage form specified for use by lenders who sell mortgages to the FNMA and the FHLMC on the secondary market also imposes such a requirement on mortgagees. There is no policy ground for objecting to the Board's requirement, but there is also no justification for it in the Act. Hence the Board's authority to impose the requirement on lenders other than federally-chartered savings associations must rest on the rather thin reed of its general power to issue rules.

Concealment of Transfers

In jurisdictions where due-on-sale clauses have been automatically enforceable or where there has been some doubt as to their enforceability, parties to real estate transactions may be tempted to avoid the consequences of the due-on-sale clause by concealing the transfer from the mortgagee. Because the Act will increase the number of enforceable due-on-sale clauses, these concealment attempts will probably increase. For example, to decrease the risk of discovery, the parties may arrange to have the transferee make the mortgage payments to the mortgagor-transferor or to a third party, who in turn will make the payment to the mortgagee in the mortgagor's name. Usually the parties continue to use the payment book originally issued to the mortgagor-transferor.

14. 47 Fed.Reg. 54,425 (codified at 12 CFR 701.21–6(d)(2)(i)).

15. 48 Fed.Reg. 51,283 (codified at 12 CFR 30.1).

For a variety of reasons these concealment strategies often fail. Some mortgagees, for example, may closely monitor the public records for evidence of new real estate recordings affecting their mortgaged properties. Ownership changes may also become apparent from the annual real estate tax statements that the mortgagee receives in its capacity as an escrow agent for real estate taxes and insurance. Similar information can be obtained when a new casualty insurance policy is issued and the mortgagee's copy reveals the new owner. Moreover, mortgagees can keep abreast of transfers through a program of regular inspection of the real estate on which they hold mortgages.

Transferees may attempt to reduce the chances of discovery by not recording the transfer. This approach not only frustrates mortgagee discovery of the transfer from an examination of the public records, but also usually prevents the revelation of a new owner incident to the issuance of new tax statements. In addition, the parties may also keep the casualty insurance policy in force in the mortgagor's name, but utilize a side agreement that purports to assign the beneficial interest in the policy to the transferee.

Even assuming that the foregoing tactics succeed in preventing mortgagee discovery of a transfer, the failure to record can create substantial problems for transferees in some states. If the transferee takes possession, in most jurisdictions that constitutes constructive notice of the transferee's interest and should protect the transferee against mortgages or other interests that are created by or arise against the mortgagor-transferor. In such situations, possession is the functional equivalent of recording. A few jurisdictions, however, require actual notice; possession alone does not qualify as constructive notice.[3] Even when possession constitutes constructive notice, "establishing the existence of that possession could require litigation, while the fact of a recorded document would not."[4] Failure to record is unacceptably risky, in our view.

If the mortgagee ultimately discovers the transfer, as will often happen, does it have a remedy against the parties to the concealment beyond a belated acceleration of the mortgage debt? The answer will depend in part on whether the parties have a duty to notify the mortgagee of the transfer. One court suggested that no such duty is implicit in the due-on-sale clause itself.[5] This conclusion is by no means inescapable. A court could conceivably impose a duty of good faith on the mortgagor that would be violated by concealment attempts. Moreover, some mortgagees have begun to include express mortgage language that requires the mortgagor-transferor to notify the mortgagee in the event of a transfer. When such language is utilized, the

---

3. See, e.g., Drey v. Doyle, 99 Mo. 459, 469, 12 S.W. 287, 289 (1889); M.G.L.A. c. 183, § 4; Comment, Possession as Notice Under Missouri Recording Act, 16 Mo.L. Rev. 142 (1951).

4. Nelson and Whitman, Real Estate Finance Law § 3.33 (2nd Ed.1985).

5. Medovoi v. American Savings & Loan Association, 89 Cal.App.3d 244, 152 Cal.Rptr. 572 (1979) (depublished).

mortgagee may have a cause of action even when a window period loan is involved. Even though the due-on-sale clause in such a loan will often prove to be unenforceable, the mortgagee has a valid interest in discovering the identity of the transferee so as to be able to assess his or her creditworthiness or the impact of the transfer on mortgage security.

Suppose there is a duty to notify the lender, or at least a duty of good faith that would be violated by active concealment efforts. What damages might the lender recover for breach? If the mortgagee had been informed at the time of the transfer and had accelerated, and if the funds could have then been re-lent at a higher rate, the mortgagee has lost this interest income. In reality, most lenders are willing to forego acceleration under due-on-sale clauses in a rising-interest market if the transferee agrees to begin paying an interest rate that is higher than that provided in the original contract but nearer to the current market rate. In a concealment case the mortgagee might show damages by proving the interest rate that it customarily demanded on transferred properties at the time the concealed transfer occurred. It is doubtful that punitive damages could be recovered even for bad faith on the mortgagor's part.[6] It would appear that only the original mortgagor can be liable for compensatory damages; the transferee who has taken subject to a mortgage has no contractual relationship with the lender, and it is hard to see any other basis for liability.

Concealment can raise serious legal problems between the mortgagor and the transferee. If the lender subsequently discovers the transfer and accelerates, the transferee may well sue his seller for damages. The suit could claim, for example, a breach of an implied warranty or covenant that the loan would not be called due. We have found no case authority for such an action, but it is not inconceivable. This implied covenant notion is, in a sense, the exact opposite of the traditional implied covenant of marketable title, for here a continuing encumbrance is desired by the buyer and bargained for by the parties. The buyer would argue that acceleration by the lender breaches this term and understanding of the sales agreement. The buyer's damages would represent the excess interest (and possibly settlement and related costs) that the buyer would incur in the future upon refinancing the property after acceleration. Moreover, if the buyer is unable to qualify for new financing and foreclosure ensues, the seller may be liable for damages incident to the buyer's loss of his or her equity in the mortgaged real estate. Conceivably the seller could be faced with two suits: one by the lender for lost interest up to the date of actual acceleration, and one by the buyer for increased interest payments or loss of the property thereafter. In any transaction in which the lender is not fully informed, the seller is well-advised to include in the sale contract language by which the transferee acknowledges the risk of future acceler-

---

6. Punitive damages are not generally available for contract breaches unless a tort has also been committed. See Restatement (Second) of Contracts § 355 (1981); 5 A. Corbin, Contracts § 1077 (1960).

ation and agrees to hold the seller harmless in the event acceleration occurs.[8]

Should a lawyer be troubled by the ethical implications of counseling a client to conceal a transfer, or of arranging the details of the transaction? At most, the concealment is a breach of contract, and the Model Code of Professional Responsibility apparently does not prohibit advising a client to breach a contract, although Disciplinary Rule 7–102(A)(7) provides that a lawyer shall not "counsel or assist his client in conduct that the lawyer knows to be illegal or fraudulent."[9] Of course, "illegal" is a slippery word, and could conceivably include contract breaches. But the opinions of the American Bar Association's Committee on Ethics and Professional Responsibility consistently treat this rule as referring only to criminal conduct or something very close to it.[10] The rule has never been regarded as applying to breaches of contract.

The lawyer who counsels concealment in the face of an enforceable due-on-sale clause may be (and we think usually is) guilty of giving poor advice, but it does not appear to be an ethical violation under the Code. We are uncomfortable with this conclusion. The Code does not adequately deal with the issue, and perhaps reflects the larger societal indecision regarding the morality of breaching contracts.[11]

C. TRANSFER OF THE MORTGAGEE'S INTEREST

Page 408, in connection with the second paragraph of Note 3, read the following case:

HAMMELBURGER v. FOURSOME INN CORP.

Court of Appeals of New York, 1981.
54 N.Y.2d 580, 446 N.Y.S.2d 917, 431 N.E.2d 278.

OPINION OF THE COURT

MEYER, Judge.

* * *

I

In 1974, the Foursome Inn Corp., owner of the Surf and Sand Inn, in Montauk, New York, borrowed $35,000 from Broadhollow Funding

---

8. See Liss, Drafting Around the Mortgage "Due on Sale" Clause in the Installment Sale of Real Estate, 62 Chi.B.Rec. 312 (1981) (suggesting various other protective clauses).

9. Model Code of Professional Responsibility EC 7–5 (1980) states the same principles in even more general terms.

10. See ABA Comm. on Ethics and Professional Responsibility, Informal Op. 1314 (1975) (perjury by client); ABA Comm. on Ethics and Professional Responsibility, Formal Op. 335 (1974) (securities fraud); ABA Comm. on Professional Ethics and Grievances, Formal Op. 281 (1952) (representation of a criminal syndicate).

11. Liss, supra note 8, appears to see no ethical problems in concealment. Id. at 312.

Corporation secured by a mortgage on the Inn premises. The mortgage was for a three-year term at an interest rate of 24% per annum and contained a provision that the mortgage principal and interest "shall become due at the option of the mortgagee * * * after default * * * in furnishing a statement of the amount due on the mortgage and whether any offsets or defenses exist against the mortgage debt." Only $32,900 was paid at closing to Foursome or for closing costs, however, the remaining $2,100 having been paid to Ira S. Schwartz, then secretary-treasurer of Broadhollow.

At Schwartz' examination before trial, conducted at Foursome's instance and a copy of which was annexed to Foursome's moving papers on the first motion hereafter referred to, he testified that he was a licensed real estate broker, that the mortgage lender was in fact Stallone Enterprises Corporation (SECO) though the mortgage was taken in Broadhollow's name because of marital problems of SECO's owner, that the $2,100 represented a 6% commission to Schwartz pursuant to a commission agreement with Foursome, and that Broadhollow serviced the mortgage for SECO before its assignment to plaintiffs and continued to do so for plaintiffs after that assignment.

The assignment to plaintiffs was made in October, 1975, 10 days after Beatrice Reilly, the president of Foursome, executed on its behalf an estoppel certificate stating that "there are no defenses or offsets to said mortgage, nor to the bond which it secures." Negotiations with Mrs. Reilly for the certificate were engaged in by both Ira Schwartz and his father, Abraham, then president of Broadhollow. Mrs. Reilly's affidavit, submitted in support of the third motion by defendant hereafter referred to, sets forth facts concerning both threats to foreclose and cajoling by the Schwartzes which suggest that she may have been misled concerning the nature of her default, the offer of a proposed extension of the mortgage, or both.

In July, 1976, Foursome defaulted on its payments. Plaintiffs then declared the entire principal balance due and instituted this foreclosure action. Foursome's answer was no more than a general denial but, subsequently, it moved for leave to amend the answer to assert the affirmative defense of criminal usury. As already noted, its moving papers on that motion included a copy of Ira Schwartz' deposition. Plaintiffs, relying on the estoppel certificate, cross-moved for summary judgment. Special Term denied the motion to amend and granted plaintiffs' cross motion for summary judgment, holding the defense not available to Foursome because waived by its execution of the estoppel certificate delivered to plaintiffs. On motion for reargument Special Term adhered to that ruling. A referee to compute was then appointed and after receipt of his report judgment of foreclosure and sale was entered. On the eve of sale, however, defendant having obtained additional counsel moved to vacate the judgment on papers, including the affidavit of Mrs. Reilly above referred to, which reiterated the criminal usury involved and set forth facts suggesting, as above noted, that she signed the estoppel certificate as a result of threats or of being misled, or both. That motion, too, was denied.

On appeal to the Appellate Division that court reversed, on the law, the orders denying the motions to amend the answer and to vacate the judgment, granted both motions, denied plaintiffs' motion for summary judgment and, acting pursuant to CPLR 3212 (subd. [b]), granted Foursome summary judgment declaring the mortgage void and dismissing the complaint. It reasoned that the societal interests protected by the public policy declared in the criminal usury statute could not be affected by estoppel based on conduct of the parties to the mortgage and, therefore, did not reach the question of duress. We conclude that (1) an estoppel certificate may waive criminal as well as civil usury; (2) duress, other invalidating circumstances, or knowledge on the part of the assignee before he takes the assignment of the criminal nature of the transaction or of the exertion of duress may, however, invalidate or negate the estoppel certificate; and (3) there are in the instant case issues of fact which cannot be resolved on motion for summary judgment. We, therefore, modify as above indicated.

II

Though he be a bona fide holder, an assignee of a nonnegotiable bond and mortgage takes subject to any defense that would have prevailed against his assignor (Beck v. Sheldon, 259 N.Y. 208, 211, 181 N.E. 360, Kommel v. Herb-Gner Constr. Co., 256 N.Y. 333, 336, 176 N.E. 413). The rule is different, however, when the mortgagor gives the assignee an estoppel certificate (Riggs v. Purssell, 89 N.Y. 608, 610; see Real Property Law, § 254, subds. 2, 7) or with notice of his rights and of the facts "does what amounts to a recognition or adoption" of the transaction "although it was originally void or voidable" (Rothschild v. Title Guar. & Trust Co., 204 N.Y. 458, 464, 97 N.E. 879; Ann., 110 ALR 451, 452, 457). The assignee's right of recovery does not depend upon the title or interest of his assignor, but upon the mortgagor's representation by his certificate or by his conduct that the mortgage is valid and existing (Miller v. Zeimer, 111 N.Y. 441, 444, 18 N.E. 716; Weyh v. Boylan, 85 N.Y. 394, 397; Payne v. Burnham, 62 N.Y. 69, 72; see Union Dime Sav. Inst. of City of N.Y. v. Wilmot, 94 N.Y. 221; Ann., 165 ALR 626, 717).

The basis for the latter rule is, of course, the doctrine of estoppel *in pais* (Payne v. Burnham, supra, 62 N.Y. at p. 73; Ferguson v. Hamilton, 35 Barb. 427, 437). It turns not upon any view of the negotiability of the certificate (Weyh v. Boylan, supra, 85 N.Y. at p. 399) or the validity of the mortgage (Valentine v. Lunt, 115 N.Y. 496, 504, 21 N.E. 209), but upon the fact that the mortgagor would, if allowed to urge the defense, "obtain an unconscientious advantage at the expense of an innocent person" (Weyh v. Boylan, supra, 85 N.Y. at p. 398; see, also, Rothschild v. Title Guar. & Trust Co., 204 N.Y. 458, 464, supra; Restatement, Contracts 2d, § 90, Comment *a*), and the long-established principle that "where one of two innocent persons must suffer by the acts of a third, he who has enabled such third person to occasion the loss, must sustain it" (National Safe Deposit Co. v. Hibbs, 229 U.S. 391, 394, 33 S.Ct. 818, 819, 57 L.Ed. 1241, quoted with approval in Bunge Corp. v. Manufacturers Hanover Trust Co., 31 N.Y.2d 223, 228). Estoppel does not render the mortgage valid but prevents "one who has represented it to be valid from asserting that it is void, to the injury of those who have acted in reliance upon the representation" (Claflin v. Boorum, 122 N.Y. 385, 389; Valentine v. Lunt, supra). The policy of the usury statute is not, however, ignored, for the innocent assignee is permitted to recover only the amount advanced with interest, rather than to enforce the mortgage for its face amount * * *.

The conduct or certificate must, however, have influenced the assignee to accept the mortgage to his injury (Payne v. Burnham, supra, 62 N.Y. at p. 73). That means not just reliance upon the existence of the certificate, but on the facts expressed by or implicit in it (Wilcox v. Howell, supra, 44 N.Y. at p. 403; see Claflin v. Boorum, supra; Weyh v. Boylan, supra; Hyde Park Terrace Co. v. Jackson Bros. Realty Co., 161 App.Div. 699, 146 N.Y.S. 1037; Ann., 110 ALR 451, 462). An assignee who takes with knowledge can no more enforce the mortgage, whether as to principal or interest, than could the usurer. Knowledge by the assignee of the usurious nature of the transaction will, therefore, defeat an estoppel claim (Riggs v. Purssell, supra; Gleason v. O'Neill, 234 App.Div. 264, 254 N.Y.S. 814; Merwin v. Romanelli, 141 App.Div. 711, 126 N.Y.S. 549).

The rules thus developed concern, it is true, so-called civil usury, as the Appellate Division noted, but were developed in relation to a statute (3 Revised Statutes [5th ed.], part 2, ch. 4, tit. 3, § 5, now part of General Obligations Law, § 5–511, subd. 1), which provided that a transaction in which interest in excess of the prescribed rate was taken "shall be void." Moreover, they became the established rules not without some hesitation and the realization that they trenched upon the policy of the usury law * * *.

* * *

[The legislature's] failure to close off the estoppel certificate avenue as a means for a usurer to realize on his illegal loan may have been an oversight, though in view of the case law history above detailed that hardly seems likely. Equally probable is it that the Legislature, recognizing the "two innocent persons" rule, was unwilling to penalize by the loss of both principal and interest an assignee who in good faith reliance on the mortgagor's assurance of the absence of any defense had purchased the obligation, because the Legislature believed limitation of the assignee's recovery to what he paid plus legal interest to be a sufficient deterrent to make purchasers of mortgages wary of professional usurers and a sufficient protection to the mortgagor who by certifying the absence of a defense has made transfer of the mortgage by the usurer possible.

So to suggest is not, as the concurrence and the Appellate Division indicate, abhorrent to public policy in any way. To the contrary, it is abhorrent to the policy of the law in the name of public interest to make an innocent assignee pay for the crime of the usurer in order to protect the borrower who, by his conduct or estoppel certificate, has misled the assignee. It is, moreover, wholly unnecessary to do so. People v. Young, 207 N.Y. 522, 101 N.E. 451, makes clear that the victim of criminal usury cannot by accepting restitution affect in any way the People's power to prosecute and that rule applies as well to estoppel by conduct or by certificate. The criminal usurer continues, therefore, to be subject to prosecution for a class E felony, the maximum prison term for which is four years. He remains subject also to civil liability for his criminal act; to the assignee who has been defrauded through the usurer's obtention of a false estoppel certificate for the difference between the face amount of the bond transferred and what he has been able to collect on it from the debtor; to the debtor from whom the usurer could have collected neither principal nor interest for the principal and interest which the debtor has been required to pay to the innocent assignee, the debtor not being *in pari delicto* with the usurer. Neither public welfare nor the public policy declared by chapter 328 of the Laws of 1965 is denigrated one whit by the limited recovery permitted to an innocent assignee; to the contrary, the public interests are vindicated fully, both civilly and criminally. Indeed, to relegate the assignee to an action against the usurer, as the concurrence suggests, is to denigrate the two innocent persons policy by turning that long-respected rule completely on its head.

* * *

Accordingly, we reject the Appellate Division's basic premise and hold that, until the Legislature otherwise provides, a valid estoppel certificate executed by a mortgagor and relied upon in good faith by the assignee of the mortgage will preclude the assertion of usury, whether civil or criminal, as a complete defense.

III

We are thus brought to consideration of the issue of duress which the Appellate Division found it unnecessary to decide. What we consider, of course, is duress as it affects execution of the estoppel certificate, and the first thing to be noted is that duress in obtaining the certificate is irrelevant unless the mortgage itself is found to be usurious and, therefore, void and unenforceable but for the estoppel. This means that the provisions of the mortgage permitting the mortgagee to accelerate principal and interest for failure to give an estoppel certificate, though sanctioned by subdivisions 2 and 7 of section 254 of the Real Property Law, will not obviate the claim that the certificate was obtained by duress.

In Wilcox v. Howell, 44 N.Y. 398, 402, supra, we held that estoppel does not operate to preclude an obligor from asserting that the instrument claimed to estop him was obtained by fraud (accord Laurel Realty

Co. v. Galasso, 6 A.D.2d 889, 177 N.Y.S.2d 1016, see Weyh v. Boylan, supra, 85 N.Y. at p. 401), and the applicability of that rule to duress has been recognized in Oleet v. Pennsylvania Exch. Bank, 285 App.Div. 411, 137 N.Y.S.2d 779; see, also, Uniform Commercial Code, § 3–305, subd. [2], par. [b]). Those holdings having been part of the decisional law complex in light of which chapter 328 of the Laws of 1965 was enacted, and the strong-arm tactics of loan-shark enforcers having played such a prominent part in the Report of the State Investigation Commission, the conclusion must be that the Legislature intended no change of prior law in this respect.

Duress in obtaining the estoppel certificate will, therefore, invalidate it. We are not unaware of the effect of that holding upon the marketability of mortgage assignments, but conclude that estoppel being essentially a doctrine arising from inequitable action or conduct, the rule should not, absent legislative change, be applied when the mortgagor's action or conduct has been coerced (cf. Mandelino v. Fribourg, 23 N.Y.2d 145, 148, 295 N.Y.S.2d 654, 242 N.E.2d 823). Whether an estoppel certificate has been obtained by duress will generally be a question of fact, turning not just upon whether there was a threat to foreclose, but upon whether the trier of fact concludes from the circumstances surrounding the bargaining between the parties to the giving of the certificate or to the conduct relied upon and relative to the bargaining positions of both that the mortgagor acted under the influence of fear and would not have done so otherwise (see Restatement, Contracts 2d, §§ 174–175; 13 Williston, Contracts [3d ed.], § 1604; 2 N.Y. PJI 900–901).

IV

The Appellate Division, applying the formula set forth in Band Realty Co. v. North Brewster, 37 N.Y.2d 460, 373 N.Y.S.2d 97, 335 N.E.2d 316, concluded that the true interest rate was 27.7% per annum and, therefore, clearly in excess of the maximum prescribed by section 190.40 of the Penal Law. However, in concluding as a matter of law that the mortgage was criminally usurious, it overlooked the facts, outlined above, testified to by Ira Schwartz, that raised a triable issue of fact concerning whether the $2,100 was in fact a legitimate commission. True, the finder's fee is a device often resorted to by unscrupulous lenders (1965 Report of State Investigation Commission, Investigation of Loan-Shark Racket, pp. 73–75). But a commission payable to Schwartz as agent for Foursome (with whom he testified he had an agreement) would not necessarily make the transaction usurious (Salvin v. Myles Realty Co., 227 N.Y. 51, 124 N.E. 94; Guardian Mut. Life Ins. Co. of N.Y. v. Kashaw, 66 N.Y. 544; cf. General Obligations Law, § 5–531; see Ann., 52 ALR2d 703; 32 N.Y. Jur., Interest & Usury, §§ 67–69). Usury must be proved by clear evidence as to all its elements and will not be presumed (Giventer v. Arnow, 37 N.Y.2d 305, 372 N.Y.S.2d 63, 333 N.E.2d 366; Brown v. Robinson, 224 N.Y. 301, 120 N.E. 694; Grannis v. Stevens, 216 N.Y. 583, 111 N.E. 263). Whether the commission was a cover for usury was, therefore, a question of fact (London Realty Co. v. Riordan, 207 N.Y. 264, 266, 100 N.E. 800) which the Appellate Division could neither assume nor decide.

* * *

For the foregoing reasons, the order of the Appellate Division should be modified and affirmed, with costs, as above indicated.

COOKE, Chief Judge (concurring).

A lender who may be criminally prosecuted for a particular loan should not be permitted to avoid the civil consequence of this wrong through the simple expedient of obtaining a waiver from the borrower. As a matter of public policy, I would hold that criminal usury is not waivable outside a judicial proceeding.

Two aspects of criminal usury are abhorrent to public policy. First, the excessive interest charged is considered repulsive to our values. It is nothing more than a thoroughly unscrupulous exploitation of another's vulnerability. Society will not condone one person's taking unfair advantage of another's weaker position (see, e.g., Barnard v. Gantz, 140 N.Y. 249, 35 N.E. 430 [undue influence]; Restatement, Contracts 2d, § 177). Second, the exaction of criminally excessive interest is, in the public's mind, inextricably linked with violent methods of collecting delinquent debts.

In response to these problems, the Legislature in 1965 made criminal those loans that bear interest exceeding 25% per annum (L.1965, ch. 328, § 1; see Penal Law, § 190.40). At the same time, the Legislature also empowered corporations to assert criminal usury as an affirmative defense (L.1965, ch. 328, § 6; see General Obligations Law, § 5–521), in part to eliminate the lenders' practice of requiring individual borrowers to incorporate so that the defense of usury could not be raised at all (N.Y. Legis.Ann., 1965, p. 50).

The majority notes the long-standing rule that civil usury can be waived as a defense. The majority then concludes that the Legislature intentionally adopted this rule in reference to criminal usury out of solicitude for the innocent assignee, although the majority admits that the omission may have been mere oversight (at p. 590, p. 923 of 446 N.Y.S.2d, p. 284 of 431 N.E.2d). So reasoning, the majority refrains from "extending" public policy as determined by the Legislature (id., at pp. 590–591, pp. 923–924 of 446 N.Y.S.2d, p. 284 of 431 N.E.2d). Today's decision is not only not reflective of public policy but, on the contrary, destroys it. If the lender can compel the individual to incorporate, there is no reason why that same individual cannot be compelled to sign a waiver of defenses. And this "compulsion" need not amount to legal duress—the same circumstances which drove the borrower to the usurious lender in the first place will also serve to motivate the execution of the waiver. With the waiver in hand, the lender may now freely negotiate the illegal contract to third parties.

The problems inherent in permitting waiver of criminal usury may be best observed by use of a hypothetical. Needing $5,000 and unable to obtain a loan from a legitimate lender, A borrows the money from B, who requires that A sign a note for $10,000 and a certificate disavowing any defenses. The note is for one year and bears interest at 22%. On its face, the note evidences a noncriminal loan. Of course, in reality the loan is criminally usurious, requiring payment of $7,200 interest on a $5,000 loan, a rate of 144% (see Band Realty Co. v. North Brewster, 37 N.Y.2d 460, 373 N.Y.S.2d 97, 335 N.E.2d 316). B does not wish to carry the loan and therefore discounts it to C for $8,500. C is unaware of the true transaction and so takes the note as a holder in due course. Given today's result, A is barred from asserting any defense and the court is required to enforce an illegal contract proscribed by penal sanction. This is untenable.

Prohibiting the waiver of criminal usury does not leave the assignee without any recourse. The assignor warrants the validity of the instrument, including that there is no defense good against him (see Uniform Commercial Code, § 3–417, subd. [2], par. [d]; Restatement, Contracts 2d, § 333, subd. [1], par. [b]). Thus, the assignee may recover from the lender, the party who should properly bear the burden for violating the law. No great procedural difficulties are presented, either. Once the borrower raises the affirmative defense, the assignee may amend the complaint to include a claim against the assignor. In this way, all parties to the instrument will be before the court and all will be bound by the determination of the nature of the transaction. In short, the assignee *will* recover—either from the borrower or the assignor.

The majority equates civil usury and criminal usury in reaching its conclusion. There is, however, a critical distinction that may be succinctly stated. Civil usury, although illegal, violates private law only. Criminal usury, however, has been deemed an injury to the public welfare as well as to private rights. The usurer who can be jailed should not be allowed to profit from the wrong by simply obtaining a waiver.

It is difficult also to accept the majority's discussion of duress. It first suggests that duress is available only if the underlying mortgage is illegal (at pp. 592–593, pp. 924–925 of 446 N.Y.S.2d, pp. 285–286 of 431 N.E.2d). Duress, however, is a real defense which always follows the document (see Uniform Commercial Code, § 3–305, subd. [2], par. [b]; Restatement, Contracts 2d, § 336, subd. [1]). Consequently the legality of the underlying transaction should have no bearing on the validity of the waiver if the latter were obtained through duress.

More noteworthy, because inconsistent with the rule announced, is the implication that the certificate will be invalid if it was obtained by threatening to enforce the legal rights set forth in the mortgage (at p. 593, n.4, p. 925 of 446 N.Y.S.2d, p. 286 of 431 N.E.2d). The majority would hold that these threats constitute duress if the mortgage is usurious so that no legal rights are provided. In so arguing, the majority has gone full circle: the borrower is estopped from asserting against an assignee the defense of criminal usury unless the waiver was obtained by threatening to enforce the usurious contract, in which case the waiver is invalid and the defense may be asserted against the assignee so as to void the contract. Thus, the borrower is allowed to do indirectly what the majority declares he or she cannot do directly—defeat the waiver and avoid the contract by raising the defense of criminal usury.

I concur, however, with the majority's conclusion that summary judgment was improperly granted. There exists a question of fact as to the legitimacy of the commission paid to Ira Schwartz. If the commission was proper, then the loan was not usurious. For that reason, the Appellate Division's order should be modified and the case remitted for trial. It cannot be overemphasized, however, that public policy as expressed by the Legislature demands that all waivers of criminal usury be declared ineffective per se.

JONES, WACHTLER and FUCHSBERG, JJ., concur with MEYER, J.

COOKE, C.J., concurs in result in a separate opinion in which JASEN and GABRIELLI, JJ., concur.

Page 423, insert the following case immediately before Giorgi v. Pioneer Title Ins. Co.:

RODGERS v. SEATTLE–FIRST NATIONAL BANK

Washington Court of Appeals, 1985.
40 Wn.App. 127, 697 P.2d 1009.

MUNSON, Judge.

Seattle-First National Bank (Seattle-First) appeals from a judgment quieting title in Mr. and Mrs. Leonard Rodgers and denying its claim for damages against Yakima Federal Savings and Loan Association (Yakima Federal) and Mr. and Mrs. Paul B. Noble. The sole issue is whether an obligor who had actual notice of an assignment of a deed of trust may be discharged upon payment to the assignor when the assignee would have told the obligor to pay the assignor if the obligor had inquired. We affirm.

The findings are unchallenged and are in large part based upon a stipulation of the parties. Columbia Pacific Mortgage, Inc., (CPM) was in the business of lending money to land developers and builders. To fund its activities, CPM obtained lines of credit from several banks, including one for $7.7 million from Seattle-First's main office in Seattle. CPM's obligation to Seattle-First was evidenced by three master promissory notes—one for land development, one for residential construction, and one for commercial construction.

To secure the line of credit, CPM assigned promissory notes and deeds of trust received from its customers to Seattle-First. The value of the instruments assigned to Seattle-First was intended to approximate or exceed CPM's outstanding indebtedness to Seattle-First. The instruments went into a "collateral pool" which was controlled by CPM; CPM could add to or subtract from the pool according to its credit needs. Any pay down or borrowing on the line of credit bore no relation to the maturity dates on the notes securing the indebtedness. That is, there was no direct relationship between payments made by debtors to CPM and payments made by CPM to Seattle-First.

CPM and Seattle-First executed a "Security Agreement-General Pledge". Seattle-First filed a financing statement, took possession of the promissory notes, and recorded the assignments of the deeds of trust. Seattle-First's security interest was thus perfected. RCW 62A.9–304 (security interest in instrument perfected by possession); 65.08.070 (recording of real property conveyances). See Freeborn v. Seattle Trust & Sav. Bank, 94 Wash.2d 336, 617 P.2d 424 (1980) (regarding assignment of vendor's interest in real estate contract).

The transaction at issue was a loan made by CPM to the Nobles to finance construction of a house. The Nobles gave CPM a nonnegotiable note and deed of trust to secure the note. These were in turn assigned to Seattle-First, who took possession of the note and recorded the assignment of the deed of trust. The note provided payments were to be made to CPM in Richland "or such other place ... as the holder of this Note may designate in writing from time to time". At no time did Seattle-First tell the Nobles to make payments directly to it.

The Nobles sold the completed house to the Rodgerses, who obtained long-term financing from Yakima Federal. Mr. Noble directed Yakima Federal to satisfy his obligation with CPM from the proceeds of the sale. Yakima Federal received a title report reflecting the assignment of the deed of trust to Seattle-First. A Yakima Federal employee telephoned Seattle-First's Richland branch, and was told that branch had no information regarding the transaction, and Yakima Federal should contact CPM. Yakima Federal did not contact Seattle-First's main office in Seattle, although that address appears on the assignment of the deed of trust. On March 27, 1980, Yakima Federal gave CPM a check for $59,139.72 to satisfy the Nobles' obligation. Yakima Federal did not demand contemporaneous production of the note or reconveyance of the deed of trust. Although Yakima Federal asked CPM about the reconveyance on several occasions, none was forthcoming. On July 10, 1980, CPM filed a bankruptcy petition.

Seattle-First did not have a mechanism to receive payments directly on loans made by CPM; CPM as the actual maker of the loans received the payments. The testimony disclosed that even if Yakima Federal had called Seattle-First's head branch, it would have been told to pay CPM. In March 1980, when the Nobles' loan was satisfied, CPM had not exceeded its credit limit with Seattle-First and Seattle-First had instructed neither CPM nor CPM's debtors to make payments directly to Seattle-First. Yakima Federal employees testified it is common in the mortgage banking industry to make an immediate payment to stop accrual of interest and then have a delay of several weeks before reconveyance of the documents by the mortgage company's creditor.

The Rodgerses and Yakima Federal commenced an action to quiet title. Seattle-First counterclaimed for foreclosure of the deed of trust and brought in the Nobles as third party defendants. Yakima Federal accepted the Nobles' tender of their defense and agreed to assume liability for any judgment against them in this action. The trial court quieted title in the Rodgerses and dismissed Seattle-First's cross claim against the Nobles. Seattle-First appeals.

Seattle-First contends Yakima Federal cannot assert payment to CPM as a defense. Seattle-First argues any final payment of a note without demanding production of it is at the obligor's risk. Assets Realization Co. v. Clark, 205 N.Y. 105, 98 N.E. 457 (1912). This is especially true because Yakima Federal had actual notice through the title report of the assignment of the deed of trust. Since Seattle-First's security interest was perfected, it argues, it had an absolute right to collect upon default by CPM.

Yakima Federal counters that, if it had contacted Seattle-First's head office branch, it would have been told to pay CPM. Since Seattle-First was not insecure in March 1980 and never intended to exercise any control over this transaction, it cannot now complain. We agree.

Seattle-First extensively cites the Uniform Commercial Code. The transaction between CPM and the Nobles deals with real estate, and therefore RCW Title 62A, Article 9, does not apply. RCW 62A.9–104(j). Nor does RCW Title 62A, Article 3, apply because the Nobles gave CPM a nonnegotiable note. However, Article 9 may apply to the "realty paper" given by CPM to Seattle-First. RCW 62A.9–102, Comment 4; *Freeborn v. Seattle Trust & Sav. Bank,* supra; J. White & R. Summers, *Uniform Commercial Code,* 890–91 (2d ed.1980). Notwithstanding, Article 9 provides little guidance because a debtor on an "instrument" is not an "account debtor", entitled to pay the assignor under RCW 62A.9–318. See RCW 62A.9–105(1)(i) (defining "instrument"); RCW 62A.9–105(1)(a) (defining "account debtor"); Restatement (Second) of Contracts § 338, comment *h,* at 80 (1981). We therefore look to the common law.

The Restatement (Second) of Contracts § 338, at 75–76 (1981), provides:

> (1) Except as stated in this Section, notwithstanding an assignment, the assignor retains his power to discharge or modify the duty of the obligor to the extent that the obligor performs or otherwise gives value until but not after the obligor receives notification that the

right has been assigned and that performance is to be rendered to the assignee.

Nonproduction of the symbolic writing at the time of payment has the same effect as receipt of notification by the obligor of an assignment.[2] Here, in addition to nonproduction of the documents, Yakima Federal had actual notice through the title report of the assignment.

The Restatement follows long-settled law that one paying a note, either negotiable or nonnegotiable, should demand production of it upon payment or risk having to pay again to the assignee. In re Columbia Pac. Mortgage, Inc., 22 B.R. 753 (W.D.Wash.1982); *Assets Realization Co. v. Clark,* supra.[3] However, there are three exceptions which may provide for discharge of an obligor in the mortgage context: (1) The assignor may offer a plausible explanation for not producing the documents. *Assets Realization Co. v. Clark,* supra. (2) The assignor may have been given authority to collect payments and thus be the agent of the assignee. Ross v. Johnson, 171 Wash. 658, 19 P.2d 101 (1933); Pfeiffer v. Heyes, 166 Wash. 125, 6 P.2d 612 (1932). (3) Through the course of dealing of the parties, the assignee may be estopped from claiming payment from the obligor or denying satisfaction of the mortgage. *Ross v. Johnson,* supra; Erickson v. Kendall, 112 Wash. 26, 191 P. 842 (1920). That is, the assignee may be the innocent party who must suffer. *Erickson v. Kendall,* supra. See generally G. Osborne, G. Nelson & D. Whitman, *Real Estate Finance Law,* 344–50 (1979).

Here, the court declined to find an agency or estoppel, but rather rested its decision on (1) the language in the note requiring the Nobles to pay CPM until notified otherwise, and (2) the recorded assignment which the court believed was intended to protect Seattle-First from general creditors and subsequent assignees, not the debtors. The court indicated, however, that estoppel or agency would be alternate grounds to deny recovery to Seattle-First.

We uphold the trial court on the alternative grounds of estoppel and

---

2. "Aside from statute, an obligor who renders performance without requiring production of such a symbolic writing takes the risk that the person receiving performance does not have possession of the writing either because he has assigned it or because his right is defective. Nonproduction has the same effect as receipt of notification of assignment or reason to know of a defect in an assignee's right. In addition, the obligor who performs without surrender or cancellation of or appropriate notation on the writing takes the risk of further obligation to an assignee who takes possession of the writing as a bona fide purchaser. The latter rule may be regarded as an application of a broader doctrine of estoppel. See Restatement, Second, Agency §§ 8B, 176." Restatement (Second) of Contracts § 338, comment *h*, at 80 (1981).

3. The rule has been severely criticized in G. Osborne, G. Nelson & D. Whitman, *Real Estate Finance Law,* 344, 346 n. 7 (1979):

While the practice as described [in *Assets Realization Co. v. Clark,* supra] may have been prevalent in New York in 1912, it is certainly not so in the latter half of the Twentieth Century. Today the note is usually unavailable when the final payment is made. The payment is generally transmitted by an attorney or title company by mail and the mortgagee is trusted and expected to mark the note "paid" and mail it to the mortgagor within a reasonable time after receipt of the payment. Certainly no inference of notice should be drawn from failure to deliver the note immediately upon the tender of the final payment.

agency.[4] Seattle-First, through its course of dealing with CPM, led Noble and Yakima Federal to believe payment to CPM would suffice. Seattle-First ignores its own testimony that if the Nobles had inquired, they would have been told to pay CPM, which is what they did.

In re Columbia Pac. Mortgage, Inc., supra, cited by Seattle-First, is distinguishable. It was merely a denial of summary judgment; if the court had been presented with this situation, where the assignee would have told the obligor to pay the assignor, it might have ruled differently.

Seattle-First argues the Nobles and Yakima Federal should have issued a dual payee check or set up an escrow account. The court found, based upon substantial evidence, an escrow is not customary in residential real estate transactions, and Seattle-First would have endorsed a dual payee check back to CPM.

The judgment is affirmed.

GREEN, C.J., and THOMPSON, J., concur.

Page 427, add to Note 3 as the fourth full paragraph:

Commentators and courts are increasingly taking the position that "real estate law does not require a recording of an assignment of the mortgage in order to perfect a security interest in the mortgage, so long as the secured party takes a written assignment of the mortgage and takes and maintains possession of the note." Krasnowiecki, Miller, and Ziff, The Kennedy Mortgage Co. Bankruptcy Case: New Light Shed on the Position of Mortgage Warehousing Banks, 56 Am.Bankruptcy L.J. 325, 332 (1982). See also Bowmar, Real Estate Interests as Security under the UCC: The Scope of Article Nine, 12 U.C.C.L.J. 99, 121 (1979); Collier, Real Estate Transactions and the Bankruptcy Code ¶ 4.05[1](1984). See First National Bank of Boston v. Larson, 17 B.R. 957 (Bkrtcy.N.J.1982) (neither the filing of a financing statement under the UCC nor the recording of the mortgage assignment is required to perfect a valid security interest in note and mortgage so long as the pledgee-lender takes possession of the note); Landmark Land Co. v. Sprague, 529 F.Supp. 971, 976–77 (S.D.N.Y.1981), reversed on other grounds 701 F.2d 1065 (2d Cir.1983). Contra, see Peoples Bank v. McDonald, 743 F.2d 413 (6th Cir.1984) (note governed by Art. 9 and must be perfected by delivery; security interest in deed of trust governed by recording act).

---

4. "... Several courts have held that when an installment note secured by a mortgage is assigned and the assignor continues to collect the payments and remit them to the mortgage[e], this course of dealing constitutes the assignor the 'secret agent' of the assignee, and payment to the assignor is good though he subsequently defaults in passing it through to the assignee. This interpretation is apparently followed even if there was never any formal agency relationship created. There is no reason the concept should not be extended to single-payment notes as well. Moreover, an agency could well be inferred even if the mortgagee-assignor defaulted at the out-set in remitting the payments to the assignee. This theory can be made equally applicable to negotiable and nonnegotiable notes. The agency relationship is too typical, too widely expected, and too consistent with business practices to be denied by the assignee who has not taken the trouble to send an appropriate notice to negate it. Absent such a notice, it should be presumed." (Footnote omitted.) G. Osborne, supra at 350.

D. DISCHARGE OF THE DEBT AND MORTGAGE: BY PAYMENT OR OTHERWISE

Page 446, in connection with Note 4, read the following case:

GEORGE H. NUTMAN, INC. v. AETNA BUSINESS CREDIT, INC.

New York Supreme Court, Special Term, 1982.
115 Misc.2d 168, 453 N.Y.S.2d 586.

MEMORANDUM

ALFRED D. LERNER, Justice.

In this action to recover a prepayment premium of $46,501.60 plus interest and other relief, defendant, Aetna Business Credit, Inc. (hereinafter "Aetna"), moves for summary judgment.

On or about September 6, 1977 Aetna loaned to plaintiff, George H. Nutman, Inc., the sum of $1,200,000. Aetna received as security for the loan a first mortgage lien on various commercial property owned by plaintiff located in Brooklyn and Queens. The Mortgage Agreement provided for monthly installments of principal and interest to be due on the first day of each month, with a five-day grace period before the mortgagor would be deemed to be in default. In addition, the Mortgage Agreement contained provisions for an interest penalty for late payments, a prepayment penalty, and an acceleration clause.

Apparently plaintiff was continually late and in arrears on its payments. On or about February 28, 1979, after plaintiff defaulted, Aetna instituted a foreclosure action. A receiver of the property was appointed. On or about August 31, 1979, the parties entered into a Stipulation of Settlement whereby Aetna agreed to discontinue the foreclosure action upon plaintiff's payment of the mortgage principal, interest and late charges in full.

On or about October 18, 1979 plaintiff sold certain of the property to Martin Paint Stores, Inc. Prior to the closing of title, Aetna prepared a "satisfaction letter" setting forth the amounts due and owing which included the prepayment premiums. When plaintiff protested the inclusion of the premium, plaintiff was notified that a "Satisfaction of Mortgage" would not be executed until plaintiff complied. Plaintiff then paid the sum and commenced the present action.

* * *

Acceleration clauses give the mortgagee the option to declare the entire mortgage debt due and payable upon the happening of a stated condition such as the default by a mortgagor in payment of principal and for interest and the right to foreclose for nonpayment. These acceleration clauses exist solely for the benefit of the mortgagee and are enforced according to their terms. (Graf v. Hope Building Corp.,

251 N.Y. 1, 171 N.E. 884.) Prepayment clauses give the mortgagor the option, upon the payment of a premium, to voluntarily terminate the mortgage prematurely. These clauses are included in mortgage agreements strictly for the benefit of the mortgagor and also will be enforced according to their terms.

The question presented herein is whether the mortgagee, after electing to accelerate the mortgage because of a default, can still exact a prepayment penalty because of the premature termination of the mortgage. The court determines that it cannot.

The election by the mortgagee herein to accelerate the mortgage and to treat the mortgage debt as due was not a voluntary act by the mortgagor sufficient to bring the prepayment penalty into operation. As the Court of Appeals has held:

> "The right to exact the bonus, so called, * * * departed from the defendant, because it had voluntarily waived it by bringing suit to foreclose the mortgage. * * * The election once made was final and not subject to change at the option of the defendant. * * * Having no right to the bonus, it still insisted on the payment thereof before it would do its legal duty. * * * In effect the defendant held plaintiff's property in its grasp through its lien thereon and would not surrender it until the unlawful exaction was complied with. * * Under these circumstances the compulsion was illegal, unjust and oppressive and the plaintiff having submitted under protest had the right to recover." (Kilpatrick v. The Germania Life Ins. Co., 183 N.Y. 163, 168–169, 75 N.E. 1124.)

In the matter herein, since plaintiff was under duress when making the prepayment penalty of $46,501.60, which it was not contractually obligated to do, it is entitled to recover that amount, plus interest.

* * *

Page 448, add as Note 8:

8. Mortgagees sometimes attempt to collect prepayment penalties incident to due-on-sale clause enforcement. State law consistently has been unsympathetic to this type of "double dipping." A few state statutes prohibit the enforcement of a prepayment penalty where prepayment is triggered by the mortgagee's enforcement of a due-on-sale clause. Several courts have reached the same result without the benefit of a statute. See e.g., Tan v. California Federal Savings & Loan Association, 140 Cal.App.3d 800, 809, 189 Cal.Rptr. 775, 782 (1983); Slevin Container Corp. v. Provident Federal Savings & Loan Association, 98 Ill.App.3d 646, 648, 54 Ill.Dec. 189, 191, 424 N.E.2d 939, 941 (1981); American Federal Savings & Loan Association v. Mid-America Service Corp., 329 N.W.2d 124, 125–26 (S.D.1983). These cases reason that once a mortgagor has exercised the due-on-sale clause and accelerated the mortgage debt, payment by the mortgagor is then legally due and by definition cannot be a "prepayment."

Moreover, a Federal Home Loan Bank Board regulation, promulgated in 1983 prohibits all lenders, whether federally chartered or not, from collecting prepayment penalties resulting from acceleration under due-on-sale clauses contained in loans secured by a home "occupied or to be occupied by the borrower." 12 C.F.R. § 591.59(b)(2). This regulation is an outgrowth of the Garn-St. Germain Depository Institutions Act of 1982 (the "Act"), which makes most due-on-sale clauses enforcible. See Chapter 5(B) supra. For an analysis of the regulation from a policy perspective, see Nelson & Whitman, Real Estate Finance Law § 6.5 (2nd Ed. 1985).

Page 460, add at the end of the Note:

THOMPSON v. GLIDDEN

Supreme Judicial Court of Maine, 1982.
445 A.2d 676.

Before McKUSICK, C.J., and NICHOLS, ROBERTS, CARTER and WATHEN, JJ.

WATHEN, Justice.

Plaintiff appeals from a decision of the Superior Court (Waldo County). The Court denied her request for relief under a support mortgage granted to her by defendants and established life estates in the parties in various rooms of the house that they share. We sustain the appeal and vacate the judgment below.

In 1967 plaintiff, who was losing her sight and hearing, deeded her house and land in Troy, Maine to defendants, who are plaintiff's adopted daughter and son-in-law. Defendants in turn gave plaintiff a support mortgage which reconveyed the property to plaintiff with the provision that if defendants fulfilled the conditions of the mortgage the conveyance would be void. The support mortgage provided that defendants would pay the insurance and taxes on the house and furnish plaintiff

> with food, clothing and shelter on said premises so long as she may live and take care of her necessities of life to the extent that she cannot take care of them herself.

The testimony presented at trial shows that the parties have lived together in the house since November 1969 although the relationship between them has deteriorated markedly since March 1978.

In February 1979 plaintiff filed a complaint alleging that defendants had breached their promise to provide her with food, clothing, shelter and the necessities of life. The complaint, which contained four counts, sought foreclosure of the support mortgage, rescission of the conveyance from plaintiff to defendants, a declaratory judgment establishing the rights and duties of the parties under the support mortgage, and the designation of defendants as trustees of the property in question for the benefit of plaintiff. A non-jury trial was held, and the rescission claim was denied at the end of the presentation of all plaintiff's evidence. After trial the presiding justice construed the support mortgage most strongly against the plaintiff to find that there had been no breach. He denied all of plaintiff's other claims for relief except that for a declaratory judgment. Relying on evidence presented concerning use of the house, the court established a life estate in plaintiff in a sitting room and bedroom. The decree gave defendants a life estate in the upper floor of the house and in the family room. The bath, laundry and kitchen were to be used jointly. Plaintiff assigns as error the trial court's construction of the support mortgage, the court's finding that there was no breach of the mortgage, and the establishment of the life estates.

Initially we note that the support mortgage is a simplistic legal response to a very complex need for financial and personal planning. Because it employs rigid conveyancing and contract concepts in an attempt to structure economic, interpersonal, and family relationships, it is not surprising that its history has been marked by conspicuous failure. Modern socio-economic conditions and changes within the structure of the family increase rather than decrease the likelihood of dispute. Judicial resolution, bound as it is to the underlying principles of property and contract law, is necessarily incomplete and formalistic.

Construction of the Mortgage

The trial court found that the support mortgage in this case was drafted by plaintiff's attorney, and finding the instrument ambiguous, the presiding justice construed it most strongly against plaintiff. Although this rule of construction is commonly accepted in commercial and business transactions, see, e.g., Hills v. Gardiner Savings Institution, Me., 309 A.2d 877 (1973), we agree with plaintiff that its application in this case is inappropriate. The instant support mortgage is not a contract of adhesion nor do the circumstances require construction against the drafter in order to meet the expectations of the party in the inferior bargaining position. Dairy Farm Leasing Co., Inc. v. Hartley, Me., 395 A.2d 1135, 1139, n.3 (1978). In fact defendants actively participated in the drafting of the documents, refusing to sign them until they had been redrafted to meet their specifications.

Moreover, a support mortgage is not an ordinary contract which requires application of the rule of strict construction against the drafter in order to ascertain the intent of the agreement. The intent, implicit in the nature of the agreement, has been aptly described by a Rhode Island court:

> One under stress of infirmity or age surrenders his property to another for relief from care and anxiety, and receives in return an assurance of support * * *. [A] feeble party has fully performed his part of the contract in the hope of security and quiet.

Grant v. Bell, 26 R.I. 288, 58 A. 951 (1904). To give effect, therefore, to the unique purpose of a support mortgage, contracts of this nature should be liberally construed in favor of the elderly grantors. Tuttle v. Burgett's Adm'r, 53 Ohio St. 498, 42 N.E. 427, 429 (1895); see also Strock v. MacNicholl, 196 Va. 734, 85 S.E.2d 263, 269 (1955).

The rule of construction utilized by the trial court must necessarily have tinctured its evaluation of the evidence presented in this case.

The court's order reveals that in determining whether there was a breach of the agreement the trial justice focused solely on whether the physical maintenance requirements of the support mortgage had been met. In considering agreements of this kind, many jurisdictions have recognized that in addition to the explicit promise of physical well being there is also an implicit promise of peace, harmony, and emotional well being:

> In addition to the physical necessities, the grantor has the right to expect reasonable personal care and the courtesies and kindness usually obtaining between individuals that have the same ties of blood or association in families of similar station as those of the contracting parties. "According to the view ordinarily taken, the agreement of a grantee to furnish his grantor support, especially where the parties expect to reside together, is to be construed as contemplating not merely physical necessities, but kindness, and personal care and attention."

Strock v. MacNicholl, 196 Va. 734, 85 S.E.2d 263, 268 (1955) (quoting Note, 112 A.L.R. 670, 708). See also, Payne v. Winters, 366 Pa. 299, 77 A.2d 407 (1951); Brinkley v. Patton, 194 Okl. 244, 149 P.2d 261 (1944); Grant v. Bell, 58 A. at 951–52. The liberal construction in favor of the grantor which we have mandated requires that any evaluation of the evidence to determine whether a breach of the support mortgage has occurred must employ this broader view. We therefore remand this case to Superior Court for a reconsideration of the evidence under the more expansive construction that we now announce.

Declaratory Relief

Plaintiff argues that the declaratory judgment granted by the court in essence reformed the agreement between the parties rather than construing it. We agree. The deed and the accompanying support mortgage which the court was asked to construe were conveyances in fee simple. In declaring the rights of the parties under these instruments, the court established life estates in separate sections of the house, thereby creating entirely different interests in the property than had been created by the original instruments. The relief sought in Count III of the complaint was not a reformation of the agreement between the parties but a declaration of the parties' rights and duties under the support mortgage. The Declaratory Judgments Act, 14 M.R.S.A. §§ 5951–5963 (1980), provides a means for parties to have their rights, status and relations under existing written instruments judicially determined. Although the Act is to be liberally construed, Hodgdon v. Campbell, Me., 411 A.2d 667 (1980), it does not authorize the reformation of agreements. Upon remand the court should confine any order under Count III to a declaration of the rights and duties of the parties under the existing instruments.

The entry is:

Judgment vacated.

Remanded to Superior Court for further proceedings consistent with the opinion herein.

NOTE

Suppose that on remand in the Thompson case, the trial court finds that a default in the mortgage exists and orders foreclosure. How much is the mortgage debt? How will the court calculate the value of the mortgagors' failure to provide the mortgagee "kindness * * * and attention"? See generally, Nelson and Whitman, Real Estate Finance Law § 2.2 (2nd Ed. 1985). Suppose further that prior to the foreclosure sale, the mortgagors choose to redeem. How do the mortgagors "pay" that part of the redemption amount that is attributable to a failure to provide "kindness * * * and attention."? Is redemption possible under these circumstances?

Chapter 6

FORECLOSURE

A. THE FORECLOSURE AMOUNT: PROBLEMS OF ACCELERATION

Page 478, add at the end of the first paragraph of Note 1:

New York courts continue to have difficulty with *Graff*. Consider, for example, the language of Karas v. Wasserman, 91 A.D.2d 812, 458 N.Y.S.2d 280, 281–82 (1982):

> Plaintiffs mistakenly rely here on the continued vitality of the majority holding in Graf v. Hope Building Corp., 254 N.Y. 1, 171 N.E. 884, to the effect that acceleration clauses in mortgages will be strictly enforced irrespective of the circumstances and nature of the default. Rather, it seems clear that the evolving subsequent case law has largely adopted the reasoning of Chief Judge Cardozo's dissenting position in *Graf*, 254 N.Y. 1, 8–15, 171 N.E. 884, supra that the equitable remedy of foreclosure may be denied in the case of an inadvertent, inconsequential default in order to prevent unconscionably overreaching conduct by a mortgagee (see Blomgren v. Tinton, 763 Corp., 18 A.D.2d 979, 238 N.Y.S.2d 435; 100 Eighth Ave. Corp. v. Morgenstern, 4 A.D.2d 754, 164 N.Y.S.2d 812; More Realty Corp. v. Mootchnick, 232 App.Div. 705, 247 N.Y.S. 712; Scelza v. Ryba, 10 Misc.2d 186, 169 N.Y.S.2d 462; Domus Realty Corp. v. 3440 Realty Co., 179 Misc. 749, 40 N.Y.S.2d 69, aff'd 266 App.Div. 725, 41 N.Y.S.2d 940). Indeed, the *Graf* dissent has recently been cited as authority for that proposition by the Court of Appeals in connection with a rent acceleration clause in a lease (Fifty States Mtg. Corp. v. Pioneer Auto Parks, 46 N.Y.2d 573, 577, 578–579, 415 N.Y.S.2d 800, 389 N.E.2d 113) and in other similar contexts (J.N.A. Realty Corp. v. Cross Bay Chelsea, 42 N.Y.2d 392, 398–400, 397 N.Y.S.2d 958, 366 N.E.2d 1313).

Page 481, insert as Notes 7 and 8:

7. Suppose a mortgage debt has been accelerated in a situation where neither state law nor mortgage language affords the mortgagor the right to defeat acceleration by a pre-foreclosure tender of arrearages. If, prior to foreclosure, the mortgagor files a Chapter 13 bankruptcy proceeding, the bankruptcy court may have ample authority to permit the mortgagor to

reinstate the mortgage by payment of arrearages. See In re Taddeo in Section G of this Chapter, infra.

8. The Federal National Mortgage Association—Federal Home Loan Mortgage Corporation (FNMA—FHLMC) mortgage—deed of trust form contains substantial limitations on the acceleration process. Not only does it require detailed mailed notice and a thirty-day grace period as a condition precedent to acceleration, it also affords the mortgagor the right to defeat acceleration until five days prior to foreclosure by the payment of arrearages and mortgagee's reasonable costs and attorney's fees. See Appendix at 1087. These provisions may be omitted from the FNMA—FHLMC form only when state law is more protective of the mortgagor with respect to pre-acceleration requirements and the ability to defeat acceleration once it has occurred. Because most institutional lenders wish to retain the option of selling their home mortgages to these two secondary market entities, they will be likely to use the FNMA—FHLMC form. Thus vast numbers of mortgagors in states that have not enacted legislation regulating acceleration, or whose legislation or case law is less restrictive than the requirements of the form, will nevertheless have substantial protection against abuse of the acceleration process.

C. JUDICIAL FORECLOSURE

2. THE OMITTED PARTY PROBLEM

Page 509, insert at the end of the Portland Mortg. Co. case:

LAND ASSOCIATES, INC. v. BECKER

Supreme Court of Oregon, 1982.
294 Or. 308, 656 P.2d 927.

Before LENT, C.J., and LINDE, TANZER, CAMPBELL, ROBERTS and CARSON, JJ.

CAMPBELL, Justice.

* * *

Land Associates, the seller of real property on a land sales contract, brought an action for judgment against its buyer on June 26, 1979, naming several others who had interests in the property as defendants. Land Associates initially requested a strict foreclosure, but in an amended complaint asked for a judicial sale. Land Associates joined those who held junior liens and judgments of record at the time it filed the complaint. After the complaint was filed, two trust deeds and a judgment against the buyer went on record. The trust deeds were recorded June 27, 1979, and July 2, 1979. The judgment was entered October 31, 1979. The people holding these three above-mentioned liens were not joined in the foreclosure action and did not intervene. On November 19, 1979, Becker, the purchaser on the contract, conveyed his interest in the property by deed to respondent E & B Investors. On

March 5, 1980, the trial court entered a stipulated decree that gave Land Associates judgment for the balance of the purchase price, attorney fees and costs and directed the sale of the property on execution by the sheriff to satisfy the judgment. The decree provided for a possible deficiency and foreclosed all property interests or rights of all defendants, except for the statutory rights of redemption.

Land Associates bought the property at the sheriff's sale on April 17, 1980, and 27 days later, on May 14, 1980, obtained an ex parte order from the court directing the sheriff to issue a deed. The record in this court indicates that only the State of Oregon waived its rights to redeem. On this same day Land Associates assigned the certificate of sale to respondent E & B Investors and conveyed the property. The sheriff issued the deed the following day. The court confirmed the sale on May 15, 1980.

The three pendente lite lien creditors mentioned above then assigned their interests to appellant Bautista on June 13, 1980. On the same day, 57 days after the sale, Bautista served her notice of intent to redeem on Land Associates and its assignee E & B Investors. The sheriff refused to proceed with the redemption without direction from the court because he had already issued a deed to Land Associates. Bautista then intervened in this action, naming Land Associates and E & B Investors, Inc. as respondents, and filed allegations in the nature of a complaint asking to set aside the order which authorized the deed and directing the sheriff to permit her to exercise her statutory right of redemption. The trial court dismissed her second amended complaint and she appealed.

The Court of Appeals affirmed this dismissal. It held that Bautista, as the assignee of unjoined junior lien creditors, had no right to statutory redemption, relying on Portland Mtg. Co. v. Creditors Prot. Ass'n., 199 Or. 432, 262 P.2d 918 (1953).

* * *

The period for statutory redemption [2] starts after the foreclosure and sale itself and is one last chance for the previous owner and any lien

---

2. Bautista claims a right to redeem under ORS 23.530 and 23.540:

"**ORS 23.530.** Property sold subject to redemption, as provided in ORS 23.520, or any part thereof separately sold, may be redeemed by the following persons:

"(1) The mortgagor or judgment debtor whose right and title were sold, or his heir, devisee or grantee, who has acquired, by inheritance, devise, deed, sale, or by virtue of any execution or by any other means, the legal title to the whole or any part of the property separately sold; provided, that in the event redemption is made by anyone acquiring the legal title after attachment, or after a judgment becomes a lien on the property, such person shall acquire no greater or better right thereby to the property so redeemed than the holder of the legal title at the time of such attachment or judgment.

"(2) A creditor having a lien by judgment, decree or mortgage on any portion of the property, or any portion of any part thereof separately sold, subsequent in time to that on which the property was sold. Such creditors, after having redeemed the property, are to be termed redemptioners."

"**ORS 23.540.** A lien creditor may redeem the property within 60 days from the date of the sale by paying the amount of the purchase money, with interest at the

creditors to regain the property. It is important to distinguish the two types of redemption—equitable redemption only exists until the interest is foreclosed, while statutory redemption only begins after the interest is foreclosed.

In the present case, the Court of Appeals relied on *Portland Mtg. Co.*, supra, indicating that while arguably Bautista might have an equitable right of redemption, she did not have a statutory right of redemption. In this it is mistaken. *Portland Mtg. Co.* concerned an attempted redemption by junior lien creditors who were not joined in the foreclosure action. This court held that they had no right to statutory right to redeem because their interest had not been foreclosed. Those creditors were lienholders of record when the initial petition was filed; because they were not joined they were not bound by the foreclosure, and a statutory right of redemption did not arise.

The present situation differs because Bautista's predecessors were not lienholders of record when the initial complaint was filed. The doctrine of lis pendens controls here. This doctrine states that the filing of a suit concerning real property is notice to people who obtain an interest in the property after the commencement of the suit that they will be bound by the outcome of the suit. Puckett v. Benjamin, 21 Or. 370, 381, 28 P. 65 (1891). It is a necessary doctrine; without it every change of ownership or lesser interest in real property would require a modification of the suit and would require continual checking of the records to be sure that someone else had not obtained property rights in the property in question. Respondents argue that the doctrine means that any change of ownership during the pendency of the suit does not have any legal effect until the outcome of the suit, but in this they are mistaken. Kaston v. Storey, 47 Or. 150, 154, 80 P. 217 (1905). The doctrine of lis pendens does not change a property owner's right to transfer interests in a property even though a foreclosure suit is pending, and it also does not stop another person from gaining an interest by becoming a lien creditor after the suit is filed, as did Bautista's predecessors in interest in the present case.

The doctrine of lis pendens, however, binds Bautista's predecessors in interest by the foreclosure suit. This is the major difference between the present case and *Portland Mtg. Co.* In *Portland Mtg. Co.*, because the lien creditors of record were not joined, they were not bound by the foreclosure; thus the statutory right of redemption did not arise and their only recourse would have been the equitable right of redemption.

The situation in the present case is just the opposite; because the interests did not arise until after the foreclosure suit started, the

rate of 10 percent per annum thereon from the time of sale, together with the amount of any taxes which the purchaser may have paid thereon, and any other sum which the judgment debtor might be required to pay for redemption, with like interest, and if the purchaser is also a creditor having a lien prior to that of the redemptioner, the amount of such lien, with interest; provided, that if objections to any sale are filed, a lien creditor may redeem within 60 days from the date of the order confirming the sale."

doctrine of lis pendens means that the holders of these interests are bound by the decree of foreclosure and thus their interests were foreclosed along with those of the buyer and the lien creditors who were joined in the suit. Because their interests were foreclosed, their statutory right of redemption then came into existence. Bautista acquired these rights by the assignment. She thus is in the class of people who can exercise the rights of statutory redemption.

* * *

Reversed and remanded.

D. POWER OF SALE FORECLOSURE

2. DEFECTS IN THE EXERCISE OF THE POWER

Page 522, read the following case in connection with Note 2:

COX v. HELENIUS

Supreme Court of Washington, En Banc, 1985.
103 Wn.2d 383, 693 P.2d 683.

UTTER, Justice.

A trustee in a deed of trust foreclosure action was made aware of an action for damages and reconveyance of the deed of trust pending against the grantee of the deed of trust. He was also aware that the grantors believed their action had halted foreclosure proceedings. Nevertheless, he initiated foreclosure proceedings and held a trustee's sale in which the grantor's home, with an equity of at least $100,000 existing in the grantor, was sold for $11,784. Olympic Properties, Ltd., appeals from summary judgment entered by the trial court against Helenius as trustee, which set aside this deed of trust foreclosure sale and dismissed an unlawful detainer action.

We hold that the suit brought by the grantor prevented the trustee's initiation of foreclosure, making the sale void. We further hold that the trustee breached his duties.

The theme of the transaction attempted parallels an action heard by Judge J.E. Wyche, a member of Washington's early judiciary. When a jury returned a verdict in a suit disputing title over 100 acres of ranch land, he threatened to set aside their verdict, stating "While I am a judge, it takes 13 men to steal a ranch." W. Airey, A History of the Constitution and Government of Washington Territory, at 312 (1945) (unpublished Ph.D. thesis available in the Washington State Library, Olympia, Washington).

The deed of trust sale in question today involves not a pioneer ranch but a swimming pool and the owner's home. In November 1981, Frank and Kathleen Cox signed a 120-month installment contract with San Juan Pool Corporation for the purchase and installation of a $9,985 pool at their home on Magnolia Boulevard in Seattle. To secure payment, the Coxes granted San Juan a security interest in their home in the form of a deed of trust.

In April 1982, shortly after installation was completed, the Coxes attempted to use the "backflush" to clear the pool. The pipes installed by San Juan collapsed, backing up sewage into the Cox residence. Although the Coxes notified San Juan immediately, the company failed to take any action to repair the pipes. The Coxes, who were without running water for 8 days due to the sewage backup, spent $4,004 to clean up and repair the sewer lines.

The Coxes hired an attorney to represent them in an action against San Juan. On June 8, 1982, she sent a letter to San Juan and its collection agency detailing the damage to the home and its cost to the Coxes. Because the Coxes' alleged damages exceeded the balance due on the note secured by the deed of trust, she requested that San Juan reconvey the deed of trust to the Coxes and pay any further damages. She instructed the Coxes to withhold payments on the note until the matter was resolved.

Kevin Helenius, the trustee under the deed of trust and attorney for San Juan, then sent the Coxes a letter notifying them they were in arrears on the note. The letter added that unless payments were received within 10 days, San Juan would commence nonjudicial foreclosure.

In response, the Coxes filed a complaint for damages and reconveyance of the deed of trust. The complaint was initially served on July 22, 1982 upon the Contractor's Registration Section of the Department of Labor and Industries, the statutory agent authorized to receive service of process upon the bonding company for San Juan Pool Corporation. Likely unaware of the Coxes' action, Helenius sent the Coxes a notice of default on July 30, 1982. On August 12, upon learning that the complaint had been served on San Juan, the Coxes' attorney sent a copy to Helenius. The summons and complaint were then filed in King County Superior Court on August 27, 1982. No notice of lis pendens was recorded. That same day Helenius filed a notice of appearance for San Juan.

On September 8, 1982, Helenius sent a notice of sale and foreclosure to the Coxes. Helenius acknowledged in his deposition that he was aware of the suit for damages at this time. The Coxes amended their complaint for damages on September 20, 1982 to include a request for an injunction restraining the trustee's sale set for December 10, 1982.

On October 19, 1982, after a motion hearing on the damage suit, Helenius and the Coxes' attorney briefly discussed the Coxes' lawsuit. The two attorneys discussed settling the case or submitting the damage claim to arbitration. The Coxes' attorney believed Helenius would not hold the sale.

The sale, however, took place as scheduled on December 10, 1982. The only persons present at the sale were Helenius, his secretary, Karen Goerz, and Bertil Granberg, president of Olympic Properties, Ltd. Granberg, formerly an attorney, was disbarred and is no longer practicing. For the past 5 years he has worked full time buying and selling real estate. Goerz had been authorized to bid on San Juan's behalf by Robert Stark, its president. Goerz bid $11,783, the amount San Juan had calculated as due on the note. Granberg bid an additional dollar. Helenius then issued a trustee deed to Olympic Properties, Ltd. At the time of the sale, the residence's worth was in the range of $200,000 to $300,000.

I

Washington's deed of trust act should be construed to further three basic objectives. See Comment, *Court Actions Contesting the Nonjudicial Foreclosure of Deeds of Trust in Washington*, 59 Wash.L.Rev. 323, 330 (1984). First, the nonjudicial foreclosure process should remain efficient and inexpensive. Peoples Nat'l Bank v. Ostrander, 6 Wash. App. 28, 491 P.2d 1058 (1971). Second, the process should provide an adequate opportunity for interested parties to prevent wrongful foreclosure. Third, the process should promote the stability of land titles.

The act contains several safeguards to ensure that the nonjudicial foreclosure process is fair and free from surprise. Prior to initiating foreclosure, it is required that a default has occurred, RCW 61.24.030(3), and that no action is pending on an obligation secured by the deed of trust, RCW 61.24.030(4). Only after giving 30 days notice and an opportunity to cure, may the trustee begin the foreclosure process. RCW 61.24.030(6).

If the grantor chooses not to cure, the grantor may take one or more of the following actions. The grantor may contest the default, RCW 61.24.030(6)(j), RCW 61.24.040(2); restrain the sale, RCW 61.24.130; or contest the sale, RCW 61.24.040(2).

We are required, when possible, to give effect to every word, clause and sentence of a statute. International Paper Co. v. Department of Rev., 92 Wash.2d 277, 281, 595 P.2d 1310 (1979), *citing* 2A C. Sands, *Statutory Construction* § 46.06, at 63 (4th ed. 1973). No part should be deemed inoperative or superfluous unless the result of obvious mistake or error. C. Sands, supra.

Using these rules of statutory construction, we conclude that an action contesting the default, filed after notice of sale and foreclosure has been received, does not have the effect of restraining the sale. RCW 61.24.130 sets forth the only means by which a grantor may preclude a sale once foreclosure has begun with receipt of the notice of sale and foreclosure. That section allows the superior court to issue a restraining order or injunction to halt a sale on any proper ground. The Coxes failed to apply for an order restraining the sale, although they requested that relief in their amended complaint. Here, however, the trial judge properly determined that the lawsuit the Coxes filed after receiving the notice of default but prior to initiation of foreclosure constituted an action on the obligation. Therefore, one of the statutory requisites to nonjudicial foreclosure was not satisfied.

In some situations, a trustee may be unaware that an action on the obligation exists at the time foreclosure proceedings are initiated. Helenius, however, had actual notice of the action underlying the debt. He filed a notice of appearance in the case for the defendant beneficiary on the same day it was filed. He later represented the beneficiary at a motion hearing.

II

Even if the statutory requisites to foreclosure had been satisfied and the Coxes had filed to properly restrain the sale, this trustee's actions, along with the grossly inadequate purchase price, would result in a void sale. See Lovejoy v. Americus, 111 Wash. 571, 574, 191 P. 790 (1920); Miebach v. Colasurdo, 102 Wash.2d 170, 685 P.2d 1074 (1984). Because the deed of trust foreclosure process is conducted without review or confirmation by a court, the fiduciary duty imposed upon the trustee is exceedingly high.

Washington courts do not require a trustee to make sure that a grantor is protecting his or her own interest. However, a trustee of a deed of trust is a fiduciary for both the mortgagee and mortgagor and must act impartially between them. G. Osborne, G. Nelson & D. Whitman, *Real Estate Finance Law* § 7.21 (1979).

> The trustee is bound by his office to present the sale under every possible advantage to the debtor as well as to the creditor. He is bound to use not only good faith but also every requisite degree of diligence in conducting the sale and to attend equally to the interest of the debtor and creditor alike.

Swindell v. Overton, 310 N.C. 707, 314 S.E.2d 512, 516 (1984). See Blodgett v. Martsch, 590 P.2d 298, 302 (Utah 1978) ("duty of the trustee under a trust deed is ... to treat the trustor fairly and in accordance with a high punctilio of honor"); McHugh v. Church, 583 P.2d 210, 213 (Alaska 1978); Spires v. Edgar, 513 S.W.2d 372 (Mo.1974); Whitlow v. Mountain Trust Bank, 215 Va. 149, 207 S.E.2d 837 (1974); Woodworth v. Redwood Empire Sav. & Loan Ass'n, 22 Cal.App.3d 347, 99 Cal.Rptr. 373 (1971).

We agree with a recent Alaska decision which emphasizes that a trustee's management responsibilities under a deed of trust are less extensive than those of trustees in other fiduciary settings. *McHugh*, 583 P.2d at 214. See also S & G Inv. Inc. v. Home Fed. Sav. & Loan Ass'n, 505 F.2d 370, 377 n. 21 (D.C.Cir. 1974). The trustee of a deed of trust is not required to obtain the best possible price for the trust property. Compare, e.g., Allard v. Pacific Nat'l Bank, 99 Wash.2d 394, 406, 663 P.2d 104 (1983). Nonetheless, the trustee must "take reasonable and appropriate steps to avoid sacrifice of the debtor's property and his interest." *McHugh,* 583 P.2d at 214.

Furthermore, after a trustee undertakes a course of conduct reasonably calculated to instill a sense of reliance thereon by the grantor, that course of conduct may not be abandoned without notice to the grantor. Lupertino v. Carbahal, 35 Cal.App.3d 742, 111 Cal.Rptr. 112, 116 (1973). Helenius should have either informed the Coxes' attorney that, in his opinion, she had failed to properly restrain the sale or have delayed foreclosure until resolution of the underlying dispute, especially since the extensive damage to the Coxes' property put the very issue of default into question. RCW 61.24.040(6) allows a trustee to continue a sale "for any cause he deems advantageous".

It appears that the dual responsibility of trustee and attorney for the beneficiary precipitated at least some of the trustee's breaches. Although the dual role this trustee had troubles us, the Legislature specifically amended the statute in 1975 to allow an employee, agent or subsidiary of a beneficiary to also be a trustee. See Laws of 1975, 1st Ex.Sess., ch. 129, § 2. The amendment furthers the general intent of the act that nonjudicial foreclosure be efficient and inexpensive, and in the ordinary case would present no problem. However, the statute may not allow attorneys to do that which the Code of Professional Responsibility prohibits. The spirit of CPR DR 5–105(B) would seem to condemn action of the nature that occurred here. Where an actual conflict of interest arises, the person serving as trustee and beneficiary should prevent a breach by transferring one role to another person. See, e.g., Mintener v. Michigan Nat'l Bank, 117 Mich.App. 633, 324 N.W.2d 110 (1982).

* * *

WILLIAM H. WILLIAMS, C.J., and BRACHTENBACH, DOLLIVER, DORE, DIMMICK, PEARSON and ANDERSEN, JJ., concur.

---

3. CONSTITUTIONAL PROBLEMS WITH THE POWER OF SALE

Page 536, Read in connection with the second paragraph of Note 1:

MENNONITE BOARD OF MISSIONS v. ADAMS

Supreme Court of the United States, 1983.
462 U.S. 791, 103 S.Ct. 2706, 77 L.Ed.2d 180.

Justice MARSHALL, delivered the opinion of the Court.

This appeal raises the question whether notice by publication and posting provides a mortgagee of real property with adequate notice of a proceeding to sell the mortgaged property for nonpayment of taxes.

I

To secure an obligation to pay $14,000, Alfred Jean Moore executed a mortgage in favor of appellant Mennonite Board of Missions (MBM) on property in Elkhart, Indiana, that Moore had purchased from MBM. The mortgage was recorded in the Elkhart County Recorder's Office on March 1, 1973. Under the terms of the agreement, Moore was responsible for paying all of the property taxes. Without MBM's knowledge, however, she failed to pay taxes on the property.

Indiana law provides for the annual sale of real property on which payments of property taxes have been delinquent for fifteen months or longer. Ind. Code § 6–1.1–24–1 *et seq.* Prior to the sale, the county auditor must post notice in the county courthouse and publish notice once each week for three consecutive weeks. § 6–1.1–24–3. The owner of the property is entitled to notice by certified mail to his last known address. § 6–1.1–24–4.[1] Until 1980, however, Indiana law did not provide for notice by mail or personal service to mortgagees of property that was to be sold for nonpayment of taxes.[2]

After the required notice is provided, the county treasurer holds a public auction at which the real property is sold to the highest bidder. § 6–1.1–24–5. The purchaser acquires a certificate of sale which constitutes a lien against the real property for the entire amount paid. § 6–1.1–24–9. This lien is superior to all other liens against the property which existed at the time the certificate was issued. Ibid.

The tax sale is followed by a two-year redemption period during which the "owner, occupant, lienholder, or other person who has an interest in" the property may redeem the property. § 6–1.1–25–1. To redeem the property an individual must pay the county treasurer a sum sufficient to cover the purchase price of the property at the tax sale, the amount of taxes and special assessments paid by the purchaser following the sale, plus an additional percentage specified in the statute. §§ 6–1.1–25–2, 6–1.1–25–3. The county in turn remits the payment to the purchaser of the property at the tax sale.

If no one redeems the property during the statutory redemption period, the purchaser may apply to the county auditor for a deed to the property. Before executing and delivering the deed, the county auditor must notify the former owner that he is still entitled to redeem the property. § 6–1.1–25–6. No notice to the mortgagee is required. If the property is not redeemed within thirty days, the county auditor may then execute and deliver a deed for the property to the purchaser,

---

1. Because a mortgagee has no title to the mortgaged property under Indiana law, the mortgagee is not considered an "owner" for purposes of § 6–1.1–24–4. First Savings & Loan Assn. of Central Indiana v. Furnish, 367 N.E.2d 596, 600, n. 14 (Ind. App.1977).

2. Ind. Code § 6–1.1–24–4.2, added in 1980, provides for notice by certified mail to any mortgagee of real property which is subject to tax sale proceedings, if the mortgagee has annually requested such notice and has agreed to pay a fee, not to exceed $10, to cover the cost of sending notice. Because the events in question in this case occurred before the 1980 amendment, the constitutionality of the amendment is not before us.

§ 6-1.1-25-4, who thereby acquires "an estate in fee simple absolute, free and clear of all liens and encumbrances." § 6-1.1-25-4(d).

After obtaining a deed, the purchaser may initiate an action to quiet his title to the property. § 6-1.1-25-14. The previous owner, lienholders, and others who claim to have an interest in the property may no longer redeem the property. They may defeat the title conveyed by the tax deed only by proving, *inter alia,* that the property had not been subject to, or assessed for, the taxes for which it was sold, that the taxes had been paid before the sale, or that the property was properly redeemed before the deed was executed. § 6-1.1-25-16.

In 1977 Elkhart County initiated proceedings to sell Moore's property for nonpayment of taxes. The County provided notice as required under the statute: it posted and published an announcement of the tax sale and mailed notice to Moore by certified mail. MBM was not informed of the pending tax sale either by the county auditor or by Moore. The property was sold for $1,167.75 to appellee Richard Adams on August 8, 1977. Neither Moore nor MBM appeared at the sale or took steps thereafter to redeem the property. Following the sale of her property, Moore continued to make payments each month to MBM, and as a result MBM did not realize that the property had been sold. On August 16, 1979, MBM first learned of the tax sale. By then the redemption period had run and Moore still owed appellant $8,237.19.

In November 1979, Adams filed a suit in state court seeking to quiet title to the property. In opposition to Adams' motion for summary judgment, MBM contended that it had not received constitutionally adequate notice of the pending tax sale and of the opportunity to redeem the property following the tax sale. The trial court upheld the Indiana tax sale statute against this constitutional challenge. The Indiana Court of Appeals affirmed. 427 N.E.2d 686 (1981). We noted probable jurisdiction, ___ U.S. ___, 103 S.Ct. 204, 74 L.Ed.2d 164 (1982), and we now reverse.

II

In Mullane v. Central Hanover Bank & Trust Co., 339 U.S. 306, 314, 70 S.Ct. 652, 657, 94 L.Ed.2d 865 (1950), this court recognized that prior to an action which will affect an interest in life, liberty, or property protected by the Due Process Clause of the Fourteenth Amendment, a State must provide "notice reasonably calculated, under all circumstances, to apprise interested parties of the pendency of the action and afford them an opportunity to present their objections." Invoking this "elementary and fundamental requirement of due process," ibid, the Court held that published notice of an action to settle the accounts of a common trust fund was not sufficient to inform beneficiaries of the trust whose names and addresses were known. The Court explained that notice by publication was not reasonably calculated to provide actual notice of the pending proceeding and was therefore inadequate to inform those who could be notified by more effective means such as personal service or mailed notice:

"Chance alone brings to the attention of even a local resident an advertisement in small type inserted in the back pages of a newspaper, and if he makes his home outside the area of the newspaper's normal circulation the odds that the information will never reach him are large indeed. The chance of actual notice is further reduced when as here the notice required does not even name those whose attention it is supposed to attract, and does not inform acquaintances who might call it to attention. In weighing its sufficiency on the basis of equivalence with actual notice we are unable to regard this as more than a feint." Id. at 315.[3]

In subsequent cases, this Court has adhered unwaveringly to the principle announced in *Mullane*. In Walker v. City of Hutchinson, 352

---

3. The decision in *Mullane* rejected one of the premises underlying this Court's previous decisions concerning the requirements of notice in judicial proceedings: that due process rights may vary depending on whether actions are *in rem* or *in personam*. 339 U.S., at 312, 70 S.Ct., at 656. See Shaffer v. Heitner, 433 U.S. 186, 206, 97 S.Ct. 2569, 2580, 53 L.Ed.2d 683 (1977). Traditionally, when a state court based its jurisdiction upon its authority over the defendant's person, personal service was considered essential for the court to bind individuals who did not submit to its jurisdiction. See, e.g., Hamilton v. Brown, 161 U.S. 256, 275, 16 S.Ct. 585, 592, 40 L.Ed. 691 (1896); Arendt v. Griggs, 134 U.S. 316, 320, 10 S.Ct. 557, 558, 33 L.Ed. 918 (1890); Pennoyer v. Neff, 95 U.S. 714, 726, 733–734, 24 L.Ed. 565 (1878) ("Due process of law would require appearance or personal service before the defendant could be personally bound by any judgment rendered."). In Hess v. Pawloski, 274 U.S. 352, 47 S.Ct. 632, 71 L.Ed. 1091 (1927), the Court recognized for the first time that service by registered mail, in place of personal service, may satisfy the requirements of due process. Constructive notice was never deemed sufficient to bind an individual in an action *in personam*.

In contrast, in *in rem* or *quasi in rem* proceedings in which jurisdiction was based on the court's power over property within its territory, see generally Shaffer v. Heitner, supra, at 196–205, 97 S.Ct., at 2575–2580, constructive notice to nonresidents was traditionally understood to satisfy the requirements of due process. In order to settle questions of title to property within its territory, a state court was generally required to proceed by an *in rem* action since the court could not otherwise bind nonresidents. At one time constructive service was considered the only means of notifying nonresidents since it was believed that "[p]rocess from the tribunals of one State cannot run into another State." Pennoyer v. Neff, supra, at 727. See Ballard v. Hunter, 204 U.S. 241, 255, 27 S.Ct. 261, 266, 51 L.Ed. 461 (1907). As a result, the nonresident acquired the duty "to take measures that in some way he shall be represented when his property is called into requisition." Id., at 262, 27 S.Ct., at 269. If he "fail[ed] to get notice by the ordinary publications which have been usually required in such cases, it [was] his misfortune." Ibid.

Rarely was a corresponding duty imposed on interested parties who resided within the State and whose identities were reasonably ascertainable. Even in actions *in rem*, such individuals were generally provided personal service. See e.g., Arendt v. Griggs, supra, at 326–327, 10 S.Ct., at 560–561. Where the identity of interested residents could not be ascertained after a reasonably diligent inquiry, however, their interests in property could be affected by a proceeding *in rem* as long as constructive notice was provided. See Hamilton v. Brown, supra, at 275, 16 S.Ct., at 592; American Land Co. v. Zeiss, 219 U.S. 47, 61–62, 65–66, 31 S.Ct. 200, 206–207, 55 L.Ed. 82 (1911).

Beginning with *Mullane*, this Court has recognized, contrary to the earlier line of cases, "that an adverse judgment *in rem* directly affects the property owner by divesting him of his rights in the property before the court." Shaffer v. Heitner, supra, 433 U.S., at 206, 97 S.Ct., at 2580. In rejecting the traditional justification for distinguishing between residents and nonresidents and between *in rem* and *in personam* actions, the Court has not left all interested claimants to the vagaries of indirect notice. Our cases have required the State to make efforts to provide actual notice to all interested parties comparable to the efforts that were previously required only in *in personam* actions. See infra, at 2714–2715.

U.S 112, 77 S.Ct. 200, 1 L.Ed.2d 178 (1956), for example, the Court held that notice of condemnation proceedings published in a local newspaper was an inadequate means of informing a landowner whose name was known to the city and was on the official records. Similarly, in Schroeder v. City of New York, 371 U.S. 208, 83 S.Ct. 279, 9 L.Ed.2d 255 (1962), the Court concluded that publication in a newspaper and posted notices were inadequate to apprise a property owner of condemnation proceedings when his name and address were readily ascertainable from both deed records and tax rolls. Most recently, in Greene v. Lindsey, 456 U.S 444, 102 S.Ct. 1874, 72 L.Ed.2d 249 (1982), we held that posting a summons on the door of a tenant's apartment was an inadequate means of providing notice of forcible entry and detainer actions. See also Memphis Light, Gas & Water Div. v. Craft, 436 U.S. 1, 13–15, 98 S.Ct. 1554, 1562–1563, 56 L.Ed.2d 30 (1978); Eisen v. Carlisle & Jacquelin, 417 U.S. 156, 174–175, 94 S.Ct. 2140, 2150–2151, 40 L.Ed.2d 732 (1974); Bank of Marin v. England, 385 U.S. 99, 102, 87 S.Ct. 274, 276, 17 L.Ed.2d 197 (1966); Covey v. Somers, 351 U.S. 141, 146–147, 76 S.Ct. 724, 727, 100 L.Ed. 1021 (1956); City of New York v. New York, N. H. & H. R. Co., 344 U.S. 293, 296–297, 73 S.Ct. 299, 301, 97 L.Ed. 333 (1953).

This case is controlled by the analysis in *Mullane.* To begin with, a mortgagee possesses a substantial property interest that is significantly affected by a tax sale. Under Indiana law, a mortgagee acquires a lien on the owner's property which may be conveyed together with the mortgagor's personal obligation to repay the debt secured by the mortgage. Ind. Code § 32–8–11–7. A mortgagee's security interest generally has priority over subsequent claims or liens attaching to the property, and a purchase money mortgage takes precedence over virtually all other claims or liens including those which antedate the execution of the mortgage. Ind. Code § 32–8–11–4. The tax sale immediately and drastically diminishes the value of this security interest by granting the tax-sale purchaser a lien with priority over that of all other creditors. Ultimately, the tax sale may result in the complete nullification of the mortgagee's interest, since the purchaser acquires title free of all liens and other encumbrances at the conclusion of the redemption period.

Since a mortgagee clearly has a legally protected property interest, he is entitled to notice reasonably calculated to apprise him of a pending tax sale. Cf. Wiswall v. Sampson, 55 U.S. 52, 67, 14 L.Ed. 322 (1852). When the mortgagee is identified in a mortgage that is publicly recorded, constructive notice by publication must be supplemented by notice mailed to the mortgagor's last known available address, or by personal service. But unless the mortgagee is not reasonably identifiable, constructive notice alone does not satisfy the mandate of *Mullane.*[4]

4. In this case, the mortgage on file with the county recorder identified the mortgagee only as "MENNONITE BOARD OF MISSIONS a corporation, of Wayne County, in the State of Ohio." We assume that the mortgagee's address could have been ascertained by reasonably diligent efforts. See Mullane v. Central Hanover

Neither notice by publication and posting, nor mailed notice to the property owner, are means "such as one desirous of actually informing the [mortgagee] might reasonably adopt to accomplish it." *Mullane,* supra, at 315, 70 S.Ct., at 657. Because they are designed primarily to attract prospective purchasers to the tax sale, publication and posting are unlikely to reach those who, although they have interest in the property, do not make special efforts to keep abreast of such notices. Walker v. City of Hutchinson, supra, at 116, 77 S.Ct., 202; New York v. New York, N. H. & H. R. Co., supra, 344, U.S., at 296, 73 S.Ct., at 301; *Mullane,* supra, 339 U.S., at 315, 70 S.Ct., 657. Notice to the property owner, who is not in privity with his creditor and who has failed to take steps necessary to preserve his own property interest, also cannot be expected to lead to actual notice to the mortgagee. Cf. Nelson v. New York City, 352 U.S 103, 107–109, 77 S.Ct. 195, 197–199, 1 L.Ed.2d 171 (1956). The County's use of these less reliable forms of notice is not reasonable where, as here, "an inexpensive and efficient mechanism such as mail service is available." Greene v. Lindsey, supra, 456 U.S., at 455, 102 S.Ct., at 1881.

Personal service or mailed notice is required even though sophisticated creditors have means at their disposal to discover whether property taxes have not been paid and whether tax sale proceedings are therefore likely to be initiated. In the first place, a mortgage need not involve a complex commercial transaction among knowledgeable parties, and it may well be the least sophisticated creditor whose security interest is threatened by a tax sale. More importantly, a party's ability to take steps to safeguard its interests does not relieve the State of its constitutional obligation. It is true that particularly extensive efforts to provide notice may often be required when the State is aware of a party's inexperience or incompetence. See, e.g., Memphis Light, Gas & Water Div. v. Craft, supra, 436 U.S., at 13–15, 98 S.Ct., at 1562–1564; Covey v. Somers, supra. But it does not follow that the State may forego even the relatively modest administrative burden of providing notice by mail to parties who are particularly resourceful.[5] Cf. New York v. New York, N. H. & H. R. Co., supra, 344 U.S., at 297, 73 S.Ct., at 301. Notice by mail or other means as certain to ensure actual notice is a minimum constitutional precondition to a proceeding which will adversely affect the liberty or property interests of *any* party, whether unlettered or well versed in commercial practice, if its name and address are reasonably ascertainable. Furthermore, a mortgagee's

Bank & Trust Co., 339 U.S. 306, 317, 70 S.Ct. 652, 658–659, 94 L.Ed. 865 (1950). Simply mailing a letter to "Mennonite Board of Missions, Wayne County, Ohio," quite likely would have provided actual notice, given "the well-known skill of postal officials and employees in making proper delivery of letters defectively addressed." Grannis v. Ordean, 234 U.S 385, 397–398, 34 S.Ct. 779, 784, 58 L.Ed. 1363 (1914). We do not suggest, however, that a governmental body is required to undertake extraordinary efforts to discover the identity and whereabouts of a mortgagee whose identity is not in the public record.

5. Indeed, notice by mail to the mortgagee may ultimately relieve the county of a more substantial administrative burden if the mortgagee arranges for payment of the delinquent taxes prior to the tax sale.

knowledge of delinquency in the payment of taxes is not equivalent to notice that a tax sale is pending. The latter "was the information which the [County] was constitutionally obliged to give personally to the appellant—an obligation which the mailing of a single letter would have discharged." Schroeder v. City of New York, supra, at 214, 83 S.Ct., at 283.

We therefore conclude that the manner of notice provided to appellant did not meet the requirements of the Due Process Clause of the Fourteenth Amendment.[6] Accordingly, the judgment of the Indiana Court of Appeals is reversed and the cause is remanded for further proceedings not inconsistent with this opinion.

It is so ordered.

Justice O'CONNOR, with whom Justice POWELL and Justice REHNQUIST join, dissenting.

Today, the Court departs significantly from its prior decisions and holds that before the State conducts *any* proceeding that will affect the legally protected property interests of *any* party, the State must provide notice to that party by means certain to ensure actual notice as long as the party's identity and location are "reasonably ascertainable." Ante, at 9. Applying this novel and unjustified principle to the present case, the Court decides that the mortgagee involved deserved more than the notice by publication and posting that were provided. I dissent because the Court's approach is unwarranted both as a general rule and as the rule of this case.

I

In Mullane v. Central Hanover Trust Co., 339 U.S. 306, 314, 70 S.Ct. 652, 657, 94 L.Ed. 865 (1950), the Court established that "[a]n elementary and fundamental requirement of due process in any proceeding which is to be accorded finality is notice reasonably calculated under all circumstances, to apprise interested parties of the pendency of the action and afford them an opportunity to present their objections." We emphasized that notice is constitutionally adequate when "the practicalities and peculiarities of the case * * * are reasonably met," id., at 314–315, 70 S.Ct., at 657. See also Walker v. City of Hutchinson, 352 U.S. 112, 115, 77 S.Ct. 200, 202, 1 L.Ed.2d 178 (1956); Schroeder v. City of New York, 371 U.S. 208, 211–212, 83 S.Ct. 279, 281–282, 9 L.Ed.2d 255 (1962); Greene v. Lindsey, 456 U.S. 444, 449–450, 102 S.Ct. 1874, 1877–1878, 72 L.Ed.2d 249 (1982). The key focus is the "reasonableness" of the means chosen by the State. *Mullane,* supra, 339 U.S., at 315, 70 S.Ct., at 657. Whether a particular method of notice is reasonable depends on the outcome of the balance between the "inter-

---

6. This appeal also presents the question whether, before the county auditor executes and delivers a deed to the tax-sale purchaser, the mortgagee is constitutionally entitled to notice of its right to redeem the property. Cf. Griffin v. Griffin, 327 U.S. 220, 229, 66 S.Ct. 556, 560–561, 90 L.Ed. 635 (1946). Because we conclude that the failure to give adequate notice of the tax sale proceeding deprived appellant of due process of law, we need not reach this question.

est of the State" and "the individual interest sought to be protected by the Fourteenth Amendment." Id., at 314, 70 S.Ct., at 657. Of course, "[i]t is not our responsibility to prescribe the form of service that the [State] * * * should adopt." *Greene,* supra, 456 U.S., at 455, n. 9, 102 S.Ct., at 1880, n. 9. It is the primary responsibility of the State to strike this balance, and we will upset this process only when the State strikes the balance, in an irrational manner.

From *Mullane* on, the Court has adamantly refused to commit "itself to any formula achieving a balance between these interests in a particular proceeding or determining when constructive notice may be utilized or what test it must meet." 339 U.S., at 314, 70 S.Ct., at 657. Indeed, we have recognized "the impossibility of setting up a rigid formula as to the kind of notice that must be given; notice will *vary* with the circumstances and conditions." *Walker,* supra, 352 U.S., at 115, 77 S.Ct., at 202 (emphasis added). Our approach in these cases has always reflected the general principle that "[t]he very nature of due process negates any concept of inflexible procedures universally applicable to every imaginable situation." Cafeteria & Restaurant Workers Union, Local 473 v. McElroy, 367 U.S. 886, 895, 81 S.Ct. 1743, 1748, 6 L.Ed.2d 1230 (1961). See also Mathews v. Eldrige, 424 U.S. 319, 334–335, 96 S.Ct. 893, 902–903, 47 L.Ed.2d 18 (1976).

A

Although the Court purports to apply these settled principles in this case, its decision today is squarely at odds with the balancing approach that we have developed. The Court now holds that *whenever* a party has a legally protected property interest, "[n]otice by mail or other means as certain to ensure actual notice is a minimum constitutional precondition to a proceeding which will adversely affect the liberty or property interests * * * if [the party's] name and address are reasonably ascertainable." Ante, at 2712. Without knowing what state and individual interests will be at stake in future cases, the Court espouses a general principle ostensibly applicable whenever *any* legally protected property interest may be adversely affected. This is a flat rejection of the view that no "formula" can be devised that adequately evaluates the constitutionality of a procedure created by a State to provide notice in a certain class of cases. Despite the fact that *Mullane* itself accepted that constructive notice satisfied the dictates of due process in certain circumstances,[1] the Court, citing *Mullane,* now holds that constructive notice can *never* suffice whenever there is a legally protected property interest at stake.

* * *

---

1. In Mullane v. Central Hanover Bank & Trust Co., 339 U.S. 306, 314, 70 S.Ct. 652, 657, 94 L.Ed. 865 (1950), we held that "[p]ersonal service has not in all circumstances been regarded as indispensable to the process due to residents, and it has more often been held unnecessary as to nonresidents."

B

The Court also holds that the condition for receiving notice under its new approach is that the name and address of the party must be "reasonably ascertainable." In applying this requirement to the mortgagee in this case, the Court holds that the State must exercise "reasonably diligent efforts" in determining the address of the mortgagee, id., at 2711, n. 4, and suggests that the State is required to make some effort "to discover the identity and the whereabouts of a mortgagee whose identity is not in the public record." Ibid. Again, the Court departs from our prior cases. In *all* of the cases relied on by the Court in its analysis, the State either actually knew the identity or incapacity of the party seeking notice, or that identity was "very easily ascertainable." *Schroeder,* supra, 371 U.S., at 212–213, 83 S.Ct., at 282. See also *Mullane,* supra, 339 U.S., at 318, 70 S.Ct., at 659; Covey v. Town of Sommers, 351 U.S. 141, 146, 76 S.Ct., at 727 (1956); *Walker,* supra, 352 U.S., at 116, 77 S.Ct., at 202–203; Eisen v. Carlisle & Jacquelin, 417 U.S. 156, 175, 94 S.Ct. 2140, 2151, 40 L.Ed.2d 732 (1974).[3] Under the Court's decision today, it is not clear how far the State must go in providing for reasonable efforts to ascertain the name and address of an affected party. Indeed, despite the fact that the recorded mortgage failed to include the appellant's address, see ante, at 2711, n. 4, the Court concludes that its whereabouts were "reasonably identifiable." Id., at 2711. This uncertainty becomes particularly ominous in the light of the fact that the duty to ascertain identity and location, and to notify by mail or other similar means, exists whenever any legally protected interest is implicated.

II

Once the Court effectively rejects *Mullane* and its progeny by accepting a *per se* rule against constructive notice, it applies its rule and holds that the mortgagee in this case must receive personal service or mailed notice because it has a legally protected interest at stake, and because the mortgage was publicly recorded. See ante, at 2711. If the Court had observed its prior decisions and engaged in the balancing required by *Mullane*, it would have reached the opposite result.

It cannot be doubted that the State has a vital interest in the collection of its tax revenues in whatever reasonable manner that it chooses: "In authorizing the proceedings to enforce the payment of the taxes upon lands sold to a purchaser at tax sale, the State is in exercise of its sovereign power to raise revenue essential to carry on the affairs of state and the due administration of the laws. * * * 'The process of taxation does not require the same kind of notice as is required in a suit

---

3. In *Mullane,* the Court contrasted those parties whose identity and whereabouts are known or "at hand" with those "whose interests or whereabouts could not with due diligence be ascertained." 339 U.S., at 317, 318, 70 S.Ct., at 658, 659. This language must be read in the light of the facts of *Mullane,* in which the identity and location of certain beneficiaries were actually known. In addition, the Court in *Mullane* expressly rejected the view that a search "under ordinary standards of diligence" was required in that case. Id., at 317, 70 S.Ct., at 659.

at law, or even in proceedings for taking private property under the power of eminent domain.'" Leigh v. Green, 193 U.S. 79, 89, 24 S.Ct. 390, 392, 48 L.Ed. 623 (1904) (quoting Bell's Gap Railroad Company v. Pennsylvania, 134 U.S. 232, 239, 10 S.Ct. 533, 535, 33 L.Ed. 892 (1890)). The State has decided to accommodate its vital interest in this respect through the sale of real property on which payments of property taxes have been delinquent for a certain period of time.[4]

The State has an equally strong interest in avoiding the burden imposed by the requirement that it must exercise "reasonable" efforts to ascertain the identity and location of any party with a legally protected interest. In the instant case, that burden is not limited to mailing notice. Rather, the State must have someone check the records and ascertain with respect to each delinquent tax payer whether there is a mortgagee, perhaps whether the mortgage has been paid off, and whether there is a dependable address.

Against these vital interests of the State, we must weigh the interest possessed by the relevant class–in this case, mortgagees.[5] Contrary to the Court's approach today, this interest may not be evaluated simply by reference to the fact that we have frequently found constructive notice to be inadequate since *Mullane*. Rather, such interest "must be judged in the light of its practical application to the affairs of men as they are ordinarily conducted." *North Laramie Land Co.,* supra, 268 U. S., at 283, 45 S.Ct., at 494.

Chief Justice Marshall wrote long ago that "it is part of common prudence for all those who have any interest in [property], to guard that interest by persons who are in situation to protect it." *The Mary,* 13 U. S. (9 Cranch) 126, 144, 3 L.Ed. 678 (1815). We have never rejected this principle, and, indeed, we held in *Mullane* that "[a] State may indulge" the assumption that a property owner "usually arranges means to learn of any direct attack upon his possessory or proprietary rights." 339 U. S., at 316, 70 S.Ct., at 658. When we have found constructive notice to be inadequate, it has always been where an owner of property is, for all purposes, *unable* to protect his interest because there is no practical way for him to learn of state action that threatens to affect his property interest. In each case, the adverse action was one that was completely unexpected by the owner, and the owner would become aware of the action only by the fortuitous occasion of reading "an advertisement in small type inserted in the back pages of a newspaper * * *. [that may] not even name those whose attention it is supposed to attract, and does not inform acquaintances who might

---

4. The Court suggests that the notice that it requires "may ultimately relieve the county of a more substantial administrative burden if the mortgagee arranges for payment of the delinquent taxes prior to the tax sale." Ante, at 2712, n. 5. The Court neglects the fact that the State is a better judge of how it wants to settle its tax debts than is this Court.

5. This is not to say that the rule espoused must cover all conceivable mortgagees in all conceivable circumstances. The flexibility of due process is sufficient to accommodate those atypical members of the class of mortgagees.

call it to attention." *Mullane,* supra, 339 U. S., at 315, 70 S.Ct., at 658. In each case, the individuals had no reason to expect that their property interests were being affected.

This is not the case as far as tax sales and mortgagees are concerned. Unlike condemnation or an unexpected accounting, the assessment of taxes occurs with regularity and predictability, and the state action in this case cannot reasonably be characterized as unexpected in any sense. Unlike the parties in our other cases, the Mennonite Board had a regular event, the assessment of taxes, upon which to focus, in its effort to protect its interest. Further, approximately 95% of the mortgage debt outstanding in the United States is held by private institutional lenders and federally-supported agencies. U. S. Dept. of Commerce, Statistical Abstract of the United States: 1982–83, 511 (103d ed.).[6] It is highly unlikely, if likely at all, that a significant number of mortgagees are unaware of the consequences that ensue when their mortgagors fail to pay taxes assessed on the mortgaged property. Indeed, in this case, the Board itself required that Moore pay all property taxes.

There is no doubt that the Board could have safeguarded its interest with a minimum amount of effort. The county auctions of property commence by statute on the second Monday of each year. Ind. Code § 6–1.1–24–2(5). The county auditor is required to post notice in the county courthouse at least three weeks before the date of sale. Ind. Code § 6–1.1–24–3(a). The auditor is also required to publish notice in two different newspapers once each week for three weeks before the sale. Ind. Code § 6–1.1–24–3(a); Ind. Code § 6–1.1–22–4(b). The Board could have supplemented the protection offered by the State with the additional measures suggested by the court below: The Board could have required that Moore provide it with copies of paid tax assessments, or could have required that Moore deposit the tax monies in an escrow account, or could have itself checked the public records to determine whether the tax assessment had been paid. Pet. for Cert. 27.

When a party is unreasonable in failing to protect its interest despite its ability to do so, due process does not require that the State save the party from its own lack of care. The balance required by *Mullane* clearly weighs in favor of finding that the Indiana statutes satisfied the requirements of due process. Accordingly, I dissent.

NOTES

1. Will *Mennonite Board of Missions* be applied retroactively? If so, what then is the state of the thousands of titles that have been derived from constitutionally defective tax foreclosure statutes? See generally, Osborne,

---

6. The Court holds that "a mortgage need not involve a complex commercial transaction among knowledgeable parties * * *." Ante, at 8. This is certainly true; however, that does not change the fact that even if the Board is not a professional money lender, it voluntarily entered into a fairly sophisticated transaction with Moore. As the court below observed: "The State cannot reasonably be expected to assume the risk of its citizens' business ventures." Pet. for Cert. 27, n.9.

Nelson and Whitman, Real Estate Finance Law § 7.29 (1979). Does the current Indiana notice provision pass constitutional muster?

2. What is the significance of *Mennonite Board of Missions* for power of sale foreclosure? Does it mean that junior lienholders are entitled at least to mailed notice? Is the fact that a particular junior lienor is sophisticated and able to normally to safeguard its interest relevant constitutionally? What are the implications of *Mennonite Board of Missions* for statutes that afford mailed notice to junior mortgagees only if they previously record a request to receive it?

Page 538, add the following after the end of Note 3:

UNITED STATES v. FORD

United States District Court, Northern District of Mississippi, 1982.
551 F.Supp. 1101.

MEMORANDUM OPINION

KEADY, District Judge.

This case was initiated on January 11, 1982, by the United States as plaintiff against John R. Ford and Barbara D. Ford seeking to evict defendants from the possession of their residential property in Itawamba County, Mississippi, on the ground that the rural housing loan made to them by Farmers Home Administration (FmHA) had been foreclosed for default in payment of the mortgage indebtedness and the property sold at foreclosure sale to the United States as the highest bidder. The named defendants answered denying validity of the foreclosure and asserted a counterclaim for injunctive relief against FmHA from conducting unlawful nonjudicial foreclosure proceedings against persons of counterclaimants' class having rural housing loans and to require FmHA to resort to judicial foreclosures. Supplemental proceedings as to the Fords resulted in the government's confession as to the invalidity of the Ford foreclosure. This resulted in dismissal of the government's original suit without prejudice.

Meanwhile, Archie L. Weatherspoon and Jessie C. Weatherspoon, husband and wife, had, pursuant to an order of the United States Magistrate entered on April 21, intervened to propound their claims against the government. The Weatherspoons, hereinafter plaintiffs, alleged in their counterclaim that their own residential property, also located in Itawamba County, was unlawfully foreclosed on February 1, 1982, in a nonjudicial sale conducted by FmHA, and that Billy O. Hughes had bought the property as highest bidder. Plaintiffs alleged that their property was foreclosed without personal notice to them or an opportunity to present their defenses to foreclosure * * *.

Thereafter the government as counterdefendant and the Weatherspoons as counterplaintiffs filed cross motions for summary judgment. Both motions were denied. On July 19, the court granted Weatherspoons' motion to stay an action in the Chancery Court of Itawamba County by Hughes seeking an injunction for the Weatherspoons to surrender possession of the house to him as the present owner. The case was set for trial on the merits August 23, and Hughes was granted leave to file a claim against the government for refund of the purchase price in event the foreclosure was voided, or, if it was held valid, against Weatherspoons for possession of the house and for reasonable rent from the date of foreclosure. To this end Hughes timely filed appropriate pleadings. The court conducted an evidentiary hearing as scheduled. * * *

* * *

The heart of the Weatherspoons' claim involves their due process rights in the context of a nonjudicial foreclosure accomplished under state law pursuant to provisions in the deed of trust. It is well settled that the Due Process Clause of the fifth amendment mandates that FmHA provide mortgagors with adequate notice and opportunity for a hearing before foreclosure of an FmHA home loan. United States v. White, 429 F.Supp. 1245, 1250 (N.D.Miss.1977); see Aetna Insurance Co. v. Hartshorn, 477 F.2d 97 (5 Cir. 1973); Rau v. Cavenaugh, 500 F.Supp. 204 (D.S.D.1980). If adequate notice and opportunity for a hearing is provided, nonjudicial foreclosure pursuant to state law is constitutionally permissible.

> The nub of the question here * * * is not the lawfulness of the statute, but whether the contractual provision is [made] valid and binding between the parties [by the initial agreement or by subsequent conduct of the borrower]. (Brackets in original).

White, supra at 1251. Therefore, provisions in the deed of trust allowing nonjudicial foreclosure can be made valid by holding an administrative hearing patterned after Goldberg v. Kelly, 397 U.S. 254, 90 S.Ct. 1011, 25 L.Ed.2d 287 (1970), or by the borrower's relinquishment of his right to a hearing either by contractual waiver, United States v. Wynn, 528 F.2d 1048 (5 Cir. 1976), or waiver by conduct. Hoffman v. United States, 519 F.2d 1160 (5 Cir. 1975).

In the instant cause no hearing was held and it appears that the Weatherspoons' waiver of their due process rights by signing the note and deed of trust was not voluntary because of the inequality of bargaining power with the FmHA. *Rau,* supra, at 207–08; *White,* supra at 1251–52. Nonetheless, we find that the Weatherspoons waived their right to a hearing by failing to respond to notices mailed to them as well as personal meeting with the county supervisor. It is manifest that the Weatherspoons were apprised of their rights and the impending foreclosure, and understood their options, yet they failed to take any action to seek a hearing and present reasons for having the foreclosure postponed. By making no effort to contact FmHA officials to be heard, the Weatherspoons waived their fifth amendment rights to a hearing.

* * *

In conjunction with their constitutional claims, the Weatherspoons point out that the deed of trust required that all written notices were to be provided to them by certified mail. Only the acceleration notice was sent by certified mail; the other notices were sent by ordinary mail. Irrespective of this requirement, the Weatherspoons actually received written notices of their constitutional and statutory rights. To hold notice ineffectual because not sent by certified mail would be to elevate form over substance. "[D]ue process is flexible and calls for such procedural protections as the particular situation demands." Morrissey v. Brewer, 408 U.S. 471, 481, 92 S.Ct. 2593, 2600, 33 L.Ed.2d 484 (1972). Since defendants received constitutionally adequate notice their argument must fail. See Lehner v. United States, 685 F.2d 1187, 1190–91 (9 Cir. 1982).

An order shall issue dismissing the Weatherspoons' claim against the government, vacating the injunction against the state chancery court proceeding, and awarding possession of the property to Billy O. Hughes as purchaser to be delivered to him on February 1, 1983, together with judgment of $3,000 as reasonable rent since the date of foreclosure.

NOTE

The principal case seems to hold that a governmental agency can utilize administrative rules in conjunction with state nonjudicial foreclosure legislation to validate a foreclosure that would otherwise be unconstitutional if carried out under such state legislation alone. Do you agree? See generally, Nelson and Whitman, Real Estate Finance Law § 7.25 (2nd Ed. 1985). The FmHA procedure utilized in the principal case did not confer hearing rights on junior lienholders. Assuming that such lienholders actually existed, have their liens been destroyed? See id. at § 7.24.

JOHNSON v. UNITED STATES DEPARTMENT OF AGRICULTURE

United States Court of Appeals, Eleventh Circuit, 1984.
734 F.2d 774.

Before RONEY, FAY and CLARK, Circuit Judges.

FAY, Circuit Judge:

This lawsuit is a class action by approximately 48,000 residents of Alabama who borrowed money from the Farmers Home Administration (FmHA) under the Rural Housing loan program of Section 502, Title V of the Housing Act of 1949, 42 U.S.C. § 1472 (1980) (the Act). Appellant, Gabriel Johnson, represents a class of mortgagors who seek to set aside the FmHA's foreclosure of their homes. Earnestine Marshall intervened to represent a class of borrowers who are threatened with foreclosure. FmHA foreclosures in Alabama are processed non-judicially. This is permissible under Alabama state law and is authorized in the mortgage contracts by a "power of sale." The class challenges this non-judicial foreclosure method on due process and equal protection bases. The United States District Court for the Southern District of Alabama denied appellants' motion for a preliminary injunction to prevent non-judicial foreclosure. We reverse.

* * *

Before going into the specific facts of the named plaintiffs, it is helpful to discuss the program under which these mortgages were made. The FmHA, a division of the Department of Agriculture, is authorized to make home loans to low-income rural families. The purpose of the Act is to provide decent housing to low-income families who otherwise lack the financial means to buy a home. 42 U.S.C. § 1441. To qualify for a Section 502 loan the borrower must have been refused credit by a private financial institution, id., and must have an income of less than approximately $15,000 in Alabama. 42 U.S.C. § 1471(b)(3); 7 C.F.R. § 1944 Ex. C, Subpt. A (1983). For this purpose, "income" is any income planned to be received in the coming year by the applicant or a member of his household. 7 C.F.R. § 1944.2(c). Pensions, social security, welfare, unemployment benefits, and child support payments are included in the income calculation. Id. at § 1944.8(c)(2)(iv), (8)(v). The Section 502 program authorizes direct loans, not grants, therefore the applicant must demonstrate repayment ability under the regulatory standards. Id. at § 1944.8(2).

* * *

The mortgage note is standardized. 7 C.F.R. § 1807; see id. § 1944.33(c). All borrowers agree to many of the usual covenants in a commercial mortgage. By signing the note, the mortgagors agree to non-judicial foreclosure in a provision commonly known as a "power of sale." Although Alabama law authorizes the use of non-judicial foreclosure, whether or not a power of sale clause is contained in the note, *Ala.Code* § 35–10–3 (1982), in this case the FmHA relies on Alabama Code Section 35–10–1 which permits non-judicial foreclosure when a power of sale is included in the note. The FmHA uses non-judicial foreclosure in approximately twenty states; in all other states, according to state law, mortgages must be foreclosed in a judicial proceeding. The manner of foreclosure is the crux of appellants' equal protection claim.

After a loan is made, an extensive regulatory scheme prescribes the manner, type and frequency of loan servicing. 7 C.F.R. § 1951. The regulations are designed to help borrowers meet their notes and to assure accurate administration of the loans. Two provisions, "interest credit" and "moratorium" relief are designed to help a low-income borrower through a fixed period of time during which he is unable to meet the mortgage obligation. The interest credit subsidy reduces the interest rate paid on the mortgage in a proportion to the borrower's income. 7 C.F.R. § 1944.34. Interest credit agreements may be entered into at the loan closing or at some later date in response to changes in the borrower's income. An interest credit subsidy has the immediate effect of reducing the amount of each monthly payment and thus perhaps, allowing the homeowner to keep his property. Administration of the interest credit subsidies is charged to the Secretary of Agriculture ("Secretary") who "may" provide this relief. 42 U.S.C. § 1490a(a)(1)(B). Most of the appellants were given interest credits.

The Act also authorizes moratoria. 42 U.S.C. § 1475. The statute contemplates that the Secretary promulgate regulations that provide for a complete suspension of interest and principal payments during a period when the borrower is unable to make payments "without unduly impairing his standard of living" and "due to circumstances beyond his control." Id. In cases of extreme hardship, the Secretary is also authorized to cancel interest that accrues during the moratorium period. Id. The moratorium is just one of many work-out plans, e.g., interest credit, reamortization, and repayment agreements, that are prescribed to help a borrower through a financially difficult time. See 7 C.F.R., § 1951 Subpt. G. The moratorium "shall" be granted if a qualifying borrower applies. Id. § 1951.313. Prior to December 9, 1981 the Secretary had promulgated 7 C.F.R. § 1951.17(2)(i) (1977) which additionally required that the borrower had had a good credit history prior to experiencing the hardship. This regulation was amended on December 9, 1981 to include only the two statutory prerequisites for eligibility. 7 C.F.R. § 1951.313 (1983). All of the loans of the representative plaintiffs had been accelerated before the 1981 amendment.

The FmHA county supervisor is responsible for servicing all Section 502 loans which includes the interest credit and moratorium provisions. Id. § 1951.307. Each step of the loan process is governed by regulation as detailed as a list of points to discuss in the initial application interview. Most communication, i.e., payments, late notices, acceleration notices, is done through prescribed forms. See 7 C.F.R. § 1951 Subpts. A & G. The county supervisor notifies each borrower of the moratorium provision when the supervisor becomes aware of a change in the borrower's circumstance and includes specific language informing the borrower of the moratorium provision in any collection letter sent after a payment is not made. Id. § 1951.312.313. The regulations do not require that a borrower be given a moratorium application and none was dispensed by FmHA officials unless requested.

Moratoria may be granted in six month intervals, extendable up to three years. If after three years the borrower is unable to resume payments, foreclosure must proceed. Id. § 1951.313(4), (15). Although the first paragraph of § 1951.313 states that a moratorium *shall* be granted if the borrower meets the two statutory prerequisites in 42 U.S.C. § 1475 infra, Section 1951.313(2) requires that the borrower apply for a moratorium and authorizes the county supervisor to grant or deny the moratorium based upon a determination that no other workout program would be adequate and that the appropriate documents reveal that payment would substantially impair the borrower's standard of living. Borrowers are notified of an adverse decision and informed of the administrative appeal process set forth in 7 C.F.R. § 1900 Subpt. B.

In 1978 Congress realized there was no real administrative appeals process for FmHA decisions under Section 502 loans. S.Rep. No. 871, 95th Cong., 2d Sess. 39–40, *reprinted in* 1978 U.S.Code Cong. & Ad. News 4773, 4812. Public Law 95–557, 42 U.S.C. § 1480(g) enacted in 1978, required the Secretary to adequately notify borrowers of the denial of moratoria and to promulgate an appeal procedure that allows borrowers to present additional information "to a person, other than the person making the original determination, who has authority to reverse the decision." Pursuant to this law, the Secretary published C.F.R. Part 1900 Subpt. B, 43 Fed.Reg. 219, Nov. 13, 1978 which provided for an informal hearing before an FmHA official who did not have an active role in servicing the borrower's account. 7 C.F.R. § 1900.57 Exh. D. The borrower must initiate the appeal process as there is no automatic review. The hearing may be tape-recorded at the appellant's expense, and an FmHA designate must take "notes" of the hearing. Id. § 1900.57(d).

If the hearing officer upholds the FmHA action taken, the appellant then has thirty days in which to request in writing that the hearing officer's decision be reviewed. Id. § 3(j). If a request for review is filed, a reviewing officer (one for each state) will examine the hearing officer's decision in light of the record. Id. § 1900.58. The reviewing officer's decision concludes the administrative appeal process and, if it upholds the FmHA action, will be retroactively effective on the date the original action was taken. A "notice of acceleration," sent to all borrowers to notify them of the FmHA plan to foreclose, also informs a borrower of the right to appeal and triggers the appeal process.

The decision to foreclose is made by the county supervisor and approved by the State Director before foreclosure is begun. In Alabama, foreclosures are done by notice to the homeowners of a repossession date and the planned sale. Unless the homeowner does not voluntarily vacate the house, in which case a judicial eviction would be filed, no judicial process is used. The FmHA appeal process is available to borrowers whether judicial or non-judicial foreclosure is contemplated. In states that require judicial foreclosure, after the FmHA appeal is completed, a lawsuit is filed by the FmHA requesting foreclosure. Before a court orders foreclosure, the FmHA must prove that it followed all applicable rules and procedures in accelerating the homeowner's loan. Thus, there is a substantial procedural advantage to borrowers who are foreclosed through the judicial process.

* * *

(a) Due Process

We begin our discussion of the merits with a reminder that we are only discussing the "likelihood" of success. See University of Texas v. Camenisch, 451 U.S. 390, 394, 101 S.Ct. 1830, 1833, 68 L.Ed.2d 175 (1981). Our ruling on the preliminary injunction, as with the district court's fact finding at the preliminary stage, has no conclusive bearing at the trial on the merits. The first issue is whether the use of non-judicial foreclosure meets the minimum requirements of due process.

A FmHA loan, once made, creates a statutory entitlement and a property interest protected by the due process clause of the Fifth Amendment. See Goldberg v. Kelly, 397 U.S. 254, 262, 90 S.Ct. 1011, 1017, 25 L.Ed.2d 287 (1970); United States v. Henderson, 707 F.2d 853, 857 (5th Cir. 1983); McCachren v. United States Dep't. of Agriculture, 599 F.2d 655, 656 (5th Cir. 1979). See also Neighbors v. Block, 564 F.Supp. 1075 (E.D.Ark.1983); United States v. Ford, 551 F.Supp. 1101 (N.D.Miss.1982); Rau v. Cavenaugh, 500 F.Supp. 204 (D.S.D.1980); United States v. White, 429 F.Supp. 1245 (N.D.Miss.1977); Ricker v. United States, 417 F.Supp. 133 (D.C.Me.1976); Law v. United States Dep't. of Agriculture, 366 F.Supp. 1233 (N.D.Ga.1973). At a minimum, due process assures notice and a meaningful opportunity to be heard before a right or interest is forfeited. Mathews v. Eldridge, 424 U.S. 319, 334, 96 S.Ct. 893, 902, 47 L.Ed.2d 18 (1976); Fuentes v. Shevin, 407 U.S. 67, 80–83, 92 S.Ct. 1983, 1994–1995, 32 L.Ed.2d 556 (1972); Sniadach v. Family Finance Corp., 395 U.S. 337, 89 S.Ct. 1820, 23 L.Ed.2d 349 (1969).

It seems that all plaintiffs have been repeatedly receiving notice of the right to apply for a moratorium in each past due notice mailed. Further, it appears that adequate notice of the appeal procedures and of pending acceleration or foreclosure have been given. The notice required by regulation meets the due process standard. Any deviations from the notice regulations that might constitute a due process violation are left to the factfinder at the trial on the merits.

The second due process requirement, a meaningful opportunity to contest an adverse decision or action, is more problematic. A fair hearing requires an impartial arbiter. See Marshall v. Jerrico, Inc., 446 U.S. 238, 242–243 & n. 2, 100 S.Ct. 1610, 1613 & n. 2, 64 L.Ed.2d 182 (1980). We have serious reservations about the neutrality of the hearing officers. The regulations establish that the hearing officer is a nearby district director. On its face, the regulation appears less than neutral. The nearby district director will be evaluating a decision to foreclose made by a peer and already approved by his boss, the state director. (Sirmon Dep. at 59–60). The Supreme Court in Schweiker v. McClure, 456 U.S. 188, 195, 102 S.Ct. 1665, 1669, 72 L.Ed.2d 1 (1982) has stated that hearing officers are presumed to be unbiased until a conflict of interest or other specific reason for disqualification is shown. It is the plaintiff's burden of proof to show a conflict of interest. Id. at 196, 102 S.Ct. at 1670. At trial, the plaintiffs may be able to further demonstrate a conflict of interest in the hearing officers. On the surface, the plaintiffs have shown a substantial likelihood that a conflict may exist that would impinge the hearing officer's impartiality.

In their brief plaintiffs also contend that a memorandum of May 20, 1982, from Neil Sox Johnson, Acting Deputy Administrator, adds an additional review by the Deputy Administrator of any hearing officer's reversal of FmHA actions. Thus if a borrower prevails, then the FmHA will get an additional appeal not available when the borrower loses the hearing. This memorandum does not comport with agency rulemaking authority and also suggests due process violations. Mr. Johnson has filed an affidavit indicating that this procedure is designated to assess the need for training among hearing officers. The district court has made no findings. The memorandum at least poses a substantial question.

The Power of Sale

The FmHA has made approximately one million housing loans. Its standard form includes a power of sale that authorizes non-judicial foreclosure in the event of default. This is permitted by Alabama Code § 35–10–1 (1980). In its brief, the FmHA makes a confusing statement concerning Alabama law and the use of non-judicial foreclosure. In fact, Section 35–10–1 permits such foreclosures *if* the underlying instrument contains a power of sale. If judicial processes were used instead, a full court proceeding would automatically be conducted before foreclosure. A valid power of sale is necessary to foreclosure under Section 35–10–1.[6]

The FmHA argues that there is no right to judicial foreclosure, but only a right to due process which the FmHA claims is met through their procedure which is functionally equivalent to a judicial foreclosure. It is true that there is no absolute right to judicial foreclosure; however, if these mortgages did not contain a power of sale FmHA would foreclose through a judicial process. Additionally, if a judicial foreclosure is the only avenue open, a hearing will occur *automatically,* unlike the FmHA procedure which requires the borrower to initiate the hearing.[7] Pretermitting whether the FmHA hearing and appeal procedure meets due process, a power of sale clause at least waives the

---

6. Alabama Code § 35–10–3 does authorize non-judicial foreclosures when the underlying instrument contains no power of sale provision. But the FmHA is not relying on this provision of the Alabama Code, probably because it presents serious due process problems when there has been no valid waiver of the right to notice and a hearing. See Fuentes v. Shevin, 407 U.S. 67, 92 S.Ct. 1983, 32 L.Ed.2d 1983 (1972); Sniadach v. Family Finance Corp., 395 U.S. 337, 89 S.Ct. 1820, 23 L.Ed.2d 349 (1969).

7. There is no right to non-judicial foreclosure, only a right to due process. Therefore, if the FmHA procedure affords due process a validly executed power of sale provision is not constitutionally required. A judicial foreclosure proceeding gives the borrower more rights than the FmHA appeal and hearing process. Judicial proceedings would occur automatically, would be before a federal magistrate or district judge, and would have lawyers representing both sides. Additionally, the burden of proof in a judicial proceeding is on the FmHA to show that they followed all applicable rules and regulations and that the borrower is in default. In an FmHA proceeding the burden of proof is on the borrower to show that the FmHA acted in error. Because a judicial foreclosure gives the borrower these additional protections not available in the FmHA proceeding, when a borrower signs the power of sale provision he is waiving the right to certain processes. Even if we find that the FmHA's procedure meets the due process minimum, borrowers are waiving other processes in the power of sale. Due process requires only an opportunity for a hearing whereas judicial foreclosure requires the hearing. See Goldberg v. Kelly, 397 U.S. 254, 90 S.Ct. 1011, 25 L.Ed.2d 287 (1970); Cf. United States v. Ford, 551 F.Supp. 1101 (N.D.Miss.1982).

automatic nature of the review. We therefore examine the validity of the power of sale clause in the standard mortgage note.

Due process rights may be waived, D.H. Overmyer Co. v. Frick Co., 405 U.S. 174, 185, 92 S.Ct. 775, 782, 31 L.Ed.2d 124 (1972), although there is a strong presumption against waiver. Gonzalez v. County of Hidalgo, 489 F.2d 1043, 1046 (5th Cir.1973). Waiver depends upon the facts of a particular case, United States v. Wynn, 528 F.2d 1048, 1050 (5th Cir.1976), and is good only if it is done in an informed manner. *Overmyer,* supra 405 U.S. at 186–87, 92 S.Ct. at 782–83.

Plaintiffs introduced an expert witness who testified that the standard FmHA mortgage, containing the power of sale, requires five years of college to understand. The expert tested the named plaintiffs and found their reading levels were substantially below that required to understand the document. The expert testified that most members of the class would be unable to comprehend the FmHA documents. Earnestine Marshall testified that she did not even read the documents.

The plaintiffs also contend that their relative bargaining position with FmHA makes these contracts adhesive. This inequality is allegedly exacerbated by the standardized mortgage used in all FmHA loans. See *Gonzalez,* 489 F.2d at 1046–47. The FmHA is a large agency and practical considerations require that a standard mortgage be issued. On the question of unequal bargaining positions, we note that the FmHA has each borrower select an attorney from a list it provides. That attorney is present at the closing to look after the borrower's interests. No evidence has been offered to show what the attorneys present at the closings did as to explaining the power of sale provisions to the borrowers. We simply cannot determine on this record whether a knowing and intelligent waiver has been made. This will be resolved by the trial court in the first instance.

Some district courts have found that the FmHA failed to prove that the plaintiffs knowingly and voluntarily agreed to the power of sale provisions. See Rau v. Cavenaugh, 500 F.Supp. 204 (D.S.D.1980); United States v. White, 429 F.Supp. 1245 (N.D.Miss.1977). Our precedent requires specific proof of a knowing and voluntary waiver of the constitutional right to due process. Gonzalez v. County of Hidalgo, 489 F.2d 1043, 1046 (5th Cir.1973). At the trial on the merits this will be a substantial question of fact.

We conclude that there is a substantial likelihood that the plaintiffs will prevail on the merits of their due process claims.

(b) Equal Protection

Plaintiffs contend that the FmHA's use of judicial foreclosure in thirty jurisdictions denies equal protection to those residents of the twenty-two jurisdictions in which the FmHA uses non-judicial foreclosure. The FmHA determines the method of foreclosure based on the law of each state or jurisdiction. On its face, the distinction between types of foreclosure is made by an external neutral factor: the law of the state. We do not doubt that using the law of the situs of real property is a rational reason for the jurisdictional distinctions between foreclosure methods.

* * *

We do not think that the choice of law question raises an equal protection claim. We have one reservation. The consent decree entered into by the FmHA in Georgia in Williams v. Butz, No. CV–176–173 (Oct. 7, 1979) (S.D.Ga.), provides that notwithstanding that Georgia law permits non-judicial foreclosure, henceforth all FmHA loans in Georgia shall be foreclosed through the judicial process. By this action, the FmHA has gone beyond the original choice to use non-judicial foreclosure in the states that permit it. The FmHA has voluntarily granted Georgia residents an additional procedure not available to residents of the other twenty-two states that allow non-judicial foreclosure. It is permissible for a federal agency to use state laws if the laws further the policy of the federal program. We question whether the use of non-judicial foreclosure furthers the policies of the Housing Act.

This issue was raised by the court *sua sponte* during oral argument. At that time the attorney for the FmHA frankly stated that the consent decree was entered into in *Williams* to appease District Court Chief Judge Anthony Alaimo who was outraged about the FmHA foreclosure practice in Georgia. Without discounting the tenacity of an extraordinary jurist, we feel comfortable in assuming that this reason does not rise to the rational purpose test the government concedes it must meet. We requested that the parties brief this issue after oral argument. In its brief, the FmHA asserts that the *Williams* consent decree was entered into because a similar action had been adversely decided in Mississippi at the time which argued poorly for their chances of success in Georgia. United States v. White, 429 F.Supp. 1245 (N.D.Miss.1977). The FmHA was also motivated by the backlog of mortgages in arrears in Georgia and was concerned that a hiatus of foreclosures for all members of the certified class in *Williams* would result in an administrative nightmare. We note that in this case *lis pendens* have been filed on all houses and that the same administrative nightmare could occur. Finally, the FmHA points out that *Williams* and *White* were decided before the FmHA had issued its hearing and appeal regulations in 1978 and that a different and perhaps more serious due process challenge was motivating the settlement. The FmHA offers no reason for its failure to request a modification of the *Williams* consent decree in light of the regulatory changes. Perhaps Judge Alaimo is still an intimidating presence—if so it is an interesting footnote to notions of separation of power.

The geographic class of persons against whom the FmHA uses non-judicial foreclosure was not defined by Congress. Congress has not spoken to the manner of foreclosure. The FmHA has decided that it will foreclose non-judicially whenever permitted with the exception of

Georgia. Our review here will not opine resolution of this issue because we have no real record and little legal argument to guide us. We do conclude that the plaintiffs have more than a possibility of prevailing on the equal protection question defined at oral argument.

* * *

We find that the district court abused its discretion by denying the motion for a preliminary injunction. We recognize that there are close legal questions, but we find that there is a substantial likelihood that the plaintiffs will prevail. We need not and do not decide that the plaintiffs will prevail on all issues as it is sufficient to note that the plaintiffs will likely prevail at least in part. We are strongly persuaded that the equities, defined as the public interest, irreparable injury, and the comparative harm, favor the granting of the preliminary injunction. The harm to the plaintiffs from the denial of the injunction so clearly outweighs the injury to the FmHA from the granting of the injunction that it would be inequitable to deny the injunction. Therefore, we REVERSE and REMAND to the district court to enter the preliminary injunction requiring that all FmHA foreclosures in Alabama be done through the judicial process until this lawsuit is decided on the merits.

NOTES

1. The Eleventh Circuit has experienced considerable difficulty in resolving due process challenges to power of sale foreclosure. In Federal Deposit Insurance Corporation v. Morrison, 568 F.Supp. 1240 (D.Ala.1983), a federal district court invalidated a power of sale foreclosure conducted under Alabama legislation that afforded a mortgagor notice by publication only. The court emphasized that if notice by publication is constitutionally deficient with respect to a mortgagee, as in *Mennonite*, it "a fortiori" is as to a mortgagor. According to the district court, under *Mennonite* the notice published * * * simply was not such as one desirous of actually informing the [mortgagor] might reasonably adopt to accomplish it. Id. at 1244. The Eleventh Circuit, however, reversed based on the following perplexing reasoning:

> Carefully tracing the boundaries of these rights, however, we find that the FDIC has nowhere infringed upon Morrison's property. Foreclosure within the contractual terms and the requirements of Alabama law did not deprive him of his equity of redemption, but only terminated it. The state in creating this interest commanded that it should exist only up to the moment when the mortgagee properly exercised the power of sale. That such a moment was undetermined when the parties signed the mortgage did not nullify the conditional nature of his equity of redemption, any more than the unpredictability of a life estate holder's death can prevent termination of his interest when he actually dies. The blame for turning the once-hypothetical foreclosure into reality lies solely with the mortgagors. It ill becomes a solvent debtor whose delinquent note has contributed to his mortgagee's ruin to complain that the FDIC, struggling to minimize the damage from East Gadsden Bank's collapse, has been a more vigilant creditor than the bank. Under Alabama law, the equity of redemption existed only in the absence of foreclosure. Because foreclosure and the equity of redemption cannot overlap, it is impossible that this foreclosure

infringed on Morrison's right. We cannot give Morrison an equity of redemption any larger than the dimensions in which Alabama chose to cut it.

Because we find no deprivation, Morrison's heavy reliance on *Mennonite* * * * is misplaced. There the Supreme Court held that Indiana had deprived a mortgagee of his property by permitting a tax sale purchaser of real estate to acquire absolute title free of the mortgagee's lien. The state inflicted this deprivation under a revenue collection statute that at the time of the execution of the mortgage was entirely inapplicable to the mortgage contract and the mortgagee's rights thereunder. *Mennonite*, which construes a mortgagee's rights in a tax sale under Indiana law, offers us little guidance in construing a mortgagor's rights in a contractual foreclosure sale under Alabama law.

747 F.2d 610, 615–616 (11th Cir. 1984). The court distinguished *Johnson* on the ground that "unlike Johnson, Morrison made no claim that a federal statutory scheme affords him any property right * * *. Morrison alleges only a deprivation of the Alabama redemption rights." Id. at 616. Do you agree with this reasoning? Can *Morrison* be reconciled with most of the other cases you have studied concerning the constitutionality of power-of-sale foreclosure? See generally Nelson and Whitman, Real Estate Finance Law §§ 7.24–7.25 (2nd Ed. 1985).

2. The Multifamily Mortgage Foreclosure Act of 1981 was enacted by Congress to provide a nonjudicial foreclosure remedy for certain multifamily residential and nonresidential mortgages held by the Secretary of Housing and Urban Development. See 12 U.S.C.A. §§ 3701–3717 (West Supp.1982). Consider the following summary and analysis of this legislation contained in 1981 U.S.Code, Cong. and Adm.News, 560–562:

The procedure contemplated is similar to the "deed of trust" foreclosure approach used in approximately half of the States. The title is procedural only and is not intended to affect substantive rights except as explicitly set out in the bill. To the extent that a mortgagee has equitable defenses, the mortgagee is free to seek injunctive relief against foreclosure in the courts.

This measure is of special importance to HUD's multifamily mortgage insurance and rehabilitation loan programs. Lengthy delays in foreclosing defaulted mortgages caused by excessive foreclosure periods in some States increase the risk of property deterioration, vandalism and waste. The resulting loss to HUD (including its mortgage insurance funds) and the taxpayer in terms of rehabilitation costs and increased management and holding expenses is substantial. Moreover, these conditions impose a severe hardship on the tenants of affected projects and on the neighborhoods in which the projects are located. The proposed legislation would ameliorate this situation by providing an efficient, equitable and, most important, relatively expeditious nonjudicial foreclosure remedy.

The availability of an expeditious foreclosure remedy also provides HUD with the flexibility needed to deal with defaulted multifamily mortgages in a manner designed to promote the best interests of the owners and residents of the projects involved, the government and the communities in which the security properties are located. In certain instances, some delay in instituting foreclosure proceedings would give a deserving mortgagor the opportunity to bring the mortgage current or cure a nonmonetary default, thereby ensuring that the interests of the mortgagor, the tenants and the government are best served. The expeditious foreclosure remedy in the bill permits such a delay while at the same time assuring that, if a relatively brief delay is later found not to have been warranted, the mortgage may be foreclosed in a timely fashion.

In addition, the nonjudicial foreclosure procedure is far less costly than foreclosures conducted under State laws requiring judicial process. The savings occasioned by this measure would accrue not only to the taxpayers but also to the defaulting property owner, since foreclosure costs are typically deducted from the mortgagor's share of sale proceeds.

Finally, the proposal relieves the courts of the burden of entertaining judicial foreclosures of mortgages subject to the Act and, since foreclosures under the Act would be nonjudicial, the Department of Justice no longer would be required to handle foreclosures of these mortgages.

The title sets forth in detail the procedures to be followed for foreclosure. The principal features of this procedure are:

The Secretary as holder of the mortgage designates a foreclosure commissioner who is empowered to sell the property involved in accordance with the requirements of the Act.

The Foreclosure Commissioner commences the foreclosure upon the request of the Secretary where a default or other breach for which foreclosure is authorized by the mortgage or applicable regulatory agreement has occurred.

The foreclosure is commenced with service of a Notice of Default and Foreclosure Sale. The Notice sets forth information relevant to the sale and is published once a week for three weeks; sent by certified mail, return receipt requested, to all lienors and, at least 21 days prior to the sale, to the present and prior owners; and, in certain cases, posted, on the property.

Specific provisions prescribe the conduct of the proceeding prior to sale, the sale itself, the allowance of foreclosure costs, the disposition of sale proceeds, the transfer of title and possession, and the record of foreclosure and sale.

Since foreclosure extinguishes property rights, the bill contains numerous provisions to protect the mortgagor of the property subject to foreclosure sale, as well as other interested parties.

Major features include the following:

The foreclosure commissioner has to be responsible, financially sound and competent to conduct the foreclosure.

The Secretary is guarantor of payment of any judgment obtained against the foreclosure commissioner.

The commissioner is specifically authorized to adjourn or cancel the sale if conditions are not conducive to a sale fair to the owner.

Even if not so provided in the mortgage instrument, the owner has the right to have the mortgage reinstated one time by bringing the mortgage current or curing a nonmonetary default; subsequent reinstatement can be made at the discretion of the Secretary.

The provisions for publication, mailing and posting of the Notice of Default and Foreclosure Sale are extensive and thorough.

Foreclosure by reason of monetary default is generally based only upon total failure to meet an installment.

No other proceeding to foreclose the mortgage is continued or initiated during the pendency of a foreclosure under the bill.

The foreclosure sale cannot be held within 30 days of the default upon which foreclosure is based.

If, subsequent to commencement of a foreclosure under the bill, a new commissioner is designated less than 48 hours prior to the time of sale, the foreclosure is terminated and must begin anew; if a new commissioner is designated more than 48 hours prior to the sale, foreclosure continues unless the commissioner finds that such continuation would unfairly affect the interests of the mortgagor.

If a sale is adjourned to another day, a new Notice of Default and Foreclosure Sale must be served.

The requirement that lienors of record be notified gives opportunity for the third parties most likely to bid or purchase at foreclosure to do so.

The requirement that sale be by public auction increases the chances of arriving at a sales price reflective of the value of the property.

Costs are limited to out-of-pocket expenses and such fees as are established by regulation.

Finally, the measure specifies that post-sale redemption periods under State law do not apply to mortgages foreclosed pursuant to the Act. This provision codifies existing practice in the multifamily programs. If these redemption periods—up to 18 months or longer in some States—were applied to these mortgages, salability of the properties involved would be seriously impaired and their rehabilitation and improvement discouraged. Such a result would increase the Federal financial exposure and frustrate achievement of the programs' objectives and the national housing goals.

This legislation is of special importance to HUD's multifamily housing programs, since it helps remedy lengthy State foreclosure procedures which have caused substantial losses to the government and the taxpayer and hardship to affected residents and neighborhoods. In addition, because of the expeditious foreclosure procedure contemplated by the bill, HUD has flexibility to deal with defaulted multifamily mortgages in a manner designed to promote the bests interests of the owners and residents of affected projects, HUD and the communities in which the security properties are located.

The above legislation probably satisfies the notice requirements of the Fifth Amendment because it not only requires that mailed notice of default and foreclosure be provided to the present owner, the original mortgagor and others who appear to be liable on the mortgage debt, but to junior lienholders as well. On the other hand, the legislation fails to afford *any* interested party a right to a hearing. In light of Ricker v. United States and similar decisions, would a foreclosure under this statute satisfy the hearing requirement of the Fifth Amendment? The legislation does confer authority on the Secretary of HUD to promulgate regulations to "carry out its provisions." 12 U.S.C.A. § 3717 (West Supp.1982). Those regulations, however, treat the hearing issue as almost an afterthought. They state simply that "HUD will provide to the mortgagor [and current owner] an opportunity to present reasons why the mortgage should not be foreclosed." 24 C.F.R. § 27.5(b). Does this provision satisfy due process requirements as to the mortgagor? As to junior lienholders? See Nelson and Whitman, Real Estate Finance Law § 7.25 (2nd Ed. 1985).

Page 561, add as Note 5:

5. Unless a very narrow judicial view of governmental action is adopted, there is a high degree of risk that the use of state power of sale statutes by direct governmental instrumentalities will result in constitutionally defective foreclosures. Does the solution to this problem lie perhaps in the promulgation by the government agency of supplementary administrative rules and procedures that correct any constitutional deficiencies contained in such state legislation? Since these deficiencies most likely vary from state to state, would it be simpler and more efficient for either Congress or the governmental agency (if the latter has the authority to do so) to enact legislation or promulgate regulations that could be used as a substitute for and not merely as a supplement to existing state power of sale legislation? See Nelson & Whitman, Real Estate Finance Law §§ 7.25, 7.30, 8.8 (2nd Ed. 1985). In fact, Congress recently enacted power of sale legislation for use by the Department of Housing and Urban Development (HUD) in foreclosing HUD-held mortgages on multi-family dwellings. For a consideration of this legislation and its possible constitutional problems, see Section D(3) supra, of this Chapter.

E. DISBURSEMENT OF FORECLOSURE SALE PROCEEDS

Page 564, add the following as Notes 3 and 4:

3. Suppose that a power of sale foreclosure yields a surplus, but that the mortgagor believes there are grounds for having the sale set aside. Would you advise the mortgagor to accept a check for the surplus? Consider the consequences for one mortgagor who did so:

> It has been held that acceptance of a surplus derived from a foreclosure sale waives the right of the mortgagor to attack the foreclosure. Flake v. Building and Loan Association, 204 N.C. 650, 169 S.E. 223 (1933); 55 Am.Jur.2d Mortgages § 665 (1971). By endorsing the check and reaping the benefits of the surplus toward the satisfaction of other debts, plaintiffs elected to ratify the sale. They may not now treat the sale as a nullity and have it set aside, or sue the trustee for wrongfully conducting the sale. *Flake,* supra.

Leonard v. Pell, 56 N.C.App. 405, 289 S.E.2d 140, 142 (1982).

4. Suppose that a foreclosure sale yields a surplus, but it is insufficient to satisfy the claims of both second and third mortgagees. Suppose further that the third mortgagee can prove that the second mortgage debt is more than adequately secured by other property of the mortgagor. Should the third mortgagee whose debt is not otherwise secured have a superior claim to the surplus? See United States v. Century Federal Savings and Loan Association, 418 So.2d 1195 (Fla.App.1982).

F. STATUTORY REDEMPTION

Page 575, add as Note 4:

4. Read the material in Section G of this Chapter, infra. Is the practical effect of *Durrett* to create de facto statutory redemption in those states that

currently do not have such legislation? How does the *Durrett* principle differ from statutory redemption?

G. OTHER STATUTORY IMPACTS ON FORECLOSURE

1. ANTI–DEFICIENCY LEGISLATION AND RELATED PROBLEMS

Page 604, add as Notes 5 and 6:

5. Agricultural mortgagors have found protection against acceleration and foreclosure by the Farmers Home Administration (FmHA) under Section 1981(a) of the Agricultural Credit Act of 1978. 7 U.S.C.A. § 1981(a). Under the foregoing provision, the Secretary of Agriculture "may permit, at the request of the borrower, the deferral of principal and interest on any outstanding loan made, insured, or held by the Secretary * * * and may forego foreclosure of any such loan, for such period as the Secretary deems necessary upon a showing by the borrower that due to circumstances beyond the borrower's control, the borrower is temporarily unable to continue making payments of such principal and interest when due without unduly impairing the standard of living of the borrower."

Section 1981(a) became the focal point of national controversy during the severe agricultural recession of the early and mid-1980's. The Secretary took the position that the section itself imposed no procedural or substantive limitations of loan acceleration and foreclosure and that the decision whether to hear individual requests under it or to implement it all was solely within his discretion. Numerous federal courts rejected these contentions and held that the FmHA is obligated to afford a mortgagor pre-acceleration notice that "he may apply for a moratorium on payment of his loan and that he be given an opportunity to demonstrate that he is eligible for it * * *" Shick v. Farmers Home Administration of United States Department of Agriculture, 748 F.2d 35, 40 (1st Cir.1984). See Matzke v. Block, 732 F.2d 799 (10th Cir.1984) (affirming on this issue 564 F.Supp. 1157 (D.Kan.1983)); Allison v. Block, 723 F.2d 631 (8th Cir.1983) (affirming 556 F.Supp. 400 (W.D.Mo.1982)); United States v. Hamrick, 713 F.2d 69 (4th Cir.1983) (per curiam); Gamradt v. Block, 581 F.Supp. 122 (D.Minn.1983); Coleman v. Block, 580 F.Supp. 194 (D.N.D.1984) and 562 F.Supp. 1353 (D.N.D.1983); Jacoby v. Schuman, 568 F.Supp. 843 (E.D.Mo.1983); Curry v. Block, 738 F.2d 1556 (11th Cir. 1984). Under this reasoning, the words "may permit" in Section 1981(a) refer to the discretion of the Secretary to grant a deferral *after* a showing by the mortgagor and does not mean that he has the authority to determine whether to enforce the section at all. Rather, the Secretary was obligated to promulgate regulations under it establishing a procedure and substantive standards for deferrals and related relief.

6. Read In re Madrid and Notes in Section G of the Chapter, infra. To what extent will the application of the *Durrett* principle reduce deficiency judgments?

3. BANKRUPTCY

Page 612, delete pages 612–616 and substitute the following:

NELSON AND WHITMAN, REAL ESTATE FINANCE LAW*

638–646 (2nd Ed. 1985)

In theory, mortgagees should be unconcerned when insolvency forces mortgagors to file bankruptcy. Indeed, protection from such occurrences is the very reason for creation of mortgage security interests. In reality, however, mortgagees' rights, contractual and statutory, are often substantially affected by federal bankruptcy law, as many learn when they are forced into bankruptcy court to defend their security interests from the trustee's attack. Familiar state laws, requiring minimal time and effort to foreclose, are often neutralized by federal bankruptcy provisions which may freeze property for years.

The Bankruptcy Code (the "Code") provides for three types of bankruptcy proceedings: Chapter 7 [2] ("straight bankruptcy"), Chapter 11,[3] and Chapter 13.[4] Straight bankruptcy entails the liquidation of the debtor's non-exempt assets to satisfy his or her creditors according to the priority and amount of their claims. Such a proceeding ultimately discharges the debtor of most pre-bankruptcy debts. It is the most common type of bankruptcy proceeding. Relief may be sought by the debtor ("voluntary") or by creditors ("involuntary"). Chapter 11 proceedings, on the other hand, provide for the reorganization of corporate and other business debtors.[5] Rehabilitation, not liquidation, is the purpose of such proceedings. Reorganization plans can result in extension of debts and broad judicial control over both secured and unsecured creditors. Finally, Chapter 13 is to some extent a Chapter 11 equivalent for individuals. Such proceedings are aimed at the rehabilitation of the debtor by extension and reduction of both unsecured and certain secured claims. Such a proceeding may be used by an individual who owes less than $100,000 in unsecured debt and $350,000 in secured debt.[6]

The most immediate impact of debtor bankruptcy on the real estate mortgagee is the automatic stay. Under section 362(a) of the Code, all foreclosure proceedings, whether judicial or power of sale, are automatically stayed by the filing of any of the three types of bankruptcy

---

* Reprinted with permission of West Publishing Co.

2. See 11 U.S.C.A. §§ 701–766.
3. See 11 U.S.C.A. §§ 1101–1174.
4. See 11 U.S.C.A. §§ 1301–1330.
5. Individuals can use Chapter 11, although the typical case is a business case. See 11 U.S.C.A. § 109(d).
6. See 11 U.S.C.A. § 109(e).

proceedings.[7] The stay is applicable whether or not the foreclosure was initiated prior to the bankruptcy petition.[8] Moreover, in Chapter 13 proceedings the stay is also applicable to foreclosure and other proceedings against third persons who have guaranteed the bankrupt's consumer debt or put up property to secure it.[9] The only significant exception from the stay is for foreclosure "actions" brought by the Secretary of HUD on federally insured mortgages on property consisting of five or more living units.[10] The impact of the stay on the real estate mortgagee can be substantial. For example, a mortgagee can be in the middle of a complex judicial foreclosure in state court, and the filing of a bankruptcy petition can bring the action to an absolute halt. Not only will any foreclosure consummated in violation of the stay be ineffective, the mortgagee risks being punished for contempt as well.[11]

Straight Bankruptcy

As we noted in the preceding section, the filing of a petition in straight bankruptcy, stays any pending or planned foreclosure proceeding. However, assuming the mortgage is valid, the trustee has a legitimate interest in the mortgaged real estate only if the mortgagor-debtor has "equity" in that real estate—the amount by which the value of the property exceeds the total amount of mortgage debt against it. If a mortgagee seeks relief from the stay and such equity does not exist, the trustee should abandon the real estate to the mortgagee who then can proceed to foreclose. If equity is found to exist, the real estate will be sold by the bankruptcy court, either (1) subject to the existing mortgages and other liens, or (2) free and clear of them. If the latter course is chosen, those liens will be transferred to the sale proceeds and satisfied in order of their priority. Suppose, for example, that E-1 has a valid first mortgage on Blackacre with a $60,000 balance and that E-2 has a valid second mortgage on it with a $15,000 balance. If the trustee determines that Blackacre is worth less than $75,000, she will release it and either lienor will be free to foreclose under state law. If, however, Blackacre proves to be worth more than $75,000, she will either sell it subject to the foregoing mortgages or free and clear of them. If she chooses the latter course, the two mortgages will attach to the sale proceeds and be satisfied in order of their priority.

Because the trustee represents the interests of the bankrupt's unsecured creditors, her primary goal is to enlarge the asset pool available to satisfy their claims. Since each mortgage invalidated usually serves that purpose, she will be especially watchful for opportunities to attack vulnerable security interests. The Code affords her an impressive

---

7. See 11 U.S.C.A. § 362(a)(4); Whelan, Lenders' Rights in Bankruptcy Stays, Mortgage Banker, Oct. 1984, 57; Nimmer, Real Estate Creditors and the Automatic Stay: A Study in Behavioral Economics, 1983 Ariz.St.L.J. 281; Nimmer, Secured Creditors and the Automatic Stay: Variable Bargain Models of Fairness, 68 Minn.L. Rev. 1 (1983).

8. See 11 U.S.C.A. § 362(a).

9. See 11 U.S.C.A. § 1301.

10. See 11 U.S.C.A. § 362(b)(8).

11. See Collier on Bankruptcy ¶ 362.11 (15th Ed. 1984).

arsenal of weapons in this regard. Perhaps most basic is section 558, which gives the trustee "the benefit of any defense available to the debtor" against the mortgagee even if the debtor waives it after the commencement of bankruptcy.[4] Thus, for example, to the extent that a debtor would be able to invalidate a mortgage based on fraud, usury, incapacity or other grounds, so too will the trustee. Also important is section 544(a)(3) which affords the trustee, irrespective of knowledge on her part, the status of a bona fide purchaser of real property from the debtor who has perfected under state law.[5] Such status can be utilized whether such a purchaser actually exists or not.[6] Consequently, the trustee will always be able to defeat any mortgage of the debtor that is unrecorded as of the commencement of bankruptcy. Because she is deemed to have perfected under state law, the type of state recording act (e.g., whether race-notice, notice or pure race)[7] and its requirements become irrelevant.

While section 544(a)(3) permits the trustee to defeat any prior unrecorded mortgage, situations may arise where it is to her advantage to be able to assert its priority. Suppose, for example, that after a mortgage on Blackacre is executed, but never recorded, a second mortgage is recorded by another creditor who, under the applicable state recording act, qualifies as a bona fide purchaser against that unrecorded mortgage. The debtor-mortgagor then files a bankruptcy petition. While section 544(a)(3), as noted earlier, allows the trustee to avoid the unrecorded mortgage, it does not prevent the second mortgage, which is admittedly valid, from being promoted in priority. However, section 551 of the Code then comes to the rescue.[8] Under the latter provision, a trustee who avoids a senior lien becomes subrogated to the rights of the senior lienor up to the amount of the senior debt. For example, suppose the unrecorded mortgage has a balance of $10,000 and the recorded second mortgage a balance of $20,000. If the real estate is sold by the bankruptcy court, the trustee, as subrogee, will have a right to $10,000 and the second mortgagee will receive $15,000.

Certain mortgages may be vulnerable to a fraudulent conveyance attack. Under section 548 of the Code,[9] transfers made by the debtor within one year of bankruptcy may be set aside by the trustee if they were made with the intent to hinder, delay or defraud any creditor to which the debtor was or became indebted.[10] Thus, for example, suppose a debtor, in order to conceal his substantial equity in Blackacre, grants mortgagee a mortgage on it within a year of filing a bankruptcy petition. The trustee will be able to set aside the mortgage. Moreover,

---

4. See 11 U.S.C.A. § 558; In re Hayes, 39 B.R. 1 (Bkrtcy.Ill.1983).

5. See 11 U.S.C.A. § 544(a)(3); Jackson, Avoiding Powers in Bankruptcy, 36 Stan.L. Rev. 725, 732–742 (1984). Collier, supra note 2 at ¶ 544.02; In re Duffy-Irvine Associates, 39 B.R. 525 (Bkrtcy.Pa.1984).

6. 11 U.S.C.A. § 544(a)(3).

7. See generally, Cunningham, Stoebuck and Whitman, Property § 11.9 (1984).

8. 11 U.S.C.A. § 551.

9. 11 U.S.C.A. § 548.

10. 11 U.S.C.A. § 548(a)(1). See Jackson, supra note 5 at 777–786.

as we explore in detail in a subsequent section,[11] the constructive fraud provision of section 548 has increasingly become the basis for setting aside certain pre-bankruptcy foreclosure sales of the debtor's real estate that yield less than its "reasonably equivalent value." The trustee may have a further fraudulent conveyance weapon. To the extent that state fraudulent conveyance law confers on unsecured creditors broader powers to avoid debtor mortgages than are afforded by its section 548 counterpart, section 544(b) of the Code empowers the trustee to take advantage of that state law, a matter which we explore further in a subsequent section of this chapter.[12]

Finally, many mortgages given within 90 days of the mortgagor's bankruptcy will be voidable by the trustee as a preference under section 547 of the Act.[13] A significant policy embodied in the bankruptcy law is that similarly situated creditors be treated equally. However, once a debtor becomes financially unstable, creditors commonly violate that policy by seeking to gain advantage vis a vis their creditor brethren. Often this entails acquiring real estate mortgages from the debtor to secure pre-existing debt. To the extent that such mortgages are granted by an insolvent mortgagor within 90 days of bankruptcy and they would otherwise enable the creditor to realize more on its claim than it otherwise would in a straight bankruptcy liquidation, they constitute voidable preferences.[14] Moreover, there is a presumption of debtor insolvency during this 90 days period.[15] Moreover, if the creditor is an "insider",[16] the preference period is one year rather than 90 days.[17]

* * *

While the foregoing trustee's powers are numerous and important, it would be a mistake to overemphasize their danger for the real estate mortgagee. Most straight bankruptcy proceedings are consummated relatively rapidly, and normally the mortgage security and lien priority will be preserved. It is true that in some instances, a trustee may delay temporarily the disposition of income-producing real estate in an attempt to accumulate some of those rents for the benefit of unsecured creditors. * * *. By and large, however, the most significant impact of a straight bankruptcy on the mortgagee will be the loss of part of all of its deficiency judgment and that should pose no problem to the prudent mortgagee who made sure initially that the debt was well-secured.

The Chapter 11 Reorganization

Because the purpose of a Chapter 11 proceeding is the rehabilitation rather than the liquidation of the debtor, the debtor typically continues

---

11. See § 8.15 infra.
12. 11 U.S.C.A. § 544(b). See e.g., In re Penn Packing Co., 42 B.R. 502 (Bkrtcy.Pa. 1984); § 8.16 infra. See generally, Note, Good Faith and Fraudulent Conveyances, 97 Harv.L.Rev. 495 (1983).
13. See 11 U.S.C.A. § 547; Jackson, supra note 5 at 756–777; Ross, The Impact of Section 547 of the Bankruptcy Code upon Secured and Unsecured Creditors, 69 Minn.L.Rev. 39 (1984).
14. Id.
15. 11 U.S.C.A. § 547(f).
16. 11 U.S.C.A. § 101(28).
17. 11 U.S.C.A. § 547(b)(4)(B).

to operate the estate as a "debtor-in-possession."[1] Parties in interest (usually creditors) may obtain the appointment of a trustee only for cause "including fraud, dishonesty, incompetence, or gross mismanagement" on the part of the debtor[2] or where appointment is otherwise in such parties' "best interests."[3] The appointment of a trustee is considered "an extraordinary remedy"[4] and there is thus a strong presumption in favor of the debtor remaining in possession, at least through the plan formulation period.[5] Moreover, the debtor-in-possession is entitled to exercise the avoidance powers of a Chapter 7 trustee.[6]

From the moment the mortgagor files a Chapter 11 petition, the mortgagee is stayed from foreclosing.[7] Usually the stay will remain in effect at least while a reorganization plan is being formulated and often during its execution. However, under section 362 of the Code, the bankruptcy court may "terminat[e], annul, modify or condition such stay (1) for cause, including the lack of adequate protection of an interest in property of such [mortgagee]; or (2) with respect to a stay of an act against property, if—(A) the [mortgagor] does not have an equity in such property; and (B) such property is not necessary to an effective reorganization."[8]

The first ground for relief has provided some difficulty for the bankruptcy courts. Some courts, for example, suggest that "adequate protection" exists if there is an "equity cushion" in the mortgaged real estate.[9] Others stress that the foregoing language is designed to protect against post-filing decline in the value of the real estate.[10] In a few instances, mortgagor failure to pay real estate taxes or to keep the mortgaged premises insured have been deemed to cause a lack of adequate protection.[11] When such adequate protection is lacking, section 361 sets out three permissible ways to provide it.[12] As summarized by Professor Kennedy, "first, the trustee may be required to make periodic cash payments to the [mortgagee] in an amount sufficient to compensate for the decrease in the value of the [mortgagee's] interest resulting from the stay. Second, the [mortgagee] may be provided with an alternative or additional lien equal in value to the decrease in the

---

1. See Collier on Bankruptcy, ¶ 1104.01 (15th Ed. 1984); 11 U.S.C.A. § 1107.

2. 11 U.S.C.A. § 1104(a)(1).

3. 11 U.S.C.A. § 1104(a)(2); Collier on Bankruptcy, ¶ 1104.01(d) (15th Ed. 1984).

4. Collier on Bankruptcy, ¶ 1104.01(b) (15th Ed. 1984).

5. Id.

6. 11 U.S.C.A. § 1107. See In re Hartman Paving, Inc., 745 F.2d 307 (4th Cir. 1984).

7. See 11 U.S.C.A. § 362(a).

8. See 11 U.S.C.A. § 362(d).

9. See e.g., In re Jamaica House, 31 B.R. 192 (Bkrtcy.Vt.1983); In re Tucker, 5 B.R. 180 (Bkrtcy.N.Y.1980); In re Penn York Manufacturing, Inc., 14 B.R. 51 (Bkrtcy.Pa.1981); Hagendorfer v. Marlette, 42 B.R. 17 (S.D.Ala.1984).

10. See e.g., In re Development, Inc., 36 B.R. 998 (Bkrtcy.Hawaii 1984); In re Riviera Inn of Wallingford, Inc., 7 B.R. 725 (Bkrtcy.Conn.1980); In re Gaim Development Corp., 9 B.R. 17 (Bkrtcy.Fla.1981); In re Palmer River Realty Inc., 26 B.R. 138 (Bkrtcy.R.I.1983); In re BBT, 11 B.R. 224 (Bkrtcy.Nev.1981); La Jolla Mortgage Fund v. Rancho El Cajon Associates, 18 B.R. 283 (Bkrtcy.Cal.1982).

11. In re Jenkins, 36 B.R. 788 (Bkrtcy. Fla.1984); In re Jamaica House, Inc., 31 B.R. 192 (Bkrtcy.Vt.1983); In re Ausherman, 34 B.R. 393 (Bkrtcy.Ill.1983).

12. 11 U.S.C.A. § 361.

value of the [mortgagee's] interest resulting from the stay. Finally, any other relief may be granted that will give the [mortgagee] realization of the 'indubitable equivalent' of its interest in property."[13] The latter alternative is a "catch-all" concept that awaits case by case development. Nevertheless, as one commentator has stressed, "[g]iving a creditor which holds security of the highest quality with an sample cushion alternative security of dubious value or of a value barely that of the debt would not meet 'indubitable equivalent' standard."[14]

The second ground for stay relief is more commonly relied upon by mortgagees. Under this approach two requirements must be satisfied. First, the mortgagor must lack equity in the mortgaged real estate and second, that real estate must not be necessary to an "effective reorganization."[15] The meaning of the term "equity" has proved especially troublesome for the bankruptcy courts. Under the predominate approach, "equity" refers to "the difference between the value of the property and all encumbrances against it."[16] A sizeable minority of decisions, however, take the position that the term "means the difference between the value of the property and the lien which is the subject of the [request for stay relief], along with any liens senior thereto."[17] Under this view, it makes no difference how many junior encumbrances are outstanding against the subject property so long as the [mortgagor] has a substantial and meaningful equity cushion over and above the senior encumbrances."[18] Because it enhances the likelihood that equity will exist and that relief from the stay will thus be denied, the minority view is especially appealing to junior lienholders. By keeping the stay in effect they postpone the day of reckoning when they must either satisfy the senior indebtedness or suffer foreclosure of their liens.[19]

13. Kennedy, Automatic Stays Under the New Bankruptcy Law, 12 U.Mich.J.L. Ref. 3.43–44 (1979). See In re Development, Inc., 36 B.R. 998 (Bkrtcy.Hawaii 1984).

14. Collier on Bankruptcy, ¶ 361.01[4] (15th Ed.1984).

15. See 11 U.S.C.A. § 362(d)(2).

16. See e.g., Stewart v. Gurley, 745 F.2d 1194 (9th Cir.1984); In re Faires, 34 B.R. 549 (Bkrtcy.Wash.1983); In re Development, Inc., 36 B.R. 998 (Bkrtcy.Hawaii 1984); In re Trina-Dee, Inc., 26 B.R. 152 (Bkrtcy.Pa.1983); In re Koopmans, 22 B.R. 395 (Bkrtcy.Utah 1982); In re Crescent Beach Inn, Inc., 22 B.R. 161 (Bkrtcy.Me. 1982); La Jolla Mortgage Fund v. Rancho El Cajon Associates, 18 B.R. 283 (Bkrtcy. Cal.1982); In re Saint Peter's School, 16 B.R. 404 (Bkrtcy.N.Y.1982); First Connecticut Small Business Investment Co. v. Ruark, 7 B.R. 46 (Bkrtcy.Conn.1980); In re Dallasta, 7 B.R. 883 (Bkrtcy.Pa.1980); Note, "Automatic Stay under the 1978 Bankruptcy Code: An Equitable Roadblock to Secured Creditor Relief," 17 San Diego L.Rev. 1113, 1123 (1980). Whelan, Lenders' Rights in Bankruptcy Stays, Mortgage Banker, Oct. 1984, 57, 58.

17. In re Faires, 34 B.R. 549 (Bkrtcy. Wash.1983). See e.g., In re Cote, 27 B.R. 510 (Bkrtcy.Or.1983); In re Palmer River Realty, Inc., 26 B.R. 138 (Bkrtcy.R.I.1983); Matter of Certified Mortgage Corp., 25 B.R. 662 (Bkrtcy.Fla.1982); Matter of Spring Garden Foliage, Inc., 15 B.R. 140 (Bkrtcy. Fla.1981); In re Wolford Enterprises, Inc., 11 B.R. 571 (Bkrtcy.Va.1981).

18. Matter of Spring Garden Foliage, Inc., 15 B.R. 140, 143 (Bkrtcy.Fla.1981).

19. "There may be many instances when the holder of a lien inferior to the lien of a plaintiff does not want relief from the stay afforded to the plaintiff. In a foreclosure a junior lienholder is faced with the possibility that unless it purchases the interests of those holders of superior liens it will lose any recovery upon its lien. The junior lienholder may prefer to negotiate with the debtor for different payment terms or a reduction in the amount due to it."

If the court finds that equity exists, it must then determine whether the mortgaged real estate is "necessary to an effective reorganization."[20] As one court has stressed, it is "not enough for a debtor to argue that the automatic stay should continue because it needs the secured property in order to propose a reorganization. If this were the test all property held by debtors could be regarded as necessary for the debtor's reorganization. The key word is 'effective'."[21] The mere fact that the real estate is essential to the survival of the mortgagor's business is insufficient.[22] Rather, the mortgagor is required to demonstrate that there is "a reasonable likelihood of a successful reorganization within a reasonable period of time."[23]

On the surface it would seem that a mortgagee should invariably prefer the "adequate protection" route to stay relief over the "no equity—necessary to an effective reorganization" approach. For example, suppose the mortgagee can establish that an "equity cushion" no longer exists in the mortgaged real estate. If such a showing is enough to show inadequate protection, why should the mortgagee run the risk that mortgagor will be able to establish that the real estate is necessary to an effective reorganization? Perhaps the answer lies in the fact that if the court finds both a lack of equity and that the property is unnecessary to an effective reorganization, it will invariably dissolve the stay because, by definition, there is no reason for the court to retain control over it. On the other hand, a finding of inadequate protection alone may simply result in a decree ordering additional protection for the mortgagee or some modification, rather than dissolution, of the stay.[24]

IN RE PALMER RIVER REALTY, INC.

United States Bankruptcy Court, District of Rhode Island, 1983.
26 B.R. 138.

EMIL F. GOLDHABER, Bankruptcy Judge:

* * * In 1955 the Plaintiffs, Antonio and Joseph Asquino, and a partner purchased real estate in Rehoboth and Seekonk, Massachusetts, and developed the Sun Valley Golf Course. The operations were conducted by three affiliated corporations: Sun Valley Country Club, Inc., operated the golf course; Sun Valley Restaurant, Inc., operated the restaurant, bar, and social activities; and Palmer River Realty, Inc., held title to the real estate, a total of approximately 238 acres.

In re Cote, 27 B.R. 510, 513 (Bkrtcy.Or. 1983).

20. 11 U.S.C.A. § 362(d)(2)(B).

21. In re Clark Technical Associates, Limited, 9 B.R. 738, 740 (Bkrtcy.Conn. 1981).

22. In re Development, Inc., 36 B.R. 998 (Bkrtcy.Hawaii 1984); In re Mikole Developers, Inc., 14 B.R. 524 (Bkrtcy.Pa.1981).

23. In re Development, Inc., 36 B.R. 998 (Bkrtcy.Hawaii 1984); In re Sundale Associates, Limited, 11 B.R. 978 (Bkrtcy.Fla. 1981). In re Smith, 42 B.R. 276 (Bkrtcy.Pa. 1984).

24. See e.g., In re Jenkins, 36 B.R. 788 (Bkrtcy.Fla.1984); In re Jamaica House, Inc., 31 B.R. 192 (Bkrtcy.Vt.1983).

Sec. G   OTHER STATUTORY IMPACTS   151

In 1972 the Plaintiffs sold their stock in the corporations to John and Thomas Pellegrino and received a cash payment of $100,000 and a promissory note for $350,000. The note was secured by a mortgage covering all of the real estate except a 3.4 acre parcel which is rented to a trucking company, and a 24 acre parcel which includes approximately four holes of the 18-hole golf course. In 1975 the Pellegrinos purchased the shares of their partner, Albert Prisco, for $50,000 cash and a promissory note for $175,000 which was secured by a second mortgage on the same property secured by the Asquinos' mortgage.

On March 12, 1982, Palmer River Realty, Inc., and Sun Valley Country Club, Inc., filed Chapter 11 petitions, and a Chapter 11 petition for Sun Valley Restaurant, Inc., was filed on November 29, 1982.

The Plaintiffs' main arguments in favor of conversion, dismissal, or relief from the stay, are that the Debtors in Possession have no equity in the mortgaged property; that the Asquinos' interest is not adequately protected; and that as of the day of the hearing, six months after the Chapter 11 filing, no plan of reorganization had been filed. The Plaintiffs therefore conclude that the Court should either grant relief from the automatic stay (pursuant to 11 U.S.C. § 362(d)) to allow them to foreclose on the mortgaged property, or dismiss or convert these cases to Chapter 7. The Debtors in Possession respond that there is plenty of equity in the mortgaged property, and that the Plaintiffs' interest is therefore adequately protected. Also, admittedly after a series of delays, a plan was filed on December 22, 1982.

Section 362(d)[3] provides for two alternative bases on which a creditor may seek relief from the automatic stay: (1) for cause, which includes lack of adequate protection; or (2) when the debtor lacks equity in the property, and the property is not necessary to an effective reorganization. Since the debtor's equity is often used to determine whether adequate protection exists, we turn first to the question of equity in the mortgaged property.

Under § 362(g) the Plaintiffs have the burden of proof on the issue of equity or the absence thereof in the subject property, and the Debtors have the burden of proof on all other issues. The Plaintiffs presented opinion evidence that the market value of the entire 238 acres owned by the Debtors (which includes two unencumbered parcels—3.4 acres now leased to a trucking company, and 24 acres [approximately 4 holes] of the golf course) is between $500,000 and $540,000 at its highest and best use as an 18-hole golf course. That portion of the property subject

---

3. 11 U.S.C. § 362(d) provides as follows:

On request of a party in interest and after notice and a hearing, the court shall grant relief from the stay provided under subsection (a) of this section, such as by terminating, annulling, modifying, or conditioning such stay—

(1) for cause, including the lack of adequate protection of an interest in property of such party in interest; or

(2) with respect to a stay of an act against property, if—

(A) the debtor does not have an equity in such property; and

(B) such property is not necessary to an effective reorganization.

to the Plaintiffs' mortgage has a substantially lower value of approximately $345,000, primarily because the exclusion of three or four holes from the 18-hole golf course effectively transforms the site into a nine-hole course. * * *

In determining whether a debtor has an equity cushion in property, bankruptcy courts have used two distinctly different approaches. What appears to be the majority view is summarized as follows: "In determining whether an 'equity cushion' exists in the subject property, all encumbrances are totalled, whether or not all the lienholders have joined in the request for relief from the stay." North East Federal Savings and Loan Ass'n v. Mikole Developers, Inc. *(In re Mikole Developers, Inc.)*, 14 B.R. 524, 525 (Bkrtcy.E.D.Pa.1981). Two recent decisions, however, have departed from this view. In Central Florida Production Credit Ass'n v. Spring Garden Foliage, Inc. *(In re Spring Garden Foliage, Inc.)*, 15 B.R. 140 (Bkrtcy.M.D.Fla.1981), the court noted that the proposition that all outstanding encumbrances must be considered in determining lack of equity "has no support by logic or by the legislative history of § 362." Id. at 143. The court concluded that if the party seeking relief was a senior encumbrancer, "it makes no difference how many junior encumbrances are outstanding against the subject property so long as the Debtor has a substantial and meaningful equity cushion over and above the senior encumbrances." Id. *Accord,* Wolford v. Wolford Enterprises, Inc. *(In re Wolford Enterprises, Inc.)*, 11 B.R. 571 (Bkrtcy.S.D.W.Va.1981).

In the case at bar, the Plaintiffs are the senior encumbrancers. The second mortgagee, the former partner of the Debtors, opposes foreclosure and has expressed a willingness to cooperate with the Debtors in their reorganization efforts. In this respect the case is strikingly similar to *In re Spring Garden Foliage, Inc.,* supra, where the court found that the second mortgage had "no relevance" to the question of equity because the holder of the second mortgage was willing to assist the debtor in a plan of reorganization. 15 B.R. at 143. Based on the facts presently before the Court, including the second mortgagee's express desire to support this reorganization attempt, we conclude that the second mortgage should not be considered in determining whether there is an equity cushion in the subject property.

At the time of filing the Chapter 11 petition, the Asquinos were scheduled as secured creditors in the amount of $252,027.16. Six payments were made between the March 12, 1982 filing date, and October 8, 1982, reducing the principal to $244,450.05. * * * Based on the record, the taxes due on the mortgaged property cannot be calculated with anything approaching certainty. The Plaintiffs first argue that the Debtors owe $39,615 in real estate taxes on the mortgaged property and then concede that this figure is based on 166 acres of property in Rehoboth, 24 acres of which are excluded from the mortgage. Id. Assuming *arguendo* that the Plaintiffs' figures are correct for the mortgage balance and taxes owed, and using the Plaintiffs' estimate of $34,000 for priority and administration expenses, interest, attorneys' fees, and costs, the total debt is approximately $318,065. This is $27,000 less than the value of $345,000 which the Plaintiffs' own real estate expert placed on the subject property. Viewing this evidence most favorably to the plaintiffs, there is at least a modest equity cushion, and testimony regarding recent improvements to the golf course and clubhouse tends to corroborate the Debtors' contention that the property is not declining in value.

Based on the finding that there is equity in the property, there is no need for a protracted analysis of whether the property is "necessary to an effective reorganization." § 362(d)(2)(B). As in *In re Spring Garden Foliage, Inc.*, supra, the subject property, which covers approximately 14 holes of the golf course, is clearly "a vital and indispensable part of the business operation of the debtor." 15 B.R. at 142.

There is authority, however, to the effect that the mere fact that the property is essential to the survival of the debtor's business is not sufficient to meet the burden of proof of § 362(d)(2)(B). In addition, the debtor must demonstrate that there is "a reasonable prospect for a successful reorganization of the going concern." North East Federal Savings and Loan Ass'n v. Mikole Developers, Inc. *(In re Mikole Developers, Inc.)*, 14 B.R. 524, 526 (Bkrtcy.E.D.Pa.1981). * * * This is a hotly contested issue in this case, and at the time of the hearing the Debtors had not yet filed a plan. The court in *In re BBT*, noting that the debtor was "not totally and wholly without possibility of reorganization," found it reasonable to allow one year for the debtor to file a plan. Id. at 237. Based on the entire record, this Court finds that the Debtors are not without hope of reorganization, and that the delay in filing a plan is not tantamount to failure to meet the burden of proof pursuant to § 362(d)(2)(B).

* * * [T]here is an alternative basis on which the Plaintiffs seek relief. Section 362(d)(1) provides that relief from the automatic stay may be granted "for cause, including the lack of adequate protection of an interest in property * * *." The "adequate protection" afforded creditors is protection against a decline in the value of their collateral as of the date of filing the petition. La Jolla Mortgage Fund v. Rancho El Cajon Associates, 18 B.R. 283, 287 (Bkrtcy.S.D.Cal.1982); Provident Bank v. BBT *(In re BBT)*, 11 B.R. 224, 232 (Bkrtcy.D.Nev.1981). Thus the discovery that the Plaintiffs' mortgage covers less than the entire 18-hole golf course, while no doubt giving them less protection than they thought they possessed, is not a decline in "adequate protection" under §§ 361–362. Indeed, the unmortgaged portion of the golf course without question enhances the adequacy of the Plaintiffs' interest in the property, since a sale of the entire 18-hole golf course would bring a significantly higher price than would a sale of only that portion which is subject to the mortgage. Also, there is credible testimony regarding significant recent improvements in the maintenance of the golf course and clubhouse, providing further protection against a decline in the value of the Plaintiffs' interest in the property. The Debtors' resumption of mortgage payments to the Plaintiffs since filing the Chapter 11

petition has also improved the Plaintiffs' position over what it was prior to the filing.

Finally, several courts have found adequate protection where there is an equity cushion. Although the equity cushion here is modest, in conjunction with the factors discussed above, the Court finds that the Debtors have met the burden of showing that the Plaintiffs are adequately protected pursuant to § 362(d)(1), at least for the present time.

Accordingly, the Plaintiffs' complaint for relief from the automatic stay is denied without prejudice. Similarly, the Plaintiffs' motion to dismiss the Chapter 11 petition or convert it to a Chapter 7 proceeding is denied, also without prejudice to the right of any party to ask for appropriate future relief.

Page 623, beginning at the Notes, delete pages 623–629 and substitute the following:

NELSON AND WHITMAN, REAL ESTATE FINANCE LAW*

650–652 (2nd Ed. 1985)

The Chapter 13 "Wage Earner" Plan

The Chapter 13 plan to some extent is to the salaried person or wage earner what Chapter 11 is to the corporate or other commercial entity. Such a proceeding may be utilized by an individual who has a regular income and owes secured debt not in excess of $350,000 and unsecured debt not exceeding $100,000.[1] The plan must be completed within three years of confirmation unless the bankruptcy court approves a longer period not to exceed five years.[2] The Chapter 13 trustee may exercise the same avoidance powers that are available to his or her straight bankruptcy counterpart.[3] However, the trustee usually is passive and the debtor typically remains in possession of the estate.[4] Even though the Act confers no general avoidance powers on the debtor, bankruptcy courts frequently authorize the debtor to exercise such powers.[5] The legislative history of Chapter 13 provides a valuable insight into its purpose and operation:

> "The purpose of chapter 13 is to enable an individual, under court supervision and protection, to develop and perform under a plan for the repayment of his debts over an extended period. In some cases, the plan will call for full repayment. In others, it may

---

* Reprinted with permission of West Publishing Co.

1. 11 U.S.C.A. § 109(e).
2. 11 U.S.C.A. § 1322(c).
3. 11 U.S.C.A. § 1302(b).
4. 11 U.S.C.A. § 1306(b): Henning, An Analysis of *Durrett* and its Impact on Real and Personal Property Foreclosures: Some Proposed Modifications, 63 N.C.L.Rev. 501, 526, n. 154 (1984).

5. See e.g., In re Dudley, 38 B.R. 666 (Bkrtcy.Pa.1984); In re Wheeler, 34 B.R. 818 (Bkrtcy.Ala.1983); Matter of Lozano, 42 B.R. 966 (D.Puerto Rico 1984); In re Worcester, 28 B.R. 910 (Bkrtcy.Cal.1983); In re Cowart, 43 B.R. 110 (Bkrtcy.Fla.1984); Henning, supra note 4 at 526, n. 154.

offer creditors a percentage of their claims in full settlement. During the repayment period, creditors may not harass the debtor or seek to collect their debts. They must receive payments only under the plan. This protection relieves the debtor from indirect and direct pressures from creditors, and enables him to support himself and his dependents while repaying his creditors at the same time.

"The benefit to the debtor of developing a plan of repayment under chapter 13, rather than opting for liquidation under chapter 7, is that it permits the debtor to protect his assets. In a liquidation case, the debtor must surrender his nonexempt assets for liquidation and sale by the trustee. Under chapter 13, the debtor may retain his property by agreeing to repay his creditors. Chapter 13 also protects a debtor's credit standing far better than a straight bankruptcy, because he is viewed by the credit industry as a better risk. In addition, it satisfies many debtors' desire to avoid the stigma attached to straight bankruptcy and to retain the pride attendant on being able to meet one's obligations. The benefit to creditors is self-evident: their losses will be significantly less than if their debtors opt for straight bankruptcy."[6]

When the debtor has completed the plan, all unsecured debts are discharged except alimony and child support obligations and those debts where the last payment is to be made after the expiration of the plan.[7] While the plan can regulate or sometimes modify the repayment of installments and arrearages on real estate mortgage debts (with the possible exception of mortgages on the debtor's principal residence) until the expiration of the plan, it cannot affect those mortgage payments coming due after its expiration date.[8] Thereafter, the debtor is required to make future payments as if no plan had existed.

Real estate mortgagees in a Chapter 13 proceeding are subject to the general stay provisions contained in section 362 of the Code.[9] In addition, there is a special stay provision protecting third parties who have guaranteed the bankrupt's debt or put up property to secure it.[10] Section 1301 provides that "a creditor may not act, or commence or continue any civil action, to collect all or any part of a consumer debt of the debtor from any individual that is liable on such debt with the debtor, or that secured such debt unless such individual became liable on or secured such debt in the ordinary course of such individual's business."[11] A "consumer debt" is one "incurred by an individual

6. H.R.Rep. No. 595, 95th Cong., 1st Sess. 118 (1977), U.S.Code Cong. & Admin. News, p. 6079.

7. 11 U.S.C.A. § 1328; See Comment, Home Foreclosures Under Chapter 13 of The Bankruptcy Reform Act, 30 U.C.L.A.L. Rev. 637, 643–646 (1983).

8. 11 U.S.C.A. § 1328(a)(1).

9. 11 U.S.C.A. § 362.

10. 11 U.S.C.A. § 1301.

11. 11 U.S.C.A. § 1301(a)(1).

primarily for a personal, family or household purpose."[12] Thus, while the stay imposed by section 362 bars a mortgagee from foreclosing against the property of the mortgagor, section 1301 stays a mortgagee who holds "consumer debt" from foreclosing against the real estate of third parties that has been used as security for the mortgagor's non-business related debt.

IN RE TADDEO

United States Court of Appeals, Second Circuit, 1982.
685 F.2d 24.

Before LUMBARD, FRIENDLY and NEWMAN, Circuit Judges.
LUMBARD, Circuit Judge:

Joseph C. and Ellen A. Taddeo live at 6 Ort Court, Sayville, New York. Three years ago they defaulted on their mortgage to Elfriede Di Pierro. Di Pierro accelerated the mortgage, declared its balance due immediately, and initiated foreclosure proceedings. The Taddeos sought refuge under Chapter 13 of the new Bankruptcy Code, staying the foreclosure action under the automatic stay, 11 U.S.C. § 365(a) (Supp. IV 1980), and proposing to cure the default and reinstate the mortgage under 11 U.S.C. § 1322(b)(5). Di Pierro is listed as the Taddeos' only creditor. She rejected the plan to cure the default, and applied for relief from the automatic stay in order to foreclose. Di Pierro contended that once she accelerated her mortgage, the Taddeos had no way to cure the default under the Bankruptcy Code except to pay the full amount as required by state law. Bankruptcy Judge Parente held that the Taddeos could cure the default and reinstate their mortgage, and denied Di Pierro's motion for relief from the stay. *In re Taddeo*, 9 B.R. 299 (Bkrtcy.E.D.N.Y.1981). Judge Pratt affirmed, 15 B.R. 273 (Bkrtcy.E.D.N.Y.1981). We affirm. We do not believe that Congress labored for five years over this controversial question only to remit consumer debtors—intended to be primary beneficiaries of the new Code—to the harsher mercies of state law.

Di Pierro originally owned the house at 6 Ort Court. On June 14, 1979, she sold the house to the Taddoes, taking in return a "purchase money second mortgage" to secure a principal balance of $13,000. The property is subject to a first lien held by West Side Federal Savings & Loan Association, which is not involved in this case. Di Pierro's second mortgage was payable over 15 years at 8.5 percent in equal monthly installments of $128.05.

Upon taking occupancy, the Taddeos notified Di Pierro that they had discovered defects in the property. On advice of counsel, the Taddeos said they would withhold mortgage payments, depositing the money instead with their attorney. The Taddeos and Di Pierro corresponded for several months without reaching an agreement. On Octo-

---

12. 11 U.S.C.A. § 101(7).

ber 5, 1979, Di Pierro wrote that she was accelerating the mortgage and declaring the entire balance due immediately. The mortgage contained the acceleration clause specifically approved in N.Y. Real Prop. § 258 Schedule M (McKinney 1968), which gives the mortgagee the option to accelerate after a default in mortgage payments.

Di Pierro commenced foreclosure proceedings in state court on October 19, 1979. The Taddeos tendered full payment of their arrears by check on October 31, 1979, but Di Pierro refused to accept payment. The state court granted summary judgment to Di Pierro and ordered a referee to determine the amount owed. After a hearing on June 30, 1980, the referee found the Taddeos liable for $14,153.48 in principal and interest plus interest subsequent to the award.

Before Di Pierro could obtain final judgment of foreclosure and sale, the Taddeos filed a Chapter 13 bankruptcy petition in the Eastern District on July 10, 1980. The court appointed Harold F. Cullen as interim trustee and Richard McCord as successor trustee. 11 U.S.C. § 1302. The petition listed Di Pierro as the only creditor, and stayed Di Pierro's foreclosure action. The Taddeos filed a plan proposing to pay off arrears on the mortgage in installments of $100 per month. The plan further proposed to restore the mortgage and its original payment schedule, with payments through McCord as trustee to Di Pierro during the 3-year life of the plan and directly to Di Pierro after the plan ended. Di Pierro objected to the plan, and petitioned for relief from the automatic stay so that she could proceed with her foreclosure action. Di Pierro contended that her rights as mortgagee could not be affected by the Chapter 13 plan. Bankruptcy Judge Parente, however, held that the Taddeos could pay their arrearages and reinstate their mortgage under this section notwithstanding Di Pierro's acceleration, analogizing § 1322(b) to 11 U.S.C. § 1124(2), which nullifies acceleration clauses in Chapter 11 corporate reorganizations. Therefore Bankruptcy Judge Parente denied Di Pierro relief from the automatic stay. District Judge Pratt affirmed on similar reasoning.

Because Di Pierro is the Taddeos' only creditor, continuance of the stay is justified only if the Taddeos' plan can in fact provide for Di Pierro's mortgage. Otherwise, the stay would serve only to delay foreclosure for delay's sake, and would not be justified. *In re Pearson*, 4 Collier Bankr. Cas.2d (MB) 57, 64 n. 8, 10 B.R. 189 (Bkrtcy.E.D.N.Y. 1981). Therefore, although the Taddeos' Chapter 13 plan is not before us for approval, the question of whether under the plan the Taddeos can pay arrearages to Di Pierro and thereby cure the default and reinstate the mortgage is squarely presented for decision.

The relevant parts of § 1322(b) read as follows:

(b) * * * the plan may—

* * *

(2) modify the rights of holders of secured claims other than a claim secured only by a security interest in real property that is the debtor's principal residence, or of holders of unsecured claims;

(3) provide for the curing or waiving or any default;

* * *

(5) notwithstanding paragraph (2) of this subsection, provide for the curing of any default within a reasonable time and maintenance of payments while the case is pending on any unsecured claim or secured claim on which the last payment is due after the date on which the final payment under the plan is due;

When Congress empowered Chapter 13 debtors to "cure defaults," we think Congress intended to allow mortgagors to "deaccelerate" their mortgage and reinstate its original payment schedule. We so hold for two reasons. First, we think that the power to cure must comprehend the power to "de-accelerate." This follows from the concept of "curing a default." A default is an event in the debtor-creditor relationship which triggers certain consequences—here, acceleration. Curing a default commonly means taking care of the triggering event and returning to pre-default conditions. The consequences are thus nullified. This is the concept of "cure" used throughout the Bankruptcy Code. Under § 365(b), the trustee may assume executory contracts and unexpired leases only if he cures defaults—but the cure need address only the individual event of default, thereby repealing the contractual consequences. Fogel, Executory Contracts and Unexpired Leases in the Bankruptcy Code, 64 Minn.L.Rev. 341, 356 (1980). See Collier on Bankruptcy § 365.04 at 365–31–32 (L. King 15th Ed.1981). See also 11 U.S.C. § 1110(a)(2); 124 Cong.Rec. H 11,102 (Sept. 28, 1978); S. 17,419 (Oct. 6, 1978) (trustee may continue in possession of aircraft and ships by curing defaults and making payments in original lease or contract); 11 U.S.C. § 1168(a)(2), H.R.Rept. 595, 95th Cong. 1st Sess. 423 (1977) (trustee may retain rolling stock if he cures default and agrees to make original payments). Such legislative history as there is supports a similar reading of § 1322(b)(5). Both the Bankruptcy Commission's Bill, see § 6–201(2) & (4) and accompanying commentary, and the Bankruptcy Judges' Bill, § 6–301(2), plainly permitted the cure and de-acceleration of residential debt accelerated prior to petition. Although H.R. 6, 95th Cong. 1st Sess. § 1322(b) (1977), which superseded these bills, omitted a proviso contained in § 6–301(2) of the Judges' Bill that made this entirely clear, it is evident that this was done because the clause was regarded as surplusage. H.R. 6 adopted language almost identical to § 6–301(2) of the Commission's Bill, which accomplished just what the Judges' Bill did, albeit in different language. In fact, H.R. 6 went beyond either of its predecessors and permitted the *modification* of debt secured by a debtor's residence. Although the Senate later adopted a prohibition against modification of the rights of holders of secured real estate debt, S. 2266 95th Cong. 2nd Sess. § 1322(b)(2), which the House accepted insofar as it related to debt secured by a debtor's principal residence, 124 Cong.Rec. H 11106 (September 28, 1978), the cure and maintain powers of paragraph (b)(5) remained unchanged. This history and the policy discussed above compel the conclusion that § 1322(b)(5) was intended to permit the cure and de-acceleration of secured long-term residential debt accelerated prior to the filing of a Chapter 13 petition.

Policy considerations strongly support this reading of the statute. Conditioning a debtor's right to cure on its having filed a Chapter 13 petition prior to acceleration would prompt unseemly and wasteful races to the courthouse. Worse, these would be races in which mortgagees possess an unwarranted and likely insurmountable advantage: wage earners seldom will possess the sophistication in bankruptcy matters that financial institutions do, and often will not have retained counsel in time for counsel to do much good. In contrast, permitting debtors in the Taddeos' position to de-accelerate by payment of the arrearages will encourage parties to negotiate in good faith rather than having to fear that the mortgagee will tip the balance irrevocably by accelerating or that the debtor may prevent or at least long postpone this by filing a Chapter 13 petition.

Secondly, we believe that the power to "cure any default" granted in § 1322(b)(3) and (b)(5) is not limited by the ban against "modifying" home mortgages in § 1322(b)(2) because we do not read "curing defaults" under (b)(3) or "curing defaults and maintaining payments" under (b)(5) to be *modifications* of claims.

It is true that § 1322(b)(5)'s preface, "notwithstanding paragraph (2)," seems to treat the power to cure in (b)(5) as a subset of the power to modify set forth in (b)(2), but that superficial reading of the statute must fall in the light of legislative history and legislative purpose. The "notwithstanding" clause was added to § 1322(b)(5) to emphasize that defaults in mortgages could be cured notwithstanding § 1322(b)(2). See 124 Cong.Rec. H 11,106 (Sept. 28, 1978); S. 17,423 (Oct. 6, 1978). But the clause was not necessary. The Senate protected home mortgages from *modification* in its last bill, S. 2266, 95th Cong., 2d Sess.; it evinced no intent to protect these mortgages from *cure*. Cf. Hearings on S. 2266 Before the Subcommittee on Improvements in Judicial Machinery of the Senate Committee on the Judiciary, 95th Cong., 1st Sess. 836 (1977) (Statement of Charles A. Horsky, Chairman, National Bankruptcy Conference (S. 2266 "is completely unclear as to whether the plan can provide for the curing of defaults and the making of current payments.") Indeed, earlier Senate bills along with House bills and the present statute listed the power to cure and the power to modify in different paragraphs, indicating that the power to cure is different from the power to modify. Testimony submitted on behalf of secured creditors distinguished between modifying a claim (by reducing payments due thereon) and curing a default (and maintaining those payments). See Hearings Before the Subcommittee on Civil and Constitutional Rights of the House Committee on the Judiciary, 94th Cong., 1st Sess. 1027 (Statement of Walter W. Vaughan on behalf of the American Bankers Association) Hearings Before the Subcommittee on Improvements in the Judicial Machinery of the Senate Committee on the Judiciary, 94th Cong., 1st Sess. 130 *(indem)*. Finally, the few cases under Chapter XIII of the old Bankruptcy Act distinguished between modifying a claim and maintaining payments thereon, see Hallenbeck v. Penn Mutual Life Insurance Co., 323 F.2d 566 (4th Cir. 1963); *In re O'Dell*, 198 F.Supp. 389, 391 (D.Kan.1961), and indicate that curing a default and maintaining payments on a claim did not modify that claim. See *In re Delaney*, 534 F.2d 645, 646–47 (5th Cir. 1976) (per curiam); *In re Howard*, 344 F.Supp. 1138 (E.D.Ark.1971).

Our reading of the statute disposes of Di Pierro's major contentions on appeal. Di Pierro argues that the Taddeos cannot use § 1322(b)(5) to cure their default and maintain payments on her mortgage because (b)(5) applies only to claims whose last payment is due after the last payment under the plan is due. Di Pierro maintains her acceleration of the mortgage makes all payments due *now*. See *In re Williams*, 11 B.R. 504 (Bkrtcy.S.D.Texas 1981); *In re Paglia*, 8 B.R. 937 (Bkrtcy.E.D. N.Y.1981). But we hold that the concept of "cure" in § 1322(b)(5) contains the power to de-accelerate. Therefore the application of that section de-accelerates the mortgage and returns it to its 15-year maturity. Alternatively, we hold that the ban on "modification" in § 1322(b)(2) does not limit the Taddeos' exercise of their curative powers under either § 1322(b)(3) or (b)(5). Therefore the Taddeos may first cure their default under (b)(3) and then maintain payments under (b)(5). See *In re Soderlund*, 7 B.R. 44 (Bkrtcy.S.D.Ohio 1980), rev'd, 18 B.R. 12 (S.D.Ohio 1981).

Di Pierro also argues that under New York law the Taddeos cannot "cure" an accelerated mortgage without paying the full amount of the claim, and further asserts that the Bankruptcy Code does not empower the Taddeos to override New York law. She asserts that Congress explicitly gave corporate debtors the power to cure defaults without regard to acceleration by passing 11 U.S.C. § 1124(2), and concludes that the absence of similar language in § 1322(b) indicates that Chapter 13 debtors cannot cure defaults unless they also cure acceleration. See *In re Williams*, 11 B.R. 504 (Bkrtcy.S.D.Tex.1981); *In re Paglia*, 8 B.R. 937 (Bkrtcy.E.D.N.Y.1981). The bankruptcy court took the opposite tack, reasoning that Congress, having provided corporate debtors with curative powers under § 1124(2), must have intended similar powers to be exercised by consumer debtors under § 1322(b) as consumers are more favored by Chapter 13 than corporate debtors are by Chapter 11.

Both rationales mistake the import of § 1124. That section determines who has the right to vote on a Chapter 11 plan. Those parties with "impaired" claims or interest can vote, and § 1124(1) declares that *any* change in legal, equitable or contractual rights creates impairment. Having defined impairment in the broadest possible terms, Congress carved out a small exception to impairment in § 1124(2) providing that curing a default, even though it inevitably changes a contractual acceleration clause, does not thereby "impair" a creditor's claim. "The holder of a claim or interest who under the plan is restored to his original position, when others receive less or get nothing at all, is fortunate indeed and has no cause to complain." S.Rep.No. 989, 95th Cong., 2d Sess. 120 (1978). Section 1124(2) merely takes away the creditor's right to vote in the event of cure; the authority to cure is found in § 1123(a)(5)(G) in plain language similar to § 1322(b). See *In re Thompson,* 17 B.R. 748, 753 (Bkrtcy.W.D.Mich.1982). In short, "curing a default" in Chapter 11 means the same thing as it does in Chapters 7 or 13: the event of default is remedied and the consequences are nullified. A state law to the contrary must fall before the Bankruptcy Code.

Di Pierro argues further that § 1322(b)(5) requires the Taddeos to cure their default "within a reasonable time," and that under New York law that time has passed. But clearly the "reasonable time" requirement refers to time after a Chapter 13 petition is filed. Otherwise Chapter 13 debtors would forfeit their right to cure merely by negotiating with their creditors, or, as in this case, litigating the right of their creditor to declare a default. The bankruptcy courts which have allowed Chapter 13 debtors to cure defaults under § 1322(b)(5) have assumed that "reasonable time" refers to time after the petition was filed. See *In re Acevedo,* 4 Collier Bankr.Cas.2d (MB) 178, 9 B.R. 852 (Bkrtcy.E.D.N.Y.1981); *In re King,* 3 Collier Bankr.Cas.2d (MB) 109, 7 B.R. 110 (Bkrtcy.S.D.Cal.1980). We find no support for Di Pierro's contention that state law must govern what constitutes a reasonable time.

Di Pierro's argument reduces in the end to an assertion that because she can accelerate her mortgage under state law, the Taddeos can cure only as provided by state law. This interpretation of § 1322(b) would leave the debtor with fewer rights under the new Bankruptcy Code than under the old Bankruptcy Act of 1898. Defaulting mortgagees would forfeit their right to cure even before the start of foreclosure proceedings, before they have hired lawyers and therefore before they knew anything about their rights under Chapter 13. Such a result would render the remedy in § 1322(b) unavailable to all but a select number of debtors. See *In re Thompson,* 17 B.R. 748, 752–53 (Bkrtcy.W. D.Mich.1982). Such a result would be totally at odds with the "overriding rehabilitative purpose of Chapter 13." *In re Davis,* 15 B.R. 22, 24 (Bkrtcy.D.Kan.), aff'd, 16 B.R. 473 (D.Kan.1981).

Affirmed.

IN RE GLENN

United States Court of Appeals, Sixth Circuit, 1985.
760 F.2d 1428

Before ENGEL and KRUPANSKY, Circuit Judges, WEICK, Senior Circuit Judge.

ENGEL, Circuit Judge.

These three appeals raise similar questions about the point in the foreclosure process at which a Chapter 13 debtor loses the right to cure a default on a real estate mortgage on his principal residence.

In each case, the debtor gave a mortgage on real estate that was subject to foreclosure proceedings. In In re Gerald David Glenn, No. 82-3821, the debtors filed their Chapter 13 petition after the mortgagee had obtained a foreclosure judgment but before the property was sold. In In re Ralph Miller, No. 83-1585, and In re Edward J. Pigloski, No. 83-1316, the debtors filed their petitions after the properties had been sold at foreclosure sales but before the statutory redemption periods had run. The debtors in all three cases seek to protect their interests in the real estate by paying off any arrearages through their Chapter 13 plans and resuming the regular mortgage payments. The mortgagee in each case has objected that this treatment is contrary to the provisions of 11 U.S.C. § 1322(b).

Each appeal also raises at least one additional issue. In *Glenn*, the debtors argue that, pursuant to 11 U.S.C. § 1322(b)(2), their Chapter 13 plan may modify the rights of their creditor because the creditor's security interest is in a parcel that includes not only their principal residence, but also fifty acres of adjoining farmland. Should they not be permitted to reinstate the terms of their mortgages, the debtors in *Miller* and *Pigloski* seek a ruling that would toll the running of the statutory redemption periods for the duration of their Chapter 13 plans. The Pigloskis also claim that they should be allowed to spread the payment of the redemption amount over the entire length of their Chapter 13 plan while the debtor in *Miller* argues that the expiration of the redemption period following the foreclosure sale would constitute a preferential transfer that may be avoided under 11 U.S.C. § 547(b).

In October 1978 the Glenns bought their home and the fifty acres of land on which it is located in Fayetteville, Ohio. They made a $20,-000.00 down payment and gave a first mortgage promissory note to the Federal Land Bank of Louisville to finance the balance of the purchase price. The Glenns also delivered a mortgage deed to the bank. The note required the payment of $2850.00 every six months and contained an acceleration clause giving the bank the option to declare the entire debt due and payable immediately should the Glenns fail to make any payments.

The Glenns subsequently failed to make some of the mortgage payments, and the bank accelerated the debt. When the Glenns failed to pay the accelerated amount, the bank commenced foreclosure proceedings. On December 18, 1981, the Court of Common Pleas of Brown County, Ohio entered a foreclosure judgment against the Glenns for $51,991.95. Later that same day, the Glenns filed their Chapter 13 petition with the bankruptcy court.

Under the terms of their Chapter 13 plan, the Glenns proposed to pay the bank the arrearage on the mortgage over a period of twenty-one months while maintaining current payments outside the plan under the original terms of the note. The bank objected to the plan, arguing that the note and mortgage had been merged and reduced to judgment and that the Glenns currently owed not just the amount they were in arrears but the entire judgment amount. The bankruptcy court overruled the bank's objection and confirmed the plan. Relying upon the rationale of the Second Circuit in In re Taddeo, 685 F.2d 24 (2d Cir.1982), the court held that 11 U.S.C. § 1322(b)(5) permitted the Glenns to deaccelerate their mortgage and reinstate the original payment schedule.

* * *

On August 5, 1980, Ralph Miller purchased a house in Detroit, Michigan, subject to an existing first mortgage, dated April 17, 1973, held by First Federal of Michigan. The sale price was $26,500.00, and the balance on the mortgage note was approximately $20,900.00.

Following repeated, lengthy lay-offs from his employment, Miller defaulted on the mortgage in 1981. First Federal commenced a foreclosure by advertisement in March 1982, and a sheriff's sale was held on May 14, 1982. First Federal purchased the property for a bid of the balance owing on the mortgage.

On November 2, 1982, before the statutory redemption period expired, Miller filed a Chapter 13 petition and plan. In his plan, Miller proposed to pay the arrearage on the mortgage and to maintain current payments on the note * * *. The bankruptcy court denied the motion, denied confirmation of the plan, and lifted the automatic stay as to First Federal, allowing the mortgagee to pursue eviction.

Miller appealed these decisions to the district court, and the parties entered into a stipulation to stay proceedings pending appeal. Judge Thornton reversed the bankruptcy court, holding that 11 U.S.C. § 1322(b)(5) permits a Chapter 13 debtor to set aside a foreclosure sale, pay any arrearage, and reinstate the terms of the mortgage when the petition is filed before the redemption period expires.

* * *

In May 1981, Edward and Mary Pigloski sought to refinance their house by entering into a loan agreement arranged by Manor Mortgage Company. The house was encumbered by an existing mortgage of $14,500.00, which the mortgagee, Standard Federal Savings & Loan Association, had threatened to foreclose. Following the directions of Manor Mortgage Company, the Pigloskis incorporated themselves and signed a wrap-around mortgage and note to Maxine Wynn. The parties dispute the amount owed on the note, and the Pigloskis claim that it is actually usurious. In any event, the Pigloskis failed to make mortgage payments to Maxine Wynn.

Mrs. Wynn commenced foreclosure by advertisement under Michigan law in October 1981, and a sheriff's sale was held on November 20, 1981.

On April 30, 1982, before the statutory redemption period expired, the Pigloskis filed a Chapter 13 petition and plan. Under their plan, the Pigloskis proposed to pay, over a period of two and one half years, all the amounts they believed were legally due and owing to Mrs. Wynn

* * *. [The bankruptcy court held against the Pigloskis.] Judge Boyle also held that a foreclosure sale extinguishes the mortgage and, as a result, is not subject to cure under section 1322(b)(5).

II.

11 U.S.C. § 1322(b) outlines the permissible contents of a wage earner plan under Chapter 13 of the Bankruptcy Code. The relevant portions of that section provide:

> (b) Subject to subsections (a) and (c) of this section, the plan may—
>
> . . . .
>
> (2) modify the rights of holders of secured claims, other than a claim secured only by a security interest in real property that is the debtor's principal residence, or of holders of unsecured claims;
>
> (3) provide for the curing or waiving of any default;
>
> . . . .
>
> (5) notwithstanding paragraph (2) of this subsection, provide for the curing of any default within a reasonable time and maintenance of payments while the case is pending on any unsecured claim or secured claim on which the last payment is due after the date on which the final payment under the plan is due;
>
> . . . .

The mortgagees do not dispute that subsection (b)(5) permits a Chapter 13 debtor to cure a default on a long-term mortgage on the debtor's principal residence. However, they contend that once the long-term debt has been accelerated, or a foreclosure judgment has been obtained, or a foreclosure sale has occurred, the claim is no longer one "on which the last payment is due after the date on which the final payment under the plan is due" and, therefore, is not subject to cure under subsection (b)(5). Moreover, they argue that allowing the debtor to cure the default and reinstate the terms of the mortgage after any of these events would violate the language of subsection (b)(2), which prohibits modification of the rights of holders of claims "secured only by a security interest in real property that is the debtor's principal residence."

The courts disagree over whether and under what circumstances section 1322(b) allows a cure once a default on a mortgage has triggered acceleration of the debt, a judgment or a sale. The bankruptcy court in In re Ivory, 32 B.R. 788 (Bankr.D.Or.1983), grouped the differing viewpoints into the following general categories:

> (1) Courts that hold that a debtor may not cure a default once a mortgage debt has been accelerated: In re Wilson, 11 B.R. 986 (Bkrtcy.S.D.N.Y.1981); Matter of LaPaglia, 8 B.R. 937 (Bkrtcy.E.D. N.Y.1981); In re Allen, 17 B.R. 119, 8 B.C.D. 945 (Bkrtcy.N.D.Ohio 1981).

(2) Courts that hold that a debtor may cure a default where the mortgage debt has been accelerated provided that no foreclosure judgment has been entered: Percy Wilson Mortgage & Finance Corp. v. McCurdy, 21 B.R. 535 (Bkrtcy.S.D.Ohio W.D.1982); In re Maiorino, 15 B.R. 254 (Bkrtcy.D.Conn.1981); In re Pearson, 10 B.R. 189 (Bkrtcy.E.D.N.Y.1981).

(3) Courts (that) hold that a debtor may cure a default where a state court judgment of foreclosure has been entered provided that no sale has taken place: In re Acevedo, 26 B.R. 994 (D.E.D.N.Y. 1982); In re James, 20 B.R. 145, 9 B.C.D. 208 (Bkrtcy.E.D.Mich. 1982); In re Brantley, 6 B.R. 178 (Bkrtcy.N.D.Fla.1980).

(4) Courts that place no express limitation on the debtor's right to cure a default after acceleration: In re Taddeo, 685 F.2d 24 (2nd Cir.1982); In re Sapp, 11 B.R. 188 (Bkrtcy.S.D.Ohio E.D.1981); In re Davis, 16 B.R. 473 (D.Kan.1981). Or after a judgment has been entered: In re Young, 22 B.R. 620 (Bkrtcy.N.D.Ill.E.D.1982); In re Breuer, 4 B.R. 499, 6 B.C.D. 136 (Bkrtcy.S.D.N.Y.1980).

(5) Courts that hold that a debtor may cure a default where a foreclosure sale has been held provided that the debtor's right of redemption under state law has not expired: In re Johnson, 29 B.R. 104 (Bkrtcy.S.D.Fla.1983); In re Chambers, 27 B.R. 687 (Bkrtcy.S.D. Fla.1983); In re Taylor, 21 B.R. 179 (Bkrtcy.W.D.Mo.1982); In re Thompson, 17 B.R. 748 (Bkrtcy.W.D.Mich.1982).

32 B.R. at 790. To the fourth group we add the following recent opinions by the Fifth and Seventh Circuits: Grubbs v. Houston First American Savings Association, 730 F.2d 236 (5th Cir.1984) (en banc) (holding that a debtor may cure a default after acceleration, but expressing no limit on the right); Matter of Clark, 738 F.2d 869 (7th Cir.1984) (holding that a debtor may cure a default after a judgment of foreclosure that does no more than judicially confirm the acceleration under state law, but expressing no opinion whether the right to cure survives a sale or a judgment of foreclosure in states where the effect of the judgment is different).

Most courts agree that section 1322(b)(5) allows the debtor to cure a default when the mortgagee has not yet accelerated the debt, see, e.g., In re Pearson, 10 B.R. at 193; In re Hartford, 7 B.R. 914 (Bankr.D.Me. 1981), and that the debtor may not reinstate the mortgage if the bankruptcy petition is filed after the state redemption period has expired, see, e.g., In re Ivory, 33 B.R. at 791; In re Thompson, 17 B.R. at 751.

The legislative history of section 1322(b) is ambiguous about the scope of the right afforded the debtor to cure a mortgage default. To encourage consumer debtor rehabilitation rather than liquidation, Congress designed Chapter 13 of the Bankruptcy Code to provide greater relief than was available under the former Bankruptcy Act. H.R.Rep. No. 595, 95th Cong., 1st Sess. 116–17 (1977), reprinted in 1978 U.S.Code

Cong. & Ad.News 5787, 5963, 6076–78. The House Report further explains the chapter's general purpose:

> The purpose of chapter 13 is to enable an individual, under court supervision and protection, to develop and perform under a plan for the repayment of his debts over an extended period. In some cases, the plan will call for full repayment. In others, it may offer creditors a percentage of their claims in full settlement. During the repayment period, creditors may not harrass (sic) the debtor or seek to collect their debts. They must receive payments only under the plan. This protection relieves the debtor from indirect and direct pressures from creditors, and enables him to support himself and his dependents while repaying his creditors at the same time.
>
> The benefit to the debtor of developing a plan of repayment under Chapter 13, rather than opting for liquidation under chapter 7, is that it permits the debtor to protect his assets. In a liquidation case, the debtor must surrender his nonexempt assets for liquidation and sale by the trustee. Under chapter 13, the debtor may retain his property by agreeing to repay his creditors. Chapter 13 also protects a debtor's credit standing far better than a straight bankruptcy, because he is viewed by the credit industry as a better risk. In addition, it satisfies many debtors' desire to avoid the stigma attached to straight bankruptcy and to retain the pride attendant on being able to meet one's obligations. The benefit to creditors is self-evident: their losses will be significantly less than if their debtors opt for straight bankruptcy.

Id. at 118, U.S.Code Cong. & Admin.News 1978, p. 6079.

One of the significant specific changes introduced by Congress in the new legislation was to allow modification of the contract rights of secured creditors under a Chapter 13 plan. H.R.Rep., supra, at 124; Bankruptcy Laws Commission's Report, H.R.Doc. 137, pt. 2, 93rd Cong., 1st Sess. 205 (1973). Nevertheless, it is evident upon examining the final language of section 1322(b)(2) that Congress contemplated a different treatment of debts secured only by mortgages on the debtor's principal residence.

One would think that when trying to liberalize the relief to debtors under Chapter 13, Congress would be particularly solicitous of the individual wage earner's ability to save his home. However, it is apparent from the language of section 1322(b) that Congress intended to give a preferred status to certain types of home mortgagees and lienholders, a policy which at first blush would seem at odds with the general thrust of the new act. The question naturally arises: why?

The legislative history says little in terms of political or social philosophy as such. However, it does reveal that the final language of section 1322(b) evolved from earlier language, incorporated in the bill apparently at the behest of representatives of the mortgage market, that would have prohibited modification of the rights of all creditors whose claims were wholly secured by mortgages on real property.

Although the earlier language did not survive, the statute as finally enacted by Congress clearly evidences a concern with the possible effects the new bankruptcy act might have upon the market for homes. If any other policy objective of Congress was adequate to compete against the objective of protecting wage earners generally, it was a policy to encourage the increased production of homes and to encourage private individual ownership of homes as a traditional and important value in American life. Congress had to face the reality that in a relatively free society, market forces and the profit motive play a vital role in determining how investment capital will be employed. Every protection Congress might grant a homeowner at the expense of the holders of security interests on those homes would decrease the attractiveness of home mortgages as investment opportunities. And as home mortgages decrease in attractiveness, the pool of money available for new home construction and finance shrinks.

On the other hand, Congress was determined not to depart too far from its expressed policy of making wage earner plans more attractive to debtors, especially as an alternative to full bankruptcy proceedings under Chapter 7. Therefore, the preferred status granted some creditors under section 1322(b)(2) was limited to holders of claims secured only by a security interest in the debtor's principal residence. No preferential treatment was given debts secured by property in addition to the debtor's principal residence. Such debts normally are incurred to make consumer purchases unrelated to the home or to enable the debtor to engage in some form of business adventure. In such circumstances the home is mortgaged not for its own sake, but for other purposes, and often is only one of several forms of security given. In a consumer purchase the creditor may also take a security interest in the goods purchased, or in a business transaction, the value of the home may be an insufficient security and, therefore, form only a part of the security package. Congress granted no extra protection for holders of these types of secured claims, presumably because any impact the bankruptcy laws might have upon them would not seriously affect the money market for home construction or purchase.

Furthermore, in sections 1322(b)(3) and (5), which permit the debtor's Chapter 13 plan to cure defaults, Congress provided no special exceptions for creditors whose claims are secured by a security interest in the debtor's residence. Congress expressly provided that subsection (b)(5), which allows the debtor to cure any default on mortgages that extended beyond the life of the Chapter 13 plan, is to operate "notwithstanding paragraph (2) of this subsection."

We wish Congress had spoken its specific intent more clearly with respect to cases involving acceleration, judgments, or sales. It did not but instead saw fit to speak only in broad terms. As is so obvious from the broad range of the cited lower court decisions, any particular result often reflects the value judgment of the particular court as to which of the two competing values should predominate, or at least which is more attractive under the specific facts of the case at hand. All courts agree that at some point in the foreclosure process, the right to cure a default is irretrievably lost; however, the statute itself provides no clear cut-off point except that which the courts may see fit to create. The closer that point of finality is to the beginning of the process, the greater is the protection accorded the mortgage holder, and, hence, the more attractive the home mortgage becomes as an investment. Conversely, the further down the line the court can reach to protect the debtor from the consequences of his default, the better the debtor's needs are met by the Chapter 13 proceedings, and the more attractive those proceedings become to such debtors.

We despair of finding any clear-cut statutory language or legislative history that points unerringly to a construction of the statute that is free from challenge. Each of the cases and each result reached therein is subject to some objection either in theory or in practice. The result we reach here is, therefore, primarily a pragmatic one—one that we believe not only works the least violence to the competing concerns evident in the language of the statute but also one that is most readily capable of use. The event we choose as the cut-off date of the statutory right to cure defaults is the sale of the mortgaged premises. We pick this in preference to a number of other potential points in the progress of events ranging from the date of first default to the day the redemption period expires following sale. We do so for the following reasons, which admittedly may form a large target for criticism:

(a) The language of the statute is, to us, plainly a compromise, as we have earlier mentioned. Picking a date between the two extremes, is likewise a compromise of sorts.

(b) The sale of the mortgaged property is an event that all forms of foreclosure, however denominated, seem to have in common. Whether foreclosure is by judicial proceeding or by advertisement, and regardless of when original acceleration is deemed to have occurred, the date of sale is a measurable, identifiable event of importance in the relationship of the parties. It is at the heart of realization of the security.

(c) Although the purchaser at the sale is frequently the security holder itself, the sale introduces a new element—the change of ownership and, hence, the change of expectations—into the relationship which previously existed.

(d) The foreclosure sale normally comes only after considerable notice giving the debtor opportunity to take action by seeking alternative financing or by negotiating to cure the default or by taking advantage of the benefits of Chapter 13. Therefore, setting the date of sale as the cut-off point avoids most of what some courts have described as the "unseemly race to the courthouse." Concededly no scheme can avoid that possibility altogether, but the time and notice requirements incident to most sales at least provide breathing room and should deter precipitate action that might be expected if the cut-off date were measured by the fact of notice of acceleration or the fact of filing suit.

(e) Any earlier date meets with the complaint that the rights conferred by the statute upon debtors to cure defaults have been frustrated.

(f) Any later date meets with the objection that it largely obliterates the protection Congress intended for mortgagees of private homes as distinguished from other secured lenders.

(g) Any later date also brings with it the very serious danger that bidding at the sale itself, which should be arranged so as to yield the most attractive price, will be chilled; potential bidders may be discouraged if they cannot ascertain when, if ever, their interest will become finalized.

In so ruling we avoid any effort to analyze the transaction in terms of state property law. Modern practice varies so much from state to state that any effort to satisfy the existing concepts in one state may only create confusion in the next. Thus, in construing this federal statute, we think it unnecessary to justify our construction by holding that the sale "extinguishes" or "satisfies" the mortgage or the lien, or that the mortgage is somehow "merged" in the judgment or in the deed of sale under state law.

* * *

NOTE

Is the Sixth Circuit correct in denying *Taddeo* de-acceleration when the Chapter 13 proceeding is filed after the sale, but during the statutory redemption period? Should it make a difference whether the foreclosure sale purchaser is a third party and not the mortgagee? Professor Zaretsky would permit *Taddeo* de-acceleration during the statutory period as to mortgagee, but not third party, purchasers. Under this reasoning, [w]hen the mortgagee is the purchaser ... the problem of de-accelerating the debt may not be significantly different after foreclosure than before... Although the mortgagee would lose its bargained-for right to receive a lump sum payment after the sale, it could not be forced to accept lesser payments than it had originally agreed to accept. See Zaretsky, Some Limits on Mortgagees' Rights in Chapter 13, 50 Brooklyn L.Rev. 433, 449 (1984). On the other hand, where a third party purchases, "it seems inequitable to require him to accept an installment redemption as would normally be proposed in a Chapter 13 plan. The protection for a purchaser at the usual foreclosure sale against the right of redemption is the knowledge that the debtor will pay the purchaser a lump sum refund of the amount paid if the debtor elects to redeem." Id. at 450.

NELSON AND WHITMAN, REAL ESTATE FINANCE LAW*

658–666 (2nd Ed.1985)

Setting Aside Pre-Bankruptcy Foreclosures

Traditionally, foreclosure sale purchasers have had relatively little to fear from subsequent mortgagor bankruptcy. Unless it could be

---

* Reprinted with permission of West Publishing Co.

established that the foreclosure violated state law or that the mortgage itself was avoidable, foreclosures were relatively secure from bankruptcy attack. To be sure, in jurisdictions that utilize statutory redemption, a trustee in bankruptcy has the right to exercise the mortgagor-debtor's redemption rights.[2] However, the bankruptcy court probably does not have general equitable authority to stay the running of the redemption period.[3] Moreover, under the weight of authority, the automatic stay does not operate to toll the running of such periods.[4] The trustee may, however, pursuant to section 108(b) of the Bankruptcy Code redeem within the later of the expiration of the redemption period or 60 days after the filing of the bankruptcy petition.[5]

However troublesome the foregoing redemption rights may be for mortgagees and other foreclosure purchasers, they do not threaten the validity of pre-bankruptcy foreclosure sales. Recent developments, however, have eroded much of the traditional protection afforded such foreclosures. We have already explored in the preceding section how the *Taddeo* concept may be used in certain Chapter 13 contexts to deaccelerate previously foreclosed mortgage debts.[6] In addition, an increasing number of courts are utilizing the fraudulent conveyance provisions of the Bankruptcy Code to set aside pre-bankruptcy foreclosures. Moreover, to a much more limited extent, such foreclosures have been subjected to successful attack as voidable preferences. These latter two developments are explored in detail in this section.

1. *The Foreclosure Sale as a Fraudulent Conveyance*

   a. The Durrett problem

   Under section 548(a) of the Bankruptcy Act not only may a trustee set aside a transfer by a debtor within a year of bankruptcy that was

---

2. See In re Rice, 42 B.R. 838 (Bkrtcy.S. D.1984); authorities cited in notes 3–5 infra this section.

3. See Johnson v. First National Bank of Montevideo, Minnesota, 719 F.2d 270 (8th Cir.1983), certiorari denied —— U.S. ——, 104 S.Ct. 1015, 79 L.Ed.2d 245 (1984); In re Martinson, 731 F.2d 543 (8th Cir. 1984). In re Martinson, 26 B.R. 648 (D.N. D.1983); In re Owens, 27 B.R. 946 (Bkrtcy. Mich.1983); In re Lally, 38 B.R. 622 (Bkrtcy.Iowa 1984).

4. See Johnson v. First National Bank of Montevideo, Minnesota, 719 F.2d 270 (8th Cir.1983), certiorari denied —— U.S. ——, 104 S.Ct. 1015, 79 L.Ed.2d 245 (1984); Bank of Commonwealth v. Bevan, 13 B.R. 989 (D.Mich.1981); In re Owens, 27 B.R. 946 (Bkrtcy.Mich.1983); In re Cucumber Creek Development, Inc., 33 B.R. 820 (D.Colo.1983). Contra: In re Shea Realty, Inc., 21 B.R. 790 (Bkrtcy.Vt.1982); In re Smith, 43 B.R. 313 (Bkrtcy.Ill.1984).

5. See In re Owens, 27 B.R. 946 (Bkrtcy. Mich.1983); In re Cucumber Creek Development, Inc., 33 B.R. 820 (D.Colo.1983). Section 108(b) provides as follows:

(b) Except as provided in subsection (a) of this section, if applicable law, an order entered in a proceeding, or an agreement fixes a period within which the debtor or an individual protected under section 1301 of this title may file any pleading, demand, notice, or proof of claim or loss, cure a default, or perform any other similar act, and such period has not expired before the date of the filing of the petition, the trustee may only file, cure, or perform, as the case may be, before the later of—

(1) the end of such period, including any suspension of such period occurring on or after the commencement of the case; and

(2) 60 days after the order for relief.

11 U.S.C.A. § 108(b).

6. See § 8.15 supra.

intended to defraud, hinder or delay present or future creditors, she may also avoid such a transfer, irrespective of debtor intent, if the debtor "received less than a reasonably equivalent value in exchange for such transfer * * * and was insolvent on the date that such transfer was made."[7] Durrett v. Washington National Insurance Co.,[8] a 1980 decision of the United States Court of Appeals for the Fifth Circuit under the predecessor to section 548(a), marked the first time that a court used the fraudulent conveyance concept to invalidate a non-collusive foreclosure sale that was otherwise valid under state law.[9] In that case, a trustee under a Texas deed of trust sold the mortgaged real estate having a fair market value of $200,000 to a third party purchaser for $115,400. Nine days later Durrett, the mortgagor, filed a petition for reorganization under the predecessor to Chapter 11 and, in his capacity as debtor-in-possession, sought to set aside the foreclosure as a fraudulent conveyance. The district court held that the foreclosure sale constituted a transfer by the debtor, but denied Durrett's request on the ground that the sale produced "a fair equivalent" of the value of the real estate. On appeal, the court of appeals agreed that a transfer had taken place, but reversed the district court on the consideration issue. The court acknowledged that two transfers had taken place—the first, when the deed of trust was executed eight years earlier and which was no longer vulnerable, and a second, when the foreclosure sale took place. The latter qualified as a transfer because, under Texas law, it passed to the purchaser the debtor-mortgagor's right to possession. Moreover, it clearly fell within the statutory period. As to the consideration issue, the court suggested that a foreclosure price of less than 70% of the property's fair market value failed to meet the "fair equivalency" test under the then existing statute.

Durrett has been followed in numerous section 548(a) cases, including a decision by the United States Court of Appeals for the Eighth Circuit.[10] It has been applied to judicial foreclosures,[11] strict foreclosures[12] and in a variety of power of sale and other non-judicial

---

7. 11 U.S.C.A. § 548(a)(2)(A), 548(a)(2)(B)(i). A debtor is "insolvent if its debts are greater than its assets, at a fair" valuation, exclusive of property exempted or transferred with actual fraudulent intent. In re Wheeler, 34 B.R. 818, 822 (Bkrtcy.Ala.1983); 11 U.S.C.A. § 101(29).

8. 621 F.2d 201 (5th Cir.1980).

9. Several pre-*Durrett* cases concluded that a noncollusive foreclosure sale that yields less than fair market value was not a fraudulent conveyance. See Merriam v. Wimpfheimer, 25 F.Supp. 405 (S.D.N.Y. 1938); Pierce v. Pierce, 16 Cal.App. 375, 117 P. 580 (1911).

10. In re Hulm, 738 F.2d 323 (8th Cir. 1984), certiorari denied __ U.S. __, 105 S.Ct. 398, 83 L.Ed.2d 331 (1984), on remand __ B.R. __ (Bkrtcy.N.D.1984); see cases in note 11–13, infra. Contra: Matter of Winshall Settlor's Trust, 758 F.2d 1136 (6th Cir.1985).

11. See In re Hulm, 738 F.2d 323 (8th Cir.1984), certiorari denied __ U.S. __, 105 S.Ct. 398, 83 L.Ed.2d 331 (1984), on remand __ B.R. __ (Bkrtcy.N.D.1984); In re Dudley, 38 B.R. 666 (Bkrtcy.Pa.1984); In re Jones, 20 B.R. 988 (Bkrtcy.Pa.1982).

12. See In re Carr, 34 B.R. 653 (Bkrtcy. Conn.1983), affirmed 40 B.R. 1007 (D.Conn. 1984); In re Berge, 33 B.R. 642 (Bkrtcy. Wis.1983), motion denied in part, granted in part 37 B.R. 705 (1983); In re Perdido

contexts.[13] The decisions involve reorganizations under Chapters 11 [14] and 13 [15] as well as liquidations under Chapter 7.[16] Moreover, the "70% rule of thumb" is being increasingly institutionalized.[17]

b. Cases Rejecting *Durrett*

Two significant cases, each using a different rationale, reject the *Durrett* approach. The first, In re Alsop,[18] involved a power of sale foreclosure under a deed of trust that occurred two days prior to the filing of a Chapter 11 petition. The debtor-in-possession sought to avoid the foreclosure as a fraudulent transfer. The Bankruptcy Court for the District of Alaska rejected *Durrett* by applying a "relation back" analysis. While the *Alsop* court conceded that a transfer occurred at the time of the foreclosure sale, it stressed that section 548(d)(1) of the Act also needed to be considered.[19] Under this latter provision, a transfer is deemed to take place when "such transfer becomes so far perfected that a bona fide purchaser from the debtor against whom such transfer could have been perfected cannot acquire an interest in the property transferred that is superior to the interest in such property of the transferee."[20] In applying the foregoing section the *Alsop* court concluded that "since under Alaska law no purchaser from [mortgagors] subsequent to [mortgagors'] execution of the deed of trust and its recordation on November 8, 1978, could have acquired an interest superior to that of the transferee at the foreclosure sale, pursuant to the provisions of § 548(d)(1) the transfer was made as of November 8, 1978. Since this date is outside the one year period established by § 548(a), the foreclosure sale is not avoidable as a fraudulent transfer."[21]

Alsop seems to misinterpret section 548(d)(1). As noted earlier, a separate transfer occurs at the time of the execution of the deed of trust and, later, at the time of the foreclosure sale.[22] The purpose of section 548(d)(1) in each context is to encourage prompt recording of the transfer instrument rather than to cause a separate and distinct

Bay Country Club Estates, Inc., 23 B.R. 36 (Bkrtcy.Fla.1982) (applying Vermont law).

13. See In re Wheeler, 34 B.R. 818 (Bkrtcy.Ala.1983); In re Smith, 24 B.R. 19 (Bkrtcy.N.C.1982); In re Richardson, 23 B.R. 434 (Bkrtcy.Utah 1982); In re Thompson, 18 B.R. 67 (Bkrtcy.Tenn.1982); Matter of Marshall, 15 B.R. 738 (Bkrtcy.N.C.1981).

14. See e.g., In re Frank, 39 B.R. 166 (Bkrtcy.N.Y.1984); In re Berge, 33 B.R. 642 (Bkrtcy.Wis.1983), motion denied in part, granted in part 37 B.R. 705 (1983).

15. See e.g., In re Dudley, 38 B.R. 666 (Bkrtcy.Pa.1984); In re Wheeler, 34 B.R. 818 (Bkrtcy.Ala.1983); In re Worcester, 28 B.R. 910 (Bkrtcy.Cal.1983).

16. See e.g., In re Richard, 26 B.R. 560 (Bkrtcy.R.I.1983); In re Smith, 24 B.R. 19 (Bkrtcy.N.C.1982); In re Richardson, 23 B.R. 434 (Bkrtcy.Utah 1982).

17. See cases in notes 10–16 supra.

18. 14 B.R. 982 (Bkrtcy.Alaska 1981), affirmed 22 B.R. 1017 (D.Alaska 1982).

19. 11 U.S.C.A. § 548(d)(1).

20. Id.

21. In re Alsop, 14 B.R. 982, 986 (Bkrtcy.Alaska 1981), affirmed 22 B.R. 1017 (D.Alaska 1982).

22. See text at note 9 infra. For the view that foreclosure is not a separate transfer, see Coppel & Kahn, Defanging *Durrett*: The Established Law of Transfer, 100 Banking L.J. 676 (1983).

transfer to relate back to an earlier one.[23] As Professor Henning has stressed:

> "Foreclosure of the deed of trust involves an involuntary conveyance of the debtor's remaining interest in the property except for a statutory right of redemption in those states that grant such a right. This involuntary conveyance constitutes a separate transfer. The most important rights affected by this second transfer are the right to possession and the debtor's equity in the property, neither of which were conveyed under the deed of trust. When a purchaser buys at the foreclosure sale, the deed of trust ordinarily will be considered discharged; if the purchaser fails to record the trustee's deed, however, he will not be protected against subsequent bona fide purchasers from the original debtor. Thus, recordation of the trustee's deed serves a different purpose than recordation of the original deed of trust because it protects a different set of rights. In this context, section 548(d)(1) refers to perfection of the interests acquired at the foreclosure sale, the second transfer, and not to perfection of the interests conveyed by the deed of trust, the first transfer. If the purchaser delays in perfecting his interest, the second transfer, like the first, can be brought forward into the avoidance period." [24]

According to Professor Henning, the "relation back" notion simply represents another way of "stating the general principle that the purchaser takes free of any interests that are subordinate to the foreclosing [mortgagee] * * * This principle, however, does not provide a satisfactory basis for fusing the two transfers for purposes of section 548(d)(1). [The latter section] should be applied strictly as a mechanism for bringing a transfer * * * forward into the avoidance period." [25]

The second major anti-*Durrett* case is In re Madrid,[26] a decision of the United States Court of Appeals for the Ninth Circuit. In that case, the bankruptcy court set aside a power of sale foreclosure in a Chapter 11 context that yielded 67% of the real estate's fair market value.[27] The Bankruptcy Appellate Panel, in reversing, did not deal with the transfer issue, but instead "'constru[ed] the reasonably equivalent value requirement of § 548(a)(2) to mean the same as the consideration

---

23. See Henning, An Analysis of *Durrett* and Its Impact on Real and Personal Property Foreclosures: Some Proposed Modifications, 63 N.C.L.Rev. 507, 512–513 (1984).

24. Id. at 513–514.

25. Id. at 513–514. In a perplexing opinion, the United States Court of Appeals for the Sixth Circuit rejected *Durrett* and appeared to base its reasoning on the relation back concept or, alternatively, on the notion that "reasonable equivalence" should be determined by when, under state law, a foreclosure can be set side based on inadequacy of the sale price. Matter of Winshall Settlor's Trust, 758 F.2d 1136 (6th Cir.1985). See also, Alden, Gross and Borowitz, Real Property Foreclosure as a Fraudulent Conveyance: Proposals for Solving the *Durrett* Problem, 38 Bus.Law. 1605, 1609–1611 (1983).

26. 725 F.2d 1197 (9th Cir.1984), certiorari denied ___ U.S. ___, 105 S.Ct. 125, 83 L.Ed.2d 66 (1984).

27. In re Madrid, 10 B.R. 795 (Bkrtcy. Nev.1981).

received at a noncollusive and regularly conducted foreclosure sale." [28] The court of appeals affirmed, but its reasoning differed from that used by the bankruptcy appellate panel and *Alsop* as well. The court of appeals eschewed the "relation back" approach even though the deed of trust had been recorded more than a year before the filing of the Chapter 11 petition. Rather, the court concluded that section 548(a)(2) was simply not intended to apply to foreclosure sales under a valid lien. The latter section and its antecedents, according to the court, instead "provide authority for the proposition that conveyances are set aside when there is actual fraud or a situation indicative of fraud." [29]

The court of appeals reasoning in *Madrid* has been called into question by a provision of the Bankruptcy Amendments and Federal Judgeship Act of 1984 which amended the Bankruptcy Act's general definition of transfer to include "foreclosure of the debtor's equity of redemption." [30] Post-enactment senatorial statements indicate that the amendment "was not intended to have any effect one way or the other on the *Durrett* issue" or on *Madrid*.[31] On the other hand, Professor Henning has concluded that while "it is unclear whether [the amendment] signifies congressional approval of *Durrett*," it "probably overrules *Madrid*." [32] Whether one agrees with the latter assessment or not, the literal language of the amendment certainly emphasizes that a foreclosure sale can constitute a transfer and, at the very least, seriously undercuts the court of appeal's reasoning in *Madrid* that section 548(a) simply does not encompass foreclosures under valid liens.

c. Impact of *Durrett*

If *Durrett* ultimately prevails nationally, it in effect will create, de facto, in every state a one year statutory redemption system.[33] For those states that currently do not have a statutory redemption scheme, the impact of *Durrett* is dramatic. However, its effect in most statutory redemption states will also be significant. This is because *Durrett* is broader in scope than state redemption statutes. First, the one year period is longer than under some state statutes. Second, while state legislation typically confers redemption rights on mortgagors and, in some instances, on junior lienholders, *Durrett* rights benefit unsecured creditors as well. Third, a party who redeems under statutory redemption usually must tender to the foreclosure purchaser the amount of the purchase price. *Durrett*, on the other hand, imposes no such cost; rather, the purchaser ultimately will be reimbursed out of the proceeds of a bankruptcy resale.

* * *

28. In re Madrid, 21 B.R. 424, 427 (Bkrtcy.App. 9th Cir.1982).

29. In re Madrid, 725 F.2d 1197, 1200 (9th Cir.1984), certiorari denied —— U.S. ——, 105 S.Ct. 125, 83 L.Ed.2d 66 (1984).

30. See section 421(i) of the Bankruptcy Amendments and Federal Judgeship Act of 1984, Pub.L. No. 98–353, 98 Stat. 333, 368 (codified at 11 U.S.C.A. § 101(44)).

31. 130 Cong.Rec. S 13771–13772 (daily ed. Oct. 5, 1984).

32. Henning, supra note 23 at 514 n. 79.

33. Id. at 509.

What is the impact on a foreclosure sale purchaser of a successful avoidance under *Durrett*? Any good faith purchaser for value obtains a lien on the real estate to the extent of value given.[43] This lien will also include the value of post-purchase improvements to the real estate.[44] Moreover, interest is probably recoverable at either the mortgage rate or a market rate.[45] It should be remembered that a Chapter 7 trustee will be seeking to enhance the value of the debtor's estate by attempting to squeeze excess value out of the recaptured real estate. Thus, she will resell the property either subject to the purchaser's lien or free and clear of it. If the latter approach is utilized, the purchaser's lien will attach to the sale proceeds. In the event, however, the real estate cannot be sold for more than the lien, it should be abandoned to the purchaser.

Proceedings under Chapters 11 and 13 pose special problems in the foregoing regard. While a Chapter 7 trustee will utilize *Durrett* to recover real estate for the purpose of prompt resale, recapture in the Chapter 11 or 13 context is typically sought to enhance the likelihood of a successful rehabilitation of the debtor. Consequently, in the latter setting the real estate could be tied up indefinitely as part of a reorganization plan. This probably does not impose an unfair burden on the mortgagee as a foreclosure purchaser. After all, so long as the reorganization plan affords him adequate protection, "he is no worse off than he would have been if bankruptcy proceedings had been commenced before foreclosure was complete."[48] This is not the case, however, where the purchaser is a third party. In effect, a *Durrett* recapture forces such a purchaser to become an involuntary lender. Even if he ultimately recoups his investment, he could be substantially prejudiced by having his funds tied up for a substantial period of time. Under such circumstances, the bankruptcy court should perhaps exercise its equitable discretion by compelling the trustee or debtor-in-possession to obtain new financing for the purpose of "cashing out" the purchaser. In any event, if *Durrett* ultimately prevails, the Bankruptcy Act probably should be amended to permit recovery of property in reorganization contexts only where an immediate resale or refinancing is likely.[49]

d. An Evaluation of *Durrett*

The reaction to *Durrett* from the real estate bar and other real estate interests has been uniformly hostile.[50] This hostility reflects a

43. 11 U.S.C.A. § 548(c); Henning, supra note 23 at 522. Value means "property, or satisfaction or securing of a present or antecedent debt of the debtor." It has been suggested that in a noncollusive regularly conducted foreclosure good faith will not be a problem. See Henning supra Note 23 at 522, n. 134. But see Note, Nonjudicial Foreclosure under Deed of Trust May Be a Fraudulent Transfer of Bankrupt's Property, 47 Mo.L.Rev. 345, 351 n. 55 (1982).

44. 11 U.S.C.A. § 550(d)(1); Henning, supra note 23 at 523, n. 137.

45. Henning, supra note 23 at 523–524.

48. Id. at 527.

49. Id.

50. Groups that opposed *Durrett* include the American Land Title Association,

variety of concerns. It has been argued that the long period of uncertainty about foreclosure title created by *Durrett* will "naturally inhibit a purchaser other than the mortgagee from purchasing at foreclosure."[51] Consequently, it is asserted, "by discouraging third-party buyers, [*Durrett*] may reduce sales prices and increase the likelihood of deficiency judgments. It will encourage secured creditors to foreclose on initial default in the hope that a quicker sale will lower the risk that the debtor will file for bankruptcy during the following year."[52]

Opposition to *Durrett* has been manifested in a variety of more tangible ways. Substantial effort has been devoted to seeking its repeal by Congress.[53] Indeed, concern about *Durrett* is reflected in the Uniform Fraudulent Transfer Act (UFTA), promulgated by the National Conference of Commissioners on Uniform State Laws in 1984.[54] Because of a fear that bankruptcy and state courts would interpret state law as incorporating *Durrett* principles,[55] the UFTA provides that "a person gives a reasonably equivalent value if the person acquires an interest of the debtor in an asset pursuant to a regularly conducted, noncollusive foreclosure sale or execution of a power of sale * * * under a mortgage, deed of trust, or security agreement."[56] The foregoing language effectively insulates from a *Durrett*-type attack noncollusive foreclosures pursuant to any state procedure, judicial or otherwise, that entails a public sale.

While the merits of *Durrett* are debatable, on balance it was probably a desirable judicial development. To be sure, as we emphasized earlier in this volume, any post-sale period of title defeasibility discourages third party bidding and, for that reason, we are doubtful about the

the Mortgage Brokers Institute, the American Council of Life Insurance, the American College of Real Estate Lawyers, the California Bankers Association, and the California Bank Clearing House Association. See Alden, Gross & Horowitz, Real Property Foreclosure as a Fraudulent Conveyance: Proposals for Solving the *Durrett* Problem, 38 Bus.Law. 1605, 1607 n. 8 (1983).

51. Abramson v. Lakewood Bank & Trust Co., 647 F.2d 547, 549 (5th Cir.1981) (Clark, J., dissenting), rehearing denied 655 F.2d 1131 (5th Cir.1981), certiorari denied 454 U.S. 1164, 102 S.Ct. 1038, 71 L.Ed.2d 320 (1982).

52. Note, supra note 43 at 351. For a comprehensive criticism of *Durrett*, see Zinman, Houle and Weiss, Fraudulent Transfers According to Alden, Gross & Horowitz: A Tale of Two Circuits, 39 Bus. Law. 977 (1984).

53. See Summary of Action of the House of Delegates, 1983 A.B.A.Proc. 1, 31 (endorsing amendment to section 548); Gold, Proposed Amendment to Clarify Status of Property Bought in Foreclosure, N.Y.L.J., Nov. 17, 1982, at col. 1 (proposed amendment to section 548). An unsuccessful attempt was made in 1983 to amend section 548 to equate reasonably equivalent value with any amount paid at a good faith foreclosure. See S. 445, 98th Cong., 1st Sess. § 360, 129 Cong.Rec. 5972 (1983). A similar attempt in 1984 also failed.

54. See Uniform Fraudulent Transfer Act (1984).

55. Section 544(b) permits the trustee to avoid any transfer that could be avoided by an unsecured creditor under state or federal nonbankruptcy law. See 11 U.S.C.A. § 544(b); In re Penn Packing Co., 42 B.R. 502 (Bkrtcy.Pa.1984). Thus, the American Bar Association Section of Real Property, Probate and Trust Law urged the ULTA Drafting Committee to include anti-*Durrett* language.

56. U.L.T.A. § 3(b).

wisdom of statutory redemption systems.[57] Moreover, to some extent *Durrett* compounds such problems. This especially may be true in those states that currently do not have statutory redemption. Even in those that do, *Durrett*, as we have seen, may extend state redemption periods and, in other significant ways, make foreclosure sales easier to avoid. On the other hand, *Durrett's* benefits to unsecured creditors outweigh the foregoing concerns. As one commentator has stressed, "there is no reason to permit secured creditors to reap the benefit of assets that might have paid off unsecured creditors."[58] This reasoning is sound in reorganizations as well as liquidations. Moreover, while admittedly strong medicine, *Durrett* in a powerful way underscores the inadequacies of a foreclosure system that normally fails to produce an adequate price for foreclosed real estate.

The foregoing, however, should not be interpreted as a wholesale endorsement of *Durrett* as a permanent part of the foreclosure landscape. Moreover, certain short-term modifications to *Durrett* are clearly in order. The burden on third party foreclosure purchasers where the subsequent bankruptcy proceeding is under, as we noted earlier, Chapter 11 or 13 is clearly undesirable and should be modified judicially or by Congress. Moreover, Congress probably should reduce either the one year pre-bankruptcy avoidance period or the post-filing time requirement for trustee action, or both of them, so that the total period of title uncertainty is no longer than that associated with most statutory redemption schemes.

IN RE WHEELER

United States Bankruptcy Court, Northern District, Alabama, 1983.
34 B.R. 818.

GEORGE S. WRIGHT, Bankruptcy Judge.

The issues presented by these facts are whether a valid nonjudicial prepetition foreclosure sale may be set aside pursuant to § 548(a)(2) or § 547(b) of the Bankruptcy Code of 1978.

FINDINGS OF FACT

(1) On or about November 29, 1971, George Taylor and Essie Mae Taylor, his wife, executed a mortgage in favor of Collateral Investment Company, which was recorded in Tuscaloosa County Probate Office, Book 1042 at Page 673, on the following described real estate situated in Tuscaloosa County, Alabama, to-wit:

> All of Lot Number Eleven (11), of and according to the Plat of the Survey of Walter Smith, known as Southside Addition, to the City of Tuscaloosa, Alabama, a map or plat of which is of record in the Office of the Judge of Probate of Tuscaloosa County, Alabama, and reference to which is made in aid of and as a part of this description.

---

57. See § 8.8 supra.

58. Henning, supra note 23 at 520.

(2) This mortgage was assigned to Federal National Mortgage Association (hereinafter FNMA) by an instrument recorded in Misc. Records Book 93 at Page 519 in Tuscaloosa County Probate Office on February 3, 1972 (Collateral remained the mortgage servicing agent for FNMA).

(3) Essie Mae Taylor died intestate on April 20, 1974, and George Taylor died intestate on October 20, 1979, leaving three heirs, the debtor and two sons, Robert Lee Taylor and Louis Herbert Taylor.

(4) Robert Lee Taylor and Louis Herbert Taylor conveyed their interest in this property to the debtor by quit-claim deed on or about May 4, 1982. This deed has not been recorded.

(5) Debtor and her children have their residence and homestead in the subject property, having lived there at all times since the property was purchased in 1971 (by debtor's parents), and at all times since the death of George Taylor on October 20, 1979.

(6) On or about August 17, 1982, the mortgage indebtedness was seriously in arrears for non-payment and on August 19, 1982, the mortgage indebtedness was accelerated and the entire balance claimed due and payable. The debtor received notice of acceleration on August 21, 1982.

(7) After proper notice the mortgage was foreclosed on October 6, 1982. FNMA purchased the property at the foreclosure sale for fifteen thousand, forty-four and $^{79}/_{100}$ ($15,044.79) Dollars, said sum representing the amount due on the mortgage and the expenses of foreclosure.

(8) On or about October 29, 1982, debtor delivered the keys to the house and property to counsel of record for Collateral Investment Company.

(9) On October 29, 1982, debtor filed a petition under Chapter 13 of the Bankruptcy Code of 1978.

(10) On December 22, 1982, FNMA filed an objection to being included in the debtor's plan and petitioned this court to approve the mortgage foreclosure sale of October 6, 1982.

(11) On December 30, 1982, debtor filed an answer to FNMA's objection to inclusion in debtor's plan and petitioned this court to set aside the foreclosure sale pursuant to § 548 and § 547 of the Bankruptcy Code.

(12) At a subsequent hearing, FNMA introduced in evidence a written appraisal report valuing the property as of December 20, 1982, at an estimated reasonable value of twenty-one thousand ($21,000.00) dollars.

(13) The debtor testified that the property had been recently appraised by a county tax appraiser at twenty-three thousand, four hundred, sixty ($23,460.00) Dollars. Debtor further testified that in her opinion the fair market value of the property was thirty thousand ($30,000.00) Dollars.

[First, the court determined that the foreclosure sale did not yield a "reasonably equivalent value" and utilized *Durrett* to hold that it constituted a fraudulent transfer.]

PREFERENTIAL TRANSFER

Section 547(b) arms the trustee with the power to avoid any transfer of the debtor's property if he can establish (1) that it was a transfer of the debtor's property, (2) to or for the benefit of a creditor, (3) for or on account of an antecedent debt, (4) made while the debtor was insolvent, (5) within 90 days before petition, and (6) which enables the creditor to receive more than he would receive under a Chapter 7 liquidation. 4 *Collier on Bankruptcy,* para. 547.01 at 547.10 (15th ed. 1982); see J. White & R. Summers, *Uniform Commercial Code,* at 1001 (2d ed. 1980).

In this case FNMA foreclosed pursuant to a power of sale contained in their mortgage. The foreclosure resulted in a transfer of the debtor's property. See § 547(e)(1). The foreclosure sale occurred on October 6, 1982 and the petition was filed October 29, 1982, well within the 90 day period of § 547. The only § 547 element at issue is whether the foreclosure sale enabled FNMA to receive more than they would receive under a Chapter 7 liquidation. The property was purchased by FNMA for $15,044.79, this sum representing the indebtedness owed on their mortgage plus the expenses of foreclosure. The court, however, has determined that this property has a market value of $24,000.00. It is clear that under a Chapter 7 liquidation, FNMA, as a fully secured creditor, would be entitled to receive the full value of their $15,044.79 claim upon the disposition of the secured property. However, FNMA would be entitled to no more than the amount of their claim. Yet, by reason of this foreclosure FNMA is receiving property with a market value several thousand dollars in excess of the amount of their claim. Thus, it becomes evident that the foreclosure sale did enable FNMA to receive more than they would receive in a Chapter 7 liquidation. The court determines that this foreclosure sale was a preferential transfer under § 547(b). See generally In re Smith, 21 B.R. 345 (Bkrtcy.M.D. Fla.1982).

NOTES

1. At least one other bankruptcy court has used the preference approach to set aside a foreclosure sale. See Matter of Fountain, 32 B.R. 965 (Bkrtcy.D.Mo. 1983). It can be argued that *Wheeler* misreads the purpose of section 547. Under this reasoning, the latter section is applicable only to the extent that a creditor gets paid up to the full amount of its debt and not in those situations where more than full payment is received. Consequently, the excess is not a preference, but rather a fraudulent transfer voidable, if at all, under section 548 or, if state law is being utilized, section 544(b). Consider, in this connection, the following commentary:

> This argument is, however, unpersuasive. For one thing, it reaches the ironic conclusion that section 547 may be used to deal with the lesser of two wrongs—namely, the transfer that gives a creditor up to the full amount of her claim—but is unavailing to the extent the transfer gives her more than

she is due. The more blameworthy creditor conduct must be dealt with, under this reasoning, only as a fraudulent conveyance. However unsatisfying such a conclusion may seem intuitively, it could nevertheless be defended if the language of section 547 either compelled such a result or was at least ambiguous. After all, Congress certainly has the prerogative to treat the problems of full payment and over payment separately. The problem with this reasoning, however, is that the language of section 547 literally applies to the *Wheeler* type fact situation. Indeed, since *Wheeler* the 1984 amendment to the Code's general definition of "transfer" to include "foreclosure of the debtor's equity of redemption" actually reinforces the application of section 547 in such foreclosure contexts. Moreover, even though *Durrett* and *Wheeler* both serve similar policy objectives, the impact of *Wheeler* on state foreclosure practice is, as we have seen, less extreme than that of *Durrett*. Thus, if one attributes to Congress an intent to deal with such problems in a manner least burdensome on state prerogatives, section 547 furthers that intent more than *Durrett*. In any event, it seems difficult to fault any court for refusing to read into the otherwise plain language of section 547 a meaning that would confer a windfall on a mortgagee at the expense of the debtor and his unsecured creditors.

Nelson and Whitman, Real Estate Finance Law 668 (2nd Ed.1985).

2. To what extent do *Durrett* and the preference approach overlap? Both serve a purpose of avoiding mortgagee windfalls and protecting mortgagors and unsecured creditors. Nevertheless, they differ significantly in their impact on the foreclosure process. Thus, "while section 547 may be asserted only against mortgagee purchasers, *Durrett* is available against third party purchasers as well. Moreover, while the *Durrett* avoidance period is one year, for section 547 it is 90 days. On the other hand, since the focus under the preference approach is on whether the mortgagee-purchaser received "more" than it would have under a Chapter 7 liquidation, unlike *Durrett,* it might be used to recapture property where more than 70% of its fair market value was paid at the foreclosure sale." Nelson and Whitman, Real Estate Finance Law 668 (2nd Ed.1985).

3. Do *Durrett* and its preference counterpart constitute a long-term solution to the problem of inadequate foreclosure sale prices? Or does the answer lie in a major structural reform of state foreclosure practices? See Nelson and Whitman, Real Estate Finance Law §§ 8.8, 8.16 (2nd Ed.1985).

MATTER OF VILLAGE PROPERTIES

United States Court of Appeals, Fifth Circuit, 1984.
723 F.2d 441.

Before GARZA, WILLIAMS and HIGGINBOTHAM, Circuit Judges.

GARZA, Circuit Judge:

I

FACTS and PROCEEDINGS BELOW

Appellant, Wolters, sold the property involved in this dispute to Southland Capital Properties, which sold the property to appellee Village Properties. The second purchase was subject to the original vendor's lien, security agreement and the deed of trust, which included a provision for collateral assignment of rents. Either Village or Southland defaulted on the underlying promissory note and Village filed Chapter 11 bankruptcy on May 5, 1980. On June 5, 1980, appellant filed a complaint to modify the automatic stay to permit foreclosure on his deed of trust on realty and security agreement on equipment.

The bankruptcy court began adjudicating appellant's complaint to modify stay on July 17, 1980. On September 1, 1980, the bankruptcy court ordered foreclosure. On September 2, 1980, the deed of trust, lien and security agreement securing the payment of Southland Capital's promissory note was foreclosed and appellant acquired possession of the apartment project.

The complaint to modify the stay was the only pleading filed by appellant in this case between the filing of the Chapter 11 petition and the foreclosure sale. Before the foreclosure sale appellant did not petition the bankruptcy court for the appointment of a receiver to collect rents for its benefit, for an order of sequestration or for any other order to impound rents.

Appellant filed a proof of claim against appellee on September 8, 1980, asserting an interest in rents collected between the alleged default and the foreclosure sale. Appellee filed an objection on January 20, 1981, on the ground that appellant was not a creditor of the appellee's estate. After a hearing on stipulated facts, the bankruptcy court entered an order denying appellant's claim on February 11, 1981. Appellant appealed to the district court on February 20, 1981. On December 6, 1982, the district court affirmed the bankruptcy court. Appellant appealed to this court on January 3, 1983.

II

ISSUE

This case presents one straight forward issue: under the Bankruptcy Code of 1978, does a mortgagee of Texas property who is the holder of a deed of trust that includes a collateral assignment of rents provision, have any secured interest in rents collected by the mortgagor between the time of default on the mortgage and a court ordered foreclosure, where the only action the mortgagee took was filing a complaint to modify the automatic stay and seek foreclosure? Texas law requires a mortgagee to take affirmative steps to secure his interest in rents collected between default and foreclosure. In Butner v. United States, 440 U.S. 48, 99 S.Ct. 914, 59 L.Ed.2d 136 (1979), the Supreme Court held that under the Bankruptcy Act of 1898 state law controls this issue. We hold that *Butner* is still good law under the Bankruptcy Code of 1978. Thus under the Bankruptcy Code we look to state law to determine the issue in this case. We find the lower court interpreted Texas law correctly and we therefore affirm its decision.

Before reaching the main issue in this case we pause to discuss Texas law concerning a mortgagee's interest in rents collected by a bankrupt estate. Texas adheres to the lien theory of mortgages. Under this theory the mortgagee is not the owner of the property and is not entitled to its possession, rental or profits. Consequently, as occurred in the case at bar, mortgagees usually assign to themselves (through the deed of trust, or other instrument) the mortgagor's interest in all rents falling due after the date of the mortgage as additional security for the mortgage debt. Texas courts have followed the common law rule that an assignment of rentals is not effective "until the mortgagee obtains possession of the property, or impounds the rents, or secures the appointment of a receiver, or takes some other similar action." Taylor v. Brennan, 621 S.W.2d 592, 594 (Tex.1981) (citing Simon v. State Mutual Life Assur. Co., 126 S.W.2d 682 (Tex.Civ.App.—Dallas 1939, writ ref'd); McGeorge v. Henrie, 94 S.W.2d 761 (Tex.Civ. App.—Texarkana 1936, no writ)).

An absolute assignment of rentals, on the other hand, automatically transfers the right to rentals when a specified condition occurs (e.g., default). An absolute assignment passes title to the rents instead of creating a security interest. In Re Ventura-Louise Properties, 490 F.2d 1141 (9th Cir.1974). Courts have been reluctant to construe assignment of rents as absolute assignments. Taylor, 621 S.W.2d at 594. Moreover, some courts and commentators have suggested that there is a presumption that clauses assigning rents create a security interest. E.G., Childs v. Shelburne Realty Co., 23 Cal.2d 263, 268, 143 P.2d 697, 700 (1943); Note, *Assignment of Rents Clauses Under California Law and in Bankruptcy; Strategy for the Secured Creditor*, 31 Hast.L.J. 1433, 1452 (1980).

In *Taylor* the Supreme Court of Texas found that an assignment clause similar to the one in the case at bar manifested an intent by the parties to create a pledge of rentals. 621 S.W.2d at 595. Applying Texas law to the case before us we find that the assignment of rents in the deed of trust only created a security interest. Thus, if state law governs this issue (instead of the Bankruptcy Code) appellant is not entitled to the rents in dispute because it did not take affirmative steps to activate that pledge. For the appellant to prevail in this case Congress must have intended that the Bankruptcy Code preempt state law on the assignment of rents. In addition, the code must provide that an assignment is automatically activated upon default.

In *Butner* the Supreme Court held that under the Bankruptcy Act of 1898 state law governed a mortgagee's interests in rents and profits earned by property in a bankrupt estate. Appellant notes that the *Butner* decision is limited to the Bankruptcy Act of 1898 and that it specifically recognized that Congress has the authority to enact a federal statute defining a mortgagee's interest in rents. 440 U.S. at 54, 99 S.Ct. at 917.

Although congress does have such power we find that they did not choose to exercise it pursuant to the Bankruptcy Code. Section 552 of the Code concerns the post-petition effect of a security interest. Section 552(b) provides:

> Except as provided in sections 363, 506(c), 544, 545, 547, and 548 of this title, if the debtor and a secured party enter into a security agreement before the commencement of the case and if the security interest created by such security agreement extends to property of the debtor acquired before the commencement of the case and to proceeds, product, offspring, rents, or profits of such property, then such security interest extends to such proceeds, product, offspring, rents or profits acquired by the estate after the commencement of the case *to the extent provided by such security agreement and by applicable non-bankruptcy law,* except to the extent that the court, after notice and a hearing and based on the equities of the case, orders otherwise.

11 U.S.C. § 552(b) (1978). (emphasis added). Section 552 is consistent with *Butner.* Its primary design is to permit creditors to take security interests in proceeds pursuant to applicable state law, such as U.C.C. Article 9 or whatever state law applies to security interests in real property. Section 552 reflects Congress' historical concern that property rights usually should be controlled by state law instead of the "mere happenstance" of bankruptcy.

Of course, section 552(b) does permit a bankruptcy judge to deviate from state law "based on the equities of the case." In the case at bar, however, the bankruptcy judge found no equitable reason for not applying the Texas law. Moreover, legislative history regarding the section indicates its purpose was to cover cases where an expenditure of the estate's funds increases the value of the collateral. H.Rep. No. 595, 95th Cong., 1st Sess. 376–77 (1977), *reprinted in* [1978] *U.S.Code. Cong. & Ad. News,* 5787, 6332–33. The House report gives as an example the situation where raw materials are converted into inventory at the expense of the estate (which would thus deplete the fund available for general unsecured creditors). Id. at 6333. In the case at bar then, section 552(b) clearly requires application of state law unless appellant can avail itself of the section 363 exception.

Section 363 defines the rights and powers of the trustee regarding the use, sale or lease of estate property and the rights of third parties with interests in the subject property. Section 363 does not create property interests, instead it protects parties with an interest in cash collateral. The section forbids a trustee from using, selling or leasing cash collateral under 363(c)(1) unless each entity with an interest in the cash collateral consents or the court, after notice and a hearing, authorizes such use pursuant to section 363. Noncash collateral can be disposed of in the ordinary course of business even if it is subject to another party's interest. A party can seek "adequate protection" if such property is to be used. § 363(c). Finally, the section requires the trustee to segregate and account for any cash collateral in his possession. § 363(c)(4).

The reference to section 363 in section 552(b) appears on its face to concern the trustee's ability to use, sell and lease secured property. Comments in the Congressional Record are instructive:

> The provision allows the court to consider the equities in each case. In the course of such consideration the court may evaluate any expenditures by the estate relating to proceeds and any related improvement in position of the secured party. Although this section grants a secured party a security interest in proceeds, products, offspring, rents, or profits, the section is explicitly subject to other sections of title 11. For example, the trustee or debtor in possession may use or lease proceeds, product, offspring, rents, or profits under section 363.

124 Cong.Rec. H. 11,097–98 (daily ed. Sept. 28, 1978); S. 17,414 (daily ed. Oct. 6, 1978), *reprinted in* 4 Collier, Collier on Bankruptcy, ¶ 552.02, at 552–5–6.

Appellant contends that section 363 is broader. Section 363(a) defines cash collateral as "cash ... or other cash equivalents in which the estate and an entity other than the estate have an interest, such as a lien or a co-ownership interest." Appellant notes that in describing cash collateral the Senate Report on the Bill on the Bankruptcy Code stated: "[t]o illustrate, rents received from real property before or after the commencement of the case would be cash collateral to the extent that they are subject to a lien." S.Rep. No. 989, 95th Cong., 2nd Sess. 55, *reprinted in* [1978] *U.S.Code Cong. & Ad.News* 5841. Appellant then points out that Congress intended that the definition of "lien" be broad and include inchoate liens. Id. at 5811. Appellant also notes that section 101(37) of the Code states that "security interest" means a lien created by an agreement. From this premise appellant reasons that:

> It should be indisputable that a lien under a collateral assignment of rents yet to be collected by the Debtor is an interest in such rents, even though, like most liens, it may need judicial enforcement. That it may need judicial enforcement does not make it any less a lien or any less an interest in the rents to be collected. Nothing in § 363 suggests that 'cash collateral', to be 'cash collateral' must already have been judicially enforced. Rather, § 363 provides the mechanism, means and procedure by which the fate of rents collected from and after commencement of bankruptcy proceedings, either for the benefit of the lien holder or for the benefit of the Trustee or Debtor in Possession, or both, as the facts unfolded.... The fact that the interest under state law is not self enforcing, does not make the collateral assignment any less a lien, or the lien any less an interest, on as yet uncollected rents.

Appellant's brief, at 18–19.

Appellee points out that section 363 defines cash collateral as "cash ... in which the estate and an entity other than the estate *have an interest.*" Appellee argues that bankruptcy courts must turn to state law to determine whether and at what time a mortgagee has an interest in the rents because it is only at that time that it becomes "cash collateral."

We agree with appellee. Whether or not appellant's lien is "any less a lien," under Texas law it is impotent with regard to rents until it is perfected. We reject appellant's unsubstantiated reasoning that Congress intended for section 363 to preempt state law which traditionally determines the property rights at dispute in this case. "[S]tate-created property rights, in a bankruptcy context, will not be destroyed by implication." In the Matter of Jeffers, 3 B.R. 49, 56 (Bkrtcy.N.O.Ind. 1980) (citing *Butner*). Moreover, the comment in Senate Report 989, on which appellant relies, provides that rents received "before or after the commencement of the case would be cash collateral *to the extent* that they are subject to a lien." This language mirrors the provision in section 552(b), which provides that a security interest will exists "to the extent provided by such security agreement and by applicable nonbankruptcy law ..." Thus if appellant's claim fails under section 552(b), 363 is to no avail.

We hold that the *Butner* decision remains unscathed by the new Bankruptcy Code. Courts addressing this issue, two dealing specifically with rent assignments, have noted its continuing validity. E.g., In Re Jenkins, 13 B.R. 721, 723 (Bkrtcy.D.Col.1981); rev'd on other grounds 19 B.R. 105, 107 (D.C.Col.1982); In Re Oak Glen R-Vee, 8 B.R. 213, 216 n. 3 (Bkrtcy.C.D.Cal.1981); In Re Gaslight Village, Inc., 6 B.R. 871, 874 (Bkrtcy.D.Conn.1980); In Re Hellenschmidt, 5 B.R. 758, 760 (Bkrtcy.Ct. D.Col.1980); In Re Wheeler, 5 B.R. 600, 603 (Bkrtcy.N.D.Ga.1980); In the Matter of Jeffers, 3 B.R. 49, 56 (Bkrtcy.N.D.Ind.1980), see, e.g., In Re Kuhn Construction Co., Inc., 11 B.R. 746 (Bkrtcy.S.D.W.Va.1981). An examination of the legislative history reveals that Congress did not intend for the Code to preempt state law determination of a mortgagee's interests in rents. This conclusion comports with "the principle of bankruptcy jurisprudence ... that federal law supercedes state law only to the extent necessary to further federal objectives." In Re Hellenschmidt, 5 B.R. 758, 760 (Bkrtcy.D.Col.1980). The policy considerations and federalism concerns that underpin the *Butner* decision are just as applicable to the new code as they were to the 1898 Act. As the Supreme Court has noted: "uniform treatment of property interests by both state and federal courts within a state serves to reduce uncertainty, to discourage forum shopping, and to prevent a party from receiving 'a windfall merely by reason of the happenstance of bankruptcy.'" *Butner*, 440 U.S., at 55, 99 S.Ct., at 918 (quoting Lewis v. Manufacturers National Bank, 364 U.S. 603, 609, 81 S.Ct. 347, 350, 5 L.Ed.2d 323 (1961)).

Thus we apply state law to determine appellant's interest in the collateral rents involved in this case. As noted, the appellant did not even attempt to obtain sequestration or take other affirmative action. He therefore has not perfected his interest. In future cases, however, federal courts may be faced with situations where a Texas mortgagee petitions for sequestration, a receiver or adequate protection but the granting of the petition is delayed or denied. We recognize that judicial enforcement of collaterally assigned rents seldom occurs in Texas. Under the Bankruptcy Code, however, such petitions need not be granted by a federal court for the Texas mortgagee to perfect his interest in rentals. It should be remembered that in *Taylor* the Texas Supreme Court held that an assignment of rentals becomes operative when the mortgagee "obtains possession of the property, or impounds the events, or secures the appointment of a receiver, *or takes some other similar action*." 621 S.W.2d at 594 (emphasis added). The filing of such a petition requires affirmative action which is equivalent to the spirit of the Taylor v. Brennan requirements. The form of the action required to perfect the mortgagee's interest is not as important as its substantive thrust-diligent action by the mortgagee which demonstrates that he would probably have obtained the rents had bankruptcy not intervened.

Giving undue weight to the procedural form of the affirmative action required by Texas law would handicap a mortgagee under the Bankruptcy Code. For example, section 105(b) of the Code prohibits appointment of a receiver. Moreover, obtaining "adequate protection" under section 363(e) is conditioned upon one having an "interest" in the property. Obviously, if a mortgage does not have such an interest under Texas law he cannot obtain "adequate protection." The logical solution is to perfect the Texas mortgagee's interest when he petitions for sequestration, a receiver, adequate protection, etc. Although some states hold that perfection should occur only upon actual possession we believe that the "or takes some other similar action" language in *Taylor* encompasses perfection of a mortgagee's interest by petitioning for sequestration and the like. In a recent case, involving California law very similar to Texas, a court held that filing an action to require the debtor to cease spending, to segregate, and to account for all rents, income etc. perfected the mortgagee's interest from the date of the filing. Although the court denied sequestration because of a $1 million dollar equity cushion, it noted that the mortgagee deserved perfection because he would have obtained the rents under California law if bankruptcy proceedings had not intervened. In Re Oak Glen R-Vee, 8 B.R. 213, 216 (Bkrtcy.C.D.Cal.1981); see also Groves v. Fresno Guarantee Savings & Loan Ass'n, 373 F.2d 440, 442–43 (9th Cir.1967); Pollack v. Sampsell, 174 F.2d 415, 418–19 (9th Cir.1949).

We also note that Congress has recognized the wisdom of allowing a security interest in rents to be perfected through mere notice. Section 546(b) provides that:

> The rights and powers of the trustee under section 544, 545, or 549 of this title are subject to any generally applicable law that permits perfection of an interest in property to be effective against an entity that acquires rights in such property before the date of such perfection. If such law requires seizure of such property or commencement of an action to accomplish such perfection, and such property has not been seized or such action has not been commenced before

the date of filing of the petition, such interest in such property shall be perfected by notice within the time fixed by such law for such seizure or commencement.

11 U.S.C. § 546(b) (Supp. II 1978).

For the foregoing reasons the decision of the lower court is AFFIRMED.

NOTE

For further consideration of *Village Properties*, see Nelson and Whitman, Real Estate Finance Law § 8.17 (2nd Ed. 1985). For an excellent and in-depth analysis of the right to rents in bankruptcy, see Randolph, The Mortgagee's Interest in Rents: Some Policy Considerations and Proposals, 29 Kan.L.Rev. 1 (1980).

Chapter 7

SOME PRIORITY PROBLEMS

D. FIXTURES

Page 660, insert as the final paragraph of Note 5:

California has adopted, with certain minor variations, the 1972 Official Text of § 9–313. See West's Ann.Cal.Comm.Code § 9313 (1980). Moreover, it has also replaced its substantially modified version of the 1972 Official Text of § 9–102 with a new version that closely approximates the 1972 Official Text. The old subsection 9102(1)(c) has been deleted in the new version. See West's Ann.Cal.Comm.Code § 9102 (1980).

Chapter 8

GOVERNMENT INTERVENTION AND PRIVATE RISK–SPREADING IN THE MORTGAGE MARKET

E. SPREADING MORTGAGE RISK—INSURERS AND GUARANTORS

Page 709, insert at foot of page.

For many years FHA charged a mortgage insurance premium (MIP) of ½ percent per year on the average outstanding balance of the loan, divided into 12 installments and paid with each mortgage payment. However in 1983, acting under new authority from Congress, FHA shifted to a system for most of its programs under which the MIP is paid entirely at the loan closing. See 24 C.F.R. § 203.259a, added by 48 Fed. Reg. 28794. It established a premium of 3.8% of the initial loan amount for loans with terms of 25 years or more; slightly smaller premiums were fixed for shorter terms. The MIP may be either paid in cash or financed by adding it to the normal mortgage amount. The new system is easier to administer and results in slightly lower monthly payments, even for mortgagors who finance the MIP. If a group of loans has a favorable loss experience, its mortgagors may receive a refund of a portion of the premiums they have paid.

Page 715, insert at the beginning of note 4.

For many years both FHA and VA were required by statute to fix maximum interest ceilings. This process was much criticized, for reasons which appear below in notes 4 and 5. After much debate on the point, Congress in 1983 repealed FHA's mandate to fix maximum rates for most of its programs. See § 424(b)(2), Housing and Urban–Rural Recovery Act of 1983, Pub.L.No. 98–181. The Section 235 subsidized homeownership program was not affected by this change. For most programs, then, FHA lenders may now offer a wide variety of financing plans, with interest rates and discounts determined by the market. VA, however, continues to set interest ceilings.

G. ALTERNATIVE MORTGAGE INSTRUMENTS

Page 740, insert as a replacement for the text, beginning at the fourth paragraph, through the end of text on page 743:

The term "VRM" has now been largely replaced with the phrase "adjustable rate mortgage" or "ARM." An ARM permits the lender to adjust the interest rate on the mortgage from time to time in accordance with fluctuations in some external index of market interest rates. Such adjustments make the mortgage loan behave for rate purposes likely a relatively short-term investment (depending on the index selected) despite its long maturity. The lender using an ARM is thus protected to some degree against potential losses which could result if its cost of funds (essentially short-term) rose sharply while the interest yield on its mortgage portfolio (essentially long-term) remained relatively fixed.

However, ARMs raise questions from the viewpoint of consumer-borrowers. Perhaps the most significant is whether the borrower can absorb and pay higher rates in the future. The answer depends in part on how a rate increase is implemented. There are at least three methods:

—Monthly payments can be increased by an amount which makes the loan fully-amortized at the new, higher rate.

—The loan maturity can be increased. (If one begins with a 30-year term, even very large increases in maturity can accommodate only small rate increases, however.)

—The increased interest can be capitalized, or added to principal. This may result in "negative amortization" much like that of the GPM, in which the loan balance rises each month rather than decreasing.

Of course, combinations of these three methods are possible.

Numerous agencies have issued regulations defining and limiting the ability of financial institutions to make ARM's. They include the FHLBB, the OCC, and the National Credit Union Administration (NCUA). The FHLBB's rules are the most important of the three, and cover the largest number of transactions. As originally adopted in 1978 they were extremely restrictive, and attempted to protect borrowers from various lender actions which were thought to be potentially overreaching or unfair. Over time, however, ARM lending by savings and loan associations has been progressively deregulated.

The most recent codification of the FHLBB rules is found in 12 C.F.R. § 545.33. The remaining restrictions apply only to loans secured by homes owned by borrower-occupants. Even there, no longer is there any minimum or maximum rate adjustment, either annually or during

Sec. G   ALTERNATIVE MORTGAGE INSTRUMENTS   191

the loan's life. Nor is there any minimum time between adjustments. However, detailed provisions govern the initial disclosure of the transaction to the borrower, and the notice which must be given of any rate changes. In addition, the FHLBB is concerned that lenders use a fair index for rate adjustments. The index must be readily available to and verifiable by the borrower and beyond the control of the lender.

In the event the monthly payments are not sufficient to cover the accruing interest on the loan, and thus "negative amortization" occurs, the FHLBB rules impose a further restriction: the loan balance may never exceed 125 percent of the original appraised value of the property unless the contract provides for readjustment of the payments at least once every five years, beginning no later than the 10th year of the loan, to a level sufficient to amortize the loan fully over its remaining term at the then-existing interest rate.

While the FHLBB has been the national leader in regulating ARM's, the OCC has also been extremely active. Under its original rules, national banks were carefully limited in the parameters of the ARM loans they could make. But the OCC has deregulated to an even greater extent than the FHLBB. Its present rules, codified at 12 C.F.R. § 29.1, govern only initial disclosure and notice of adjustments. They include restrictions on the choice of index identical to those found in the FHLBB rules described above, but they impose no limitations at all on negative amortization.

The NCUA, initially perhaps the most paternalistic of the three agencies, finally moved to the opposite extreme in 1984. Its regulations, found in 12 C.F.R. § 701.21(g), contain virtually no restrictions at all on ARM lending (or, for that matter, other forms of alternative mortgage loans). Thus, there are no limits, analogous to those imposed by the FHLBB, on choice of index or on negative amortization.

The Federal Housing Administration was a late-comer to ARM activity; its Congressional authority to insure ARM's was not granted until 1983; see § 443, Housing and Urban-Rural Recovery Act of 1983, Pub.L. No. 98–181. It was limited by statute to ten percent of the aggregate number of mortgages insured by FHA in any fiscal year. Unlike the financial regulatory agencies discussed above, which elected to approve a broad spectrum of ARM formats for institutional lenders, FHA defined the parameters of its ARM rather strictly. See 24 C.F.R. § 203.49. This is an understandable approach, since FHA ultimately bears the full risk of default on loans it insures.

Under FHA's interim ARM rules, adjustments must be made annually, and may not result in rate increases of more than one percent. The rate may not change more than 5 percent (up or down) over the life of the loan. The index selected by FHA is the weekly average yield on U.S. Treasury securities, adjusted to a constant maturity of one year. While the statute allows rate changes to be paid by increased monthly payments, extensions of loan maturity up to 40 years, or increases in principal balance, FHA's interim rule permits only payment increases.

This eliminates any possibility of negative amortization, which FHA obviously felt would be unacceptably risky. However, the rule allows the lender to "carry over" index changes which would produce a rate increase greater than one percent, and apply them in a future year. The rule also contains provisions on disclosure and notice of adjustment.

Many of the conventional ARM loans made in recent years have incorporated a GPM feature; that is, the documents contain a schedule of rising monthly payments for the first five or ten years of the loan, which must be followed irrespective of any interest rate changes. The FHA ARM, however, appears not to contemplate such a feature, but instead provides for payment changes only in accordance with fluctuations in the index rate.

Page 744, add to Note 4:

The FHLBB authorizes PLAM's. 12 C.F.R. § 545.33(e)(2) permits changes in either payment or loan balance to "reflect a change in a national or regional index that measures the rate of inflation or the rate of change in consumer disposable income." No other federal agency has explicitly approved PLAM's, although they appear to be permissible under the NCUA's rules.

Note that the FHLBB also permits ARM's in which the interest rate is adjusted in accordance with an index of inflation or the rate of change in consumer income. Such an ARM's interest rate, in effect, would reflect changes in actual inflation rather than the expectations of the lender as of the date the loan was made.

Page 744, add to Note 5:

The FHLBB is the only major regulatory agency which specifically authorizes SAM's. 12 C.F.R. § 545.32(b)(3), as amended by 47 Fed.Reg. 36618 (Aug. 23, 1982), states that interest may be received in the form of a percentage "of the amount by which the current market value of the property, during the loan term or at maturity, exceeds the original appraised value." See also 12 C.F.R. § 555.19.

The FHLBB regulation does not require the lender to refinance the SAM loan at its maturity, and does not indicate how the market value of the property is to be determined. These matters are subject to negotiation between borrowers and lenders.

Page 746, insert before Notes:

The VA was authorized to guarantee GPM loans by the Veterans' Disability Compensation, Housing, and Memorial Benefits Amendments of 1981, Pub.L. 97–66. It currently permits only one type of GPM which is the equivalent of the FHA § 245(a) Plan 3—i.e., payments increase at 7.5% per year for five years. The regulations require that the loan balance never exceed 100% of the original appraised value of the property; this means that the original loan amount will depend on the interest rate, since at higher rates the amount by which the balance increases in the early years is greater. The statute permits VA to recognize an appreciation in value of 2.5% per year, up to 115% of original value, but VA has not implemented this concept. VA GPM's may be used only for single-family housing, and cannot be used to

Sec. G ALTERNATIVE MORTGAGE INSTRUMENTS 193

refinance existing mortgages. See generally DVB Circular 26-31-36, published in 46 Fed.Reg. 60124 (December 8, 1981).

The FHLBB authorizes GPM's under 12 C.F.R. § 545.33, as amended, 47 Fed.Reg. 36618 et seq. (August 12, 1982). This amendment imposes no major limitations on GPM's. It permits payment adjustments "made pursuant to a formula, or to a schedule specifying the percentage or dollar change in the payment and set forth in the contract." 12 C.F.R. § 545.33(e)(2). It also permits a loan contract to "provide for the deferral and capitalization of a portion of interest." 12 C.F.R. § 545.33(c). The outstanding balance may not exceed 125% of the original appraised value of the property, unless the contract also provides for payment adjustments at least every 5 years, beginning no later than the 10th year of the loan, in an amount sufficient to amortize the remaining balance over the remaining term by constant payments. 12 C.F.R. § 545.33(d). Virtually all GPM plans in common use easily meet this requirement.

Page 748, add to Note 4:

The FHLBB specifically authorizes the classic version of the RAM; it allows associations to defer "all interest on loans to natural persons secured by borrower-occupied property and on which periodic advances are being made." 24 CFR § 545.33(c).

Page 748, insert after Note 4:

Several additional forms of mortgages have come into fairly common use recently.

1. *Mortgage Buy-Downs and Pledged Accounts.* If a mortgage lender or investor is given a substantial front-end payment, it will be willing to reduce the interest rate which it considers acceptable. This principle is familiar in VA loans, most of which have interest rates fixed by federal regulation at below-market levels. Lenders are willing to make such loans only because they receive front-end payments, termed "discount points", which are usually paid by home sellers. The mortgage buy-down is another illustration of the same principle. If a builder or seller is sufficiently eager to market a property, he may be willing to make a substantial front-end payment to the lender to induce the lender to offer the loan at a lower-than-market interest rate. In most buy-down programs offered by lenders in recent years, the interest rate reduction has been on the order of 1% to 3%, and has been scheduled to phase out (i.e., to rise to the market rate) over a period of 1 to 3 years. Thus the buy-down program requires a smaller front-end fee than would be required if the interest rate were to be reduced for the entire life of the loan.

A pledged account is similar to a buy-down, except that the funds for the front-end payment usually come from a savings account owned by the borrower/buyer rather than cash paid by the seller of the property. The borrower may pay the amount of the account at the time of closing, or may "pledge" or assign the account to the lender under an agreement by which the lender can draw down the funds in the account over a period of time—generally the same period as the time during which the interest rate reduction is in effect.

A buy-down or pledged account program may well require no specific legislation or regulatory authorization. The Federal National Mortgage Association (FNMA) and the Federal Home Loan Mortgage Corporation (FHLMC) have recently purchased numerous buy-down loans; the interest rate on these loans may be either fixed or adjustable under one of the "ARM" plans discussed below. FHA has specifically approved buy-downs, including those on fixed-payment loans and on loans under GPM Plan 4, discussed above. Under FHA's program, the interest cannot be reduced more than 3% (e.g., from 12.5% to 9.5%), and interest increases must occur on the anniversary date of the loan's origination.

See generally Wang & Peterson, Toward Affordability: Buydown and Pledged Account Loans, 42 Mortgage Banker 9 (August 1982).

2. *The Growing-Equity Mortgage (GEM).* If a mortgage loan is made for a shorter term than the traditional 30-year maturity, the monthly payments are significantly increased. However, the average life of that loan will also be shorter than that of a 30-year loan. The average life takes into account not only the normal monthly payments, but also prepayments due to home sales, foreclosures, and other causes. The average life of a 30-year loan is probably on the order of 9 years, while that of a 15-year loan is perhaps closer to 6 years.

If a loan is originated at a discount (i.e., a front-end payment of the type described in (1.) above), the impact of that discount in reducing the required interest rate depends on the expected life of the loan; the shorter the life, the greater the impact of the discount. Hence, a lender might be willing to make a 15-year loan (with a significant discount) at a considerably lower interest rate than a 30-year loan with the same discount. There has been a noticeable trend for lenders and borrowers to see this approach as mutually advantageous.

The concept can be carried one step father; the original payments can be based on a 30-year term, but the loan documents can provide for annual increases in monthly payments. Typical agreements call for increases of, say, 4% to 7% each year. The interest rate is fixed for the loan's life, and these additional monthly payments are credited entirely to principal. Hence the loan may be paid off in, say 12 years even without considering prepayments or foreclosures. In effect, it is a 30-year loan with built-in gradual prepayments. Again, the interest rate can be significantly lower—typically on the order of 1.5% to 2% below the market rate for standard 30-year loans. The rate reduction is in part a result of the impact of discounting, discussed above, and in part a result of the normal term structure of interest rates, under which the market demands higher rates for longer maturities.

The GEM represents an attempt to increase affordability and also to mitigate the negative market impact of high interest rates, both by reducing interest levels and by reducing the period that a borrower is exposed to high interest.

FNMA and FHMLC have purchased large numbers of stepped-payment GEM's. FHA authorizes stepped-payment GEM's with annual payment increases up to 5%; see 24 CFR § 203.47.

3. *The Shared-Equity Mortgage (SEM)*. In a SEM, there are two owners of the property. One is the occupant and the other is commonly (but not necessarily) a wealthy relative who is willing to assist the occupant with the purchase. This co-mortgagor is entitled by agreement with the occupant to share in the appreciation which is realized when the property is later sold. In return, the co-mortgagor agrees to make some specific fraction of the monthly mortgage payments.

SEM's can take a wide variety of forms. They have been made more popular by the willingness of FHA, since April 1982, to grant loans up to 97% of the first $25,000 of value and 95% of the excess value, where co-mortgagors are involved. Previously, FHA treated such cases as non-owner-occupant loans, which have a maximum loan-to-value ratio of 85%. FHA imposes the following requirements for eligibility at the higher ratio:

(a) The co-mortgagor's proportion of monthly payments and of equity ownership must be the same. (The down payment can be allocated differently, however.)

(b) The occupant must pay at least 55% of the monthly payment.

(c) The occupant must have the right to buy out the co-mortgagor on 30 days' notice, with the price to be determined by an FHA-approved appraiser.

(d) Either party may sell his interest after giving the other a 30-day option to purchase it.

(e) The co-mortgagor may not force the sale or refinancing of the property except in the event of default by the occupant.

Preemption of State Law Limitations on Alternative Mortgage Instruments

The federal agencies which regulate financial institutions have authorized, in recent years, the use of numerous new types of mortgage instruments which involve such features as adjustable interest rates, graduated payments, and the like. However, this authority has extended only to federally-chartered institutions, since state-chartered banks, savings and loan associations, and credit unions, even if they have federal deposit insurance, derive their lending authority from state law and regulations. State regulators commonly attempted to issue regulations similar to those of the federal agencies in order to give their institutions parity in lending authority, but frequently their efforts were comparatively slow, were inhibited by state statutes, and contained limitations not found in the analogous federal regulations. The result was a lack of parity between federally-chartered and state-chartered lenders.

Congress addressed this problem in Title VIII of the Depository Institutions Amendments of 1982, known as the "Alternative Mortgage Transaction Parity Act of 1982". It authorized all types of state-chartered financial institutions to make mortgage loans of the kinds approved by federal agencies for the same types of federally-chartered agencies. Thus, state law limitations on alternative mortgage loans became irrelevant except to the extent that they were broader than the analogous federal regulations.

The main features of the federal Act are as follows:

Property types covered. To be covered by the Act, the loan must be secured by residential real estate, co-op stock, or a manufactured home. Thus, loans on commercial or other nonresidential property are not included.

Mortgage types covered. The Act covers all forms of adjustable-interest loans, whether the adjustment is explicit or is in the form of a renegotiation or roll-over provision. It covers loans with variations in term, repayment, or other features, and hence probably applies to GPM's. Shared equity and shared appreciation mortgages are explicitly covered. To be covered the loan must be funded or extended after October 15, 1982. Also covered are extensions, renewals, refinancings, and modifications after October 15, 1982, of loans originally made prior to that date if the borrower consents in writing.

Lenders covered. All depository institutions, HUD-approved lenders, and persons regularly in the business of extending credit on the security of property of the types mentioned in (a), above, are covered. Note that this includes mortgage bankers and similar businesses which are typically unregulated by either state or federal law. Transferees on the secondary mortgage market from these lenders are also covered.

Federal regulations applicable. State-chartered banks must conform to the regulations of the OCC; state credit unions must conform to the regulations of the NCUA. All other lenders (including both savings associations and unregulated lenders such as mortgage bankers) must conform to the FHLBB's regulations.

Reimposition of state law. A state may reimpose state law by either a legislative act or a referendum vote indicating that it does not want the federal Act to apply. Such action must occur prior to October 15, 1985. If state law is reimposed, in this way, any loan made or agreed to be made after October 15, 1982 and prior to the state's action is still covered by the federal Act. So is any extension, renewal, refinancing, or modification of a pre-October 15, 1982 loan which occurs prior to the state's reimposition of state law.

Federal agency regulations. The OCC, NCUA, and FHLBB are required to identify and publish the portions of their alternative mortgage regulations which are either inappropriate for or need amendments to work properly with non-federally-chartered lenders. See e.g., 47 Fed.Reg. 55911 (Dec. 14, 1982) (OCC); 47 Fed.Reg. 54424 (Dec. 3, 1982) (NCUA).

Manufactured homes. The FHLBB was required by a federal statute in 1980 (§ 501(c)(1) of the Depository Institutions Deregulation and Monetary Control Act of 1980) to issue regulations for consumer protection purposes dealing with balloon payments, prepayments, etc., on manufactured homes. The regulations are found in 12 C.F.R. § 590.4. The Act provides that this requirement no longer applies to transactions "which are subject to this title" * * * which presumably means all alternative mortgage loans, whether made by federal or state lenders. The reference is ambiguous.

Part III

REAL ESTATE DEVELOPMENT

Chapter 10

PLANNED UNIT DEVELOPMENTS, CONDOMINIUMS, AND COOPERATIVES

B. CONDOMINIUMS

Page 914, insert following Note 4:

The original FHA Model Act was quite inflexible in its treatment of assessments for common area expenses. These assessments were required to be allocated on the same basis as the common area ownership (see Section 10), which in turn was required to be based on the relative value of the units. In a PUD, by contrast, there is no controlling statute and allocation of expenses can be made on any reasonable basis. The following case suggests that a condominium project can have some of the flexibility of a PUD by providing for two different associations having similar but distinct functions, with only one of them subject to the condominium statute.

HOBSON v. HILLTOP PLACE COMMUNITY ASSOCIATION

Supreme Court of New Hampshire, 1982.
122 N.H. 1023, 453 A.2d 841.

BOIS, Justice.

This is an interlocutory transfer without ruling from the Superior Court (Johnson, J.). The plaintiffs, owners of condominium units in the Hilltop Place Condominiums project, challenge the manner in which the defendant homeowners' association has assessed them for certain expenses relating to the maintenance of the "common areas" of the condominiums. We hold that the defendant's method of assessment is lawful.

The instant dispute arises from a rather complex factual context. Hilltop Place is a one-hundred-forty-seven-unit residential condominiums complex, consisting of six individual condominium structures, known as "clusters," each of which is situated on its own separate parcel of land. Each condominium cluster was created in accordance with RSA chapter 479–A, the "Unit Ownership of Real Property" statute, and each cluster has its own declaration, by-laws, and cluster owners' association. Each cluster is thus responsible for managing its own affairs and for maintaining all common areas within its confines. The common expenses of each cluster are apportioned according to the percentage interests of each owner.

The defendant Hilltop Place Community Association (HPCA) is distinct from the individual cluster owners' associations. The defendant is a non-profit corporation which was established under RSA chapter 292 to promote the recreational and cultural interests and the health, safety and social welfare of all one hundred forty-seven unit owners. As such, it owns and manages "community property" consisting of roads which connect the clusters, a recreational building, and lands interspersed between the clusters. All unit owners are required to become members of HPCA, which is operated, pursuant to a declaration, by a board of directors elected by the members. The HPCA declaration states that HPCA expenses are to be assessed equally against each owner.

Because of its corporate status, HPCA, unlike the cluster owners' associations, is not subject to the condominium ownership statute, RSA chapter 479–A. In short, HPCA is a corporate entity which owns and manages the "community property," obtaining funding through equal assessments against its members. On the other hand, the cluster associations are condominium entities which manage their respective "common areas," obtaining the requisite funds through proportional assessments levied on the unit owners.

In order to establish reasonable uniformity in the maintenance and management of the Hilltop Place Project, each cluster has delegated its "common area" managerial functions to HPCA. As a result, HPCA now has two functions: to manage its own "community property" and to administer the "common area" of each cluster.

By vote of its directors, HPCA has established a standard formula for allocating HPCA managerial expenses. Approximately fifteen to twenty percent of the expenditures go to management of "community property." These expenses are assessed equally upon each of the one hundred forty-seven units, as required under HPCA's declaration. The remaining eighty to eighty-five percent of HPCA's managerial expenditures are allocated towards the management of the cluster "common areas." Each cluster must pay its share of this amount on a monthly basis. To obtain these funds, each cluster, in accordance with RSA 479–A:9, requires its unit owners to contribute sums which are proportionate to their ownership interests.

The particular HPCA practices which have given rise to this controversy are as follows. At various times, HPCA's assessments have yielded insufficient funds to meet its managerial expenses. In such situations, HPCA has paid for these expenses from surplus working capital which it raises through equal assessments against its members. Thus, some of HPCA's surplus working capital has been used on occasion to maintain the clusters' "common areas." The cluster owners' associations have reimbursed HPCA for these advances when making their monthly installment payments.

In addition to assessing its members for surplus working capital, HPCA has required its members to contribute, equally towards the purchase of various maintenance equipment. While HPCA originally employed an outside contractor to carry out its grounds maintenance duties, it decided to terminate this practice in September 1977 and to perform the work itself thereafter. HPCA subsequently purchased grounds maintenance equipment costing approximately $32,000, paid for in equal amounts by its members.

The plaintiffs, who are all owners of units in cluster three, claim that the manner in which HPCA assessed the equipment and working surplus capital expenses violated RSA chapter 479-A and the general scheme of organization of Hilltop Place.

Because the plaintiffs base their argument largely upon RSA chapter 479-A, a brief discussion of the relevant provisions will be helpful. RSA 479-A:5 states that the percentage of an individual's ownership interest in a condominium is computed by comparing the value of his unit with the value of the condominium as a whole. Under the statute, each unit owner shall be entitled to an undivided interest in the "common areas" of the condominium according to his ownership percentage. Id. RSA 479-A:1 VI defines "common areas" to include "all other parts of the property" which, pursuant to RSA 479-A:1 XIII, encompasses "articles of personal property intended for use in connection with * * * [the total condominium property]."

We have already noted that RSA 479-A:9 requires that "common expenses" shall be allocated according to each owner's undivided interest percentage. RSA 479-A:1 VII defines "common expenses" to include "all sums lawfully assessed against the unit owners by the association of unit owners" and "all expenses of administration, maintenance, repair or replacement of the common areas * * *."

With these statutory provisions in mind, we first address the plaintiffs' argument that the assessments relating to the purchase of the grounds maintenance equipment were unlawful. The plaintiffs claim, pursuant to RSA 479-A:5, that the equipment should be owned *proportionally* rather than *equally* by all the unit owners because it is part of the "common areas" as defined by RSA 479-A:1 VI, XIII. Likewise, the plaintiffs claim that the purchase of the equipment was a "common expense" under RSA 479-A:9. The plaintiffs therefore argue that HPCA should not have assessed the equipment expenses on an equal basis, but rather should have charged the unit owners in proportion to their percentages of undivided interests in the respective clusters.

It is clear that any personal property owned or leased by each individual condominium cluster for the purposes of property maintenance would have been subject to the various provisions of RSA chapter 479–A. Proportional payment for and ownership of such "common area" property would therefore have been mandatory under the statute. But the plaintiffs fail to observe the fundamental difference between such a scenario and their own. HPCA was set up and is operated as a non-profit corporation. As a corporate entity, it is subject to the provisions of RSA chapter 292, not RSA chapter 479–A.

The fact that all condominium owners in the six separate condominium clusters must become members in HPCA does not mean that HPCA is a condominium project subject to the provisions of RSA 479–A, rather than a separate corporation. Certainly, the unit owners in each cluster might have decided to maintain each cluster's grounds individually. Had they purchased maintenance equipment to that end, it would have been subject to the proportional ownership strictures of RSA chapter 479–A.

In this case, however, cluster three, in its declaration and by-laws, legally delegated its managerial and maintenance duties to HPCA. The delegation of these duties was reaffirmed in subsequent amendments signed by owners holding seventy-five percent of the voting power of the cluster. HPCA's role in maintaining the "common area" was thereby akin to that of an independent contractor, and the unit owners had no rights in the HPCA equipment by virtue of their ownership interests in the clusters. Their relationship to HPCA and their rights in its property were governed by their membership in HPCA individually. Correspondingly, while the routine maintenance fees charged to a cluster by HPCA are "common expenses" which must be allocated proportionally against the unit owners, see Pepe v. Whispering Sands Condominium Ass'n, 351 So.2d 755, 757 (Fla.App.1977), we hold that the purchase of equipment *by HPCA* was *an expense of HPCA* and not a *"common expense" of the clusters*. Because we find that the purchase of the equipment was not a "common expense," we conclude that HPCA was not required to allocate the cost of the equipment on a proportionate basis.

The plaintiffs also assert that HPCA had no authority to purchase the maintenance equipment solely for the account of HPCA and that this action constituted a breach of its fiduciary duty to the unit owners. We disagree. The declaration and articles of association of HPCA provide the corporation with a broad range of authority. The declaration specifically empowers HPCA to "purchase * * * any property or other facilities in the course of its administration * * * of the Community Property" and "to perform services * * * for one or more of the Hilltop Cluster Associations * * *." The articles of association state that HPCA has the authority "[t]o do any other thing * * * to promote the common benefits and enjoyments of the members."

We hold that the purchase of maintenance equipment by HPCA promoted the general welfare of its members and was consistent with its established powers. Cf. Peoples Laundry Co. v. Dubeau, 80 N.H. 544, 546, 119 A. 706, 707 (1923). See generally Herbert v. Sullivan, 37 F.Supp. 468, 469 (D.N.H.), aff'd, 123 F.2d 477, 478 (1st Cir. 1941), cert. denied, 315 U.S. 803, 62 S.Ct. 632, 86 L.Ed. 1203 (1942).

In addition to challenging the purchase of the grounds maintenance equipment, the plaintiffs contest HPCA's method of raising surplus working capital. The plaintiffs argue that HPCA's use of surplus working capital, raised through equal assessments against its members, for maintenance of the cluster "common areas" was improper because the cluster declarations require "common area" maintenance expenses to be assessed in accordance with the unit owners' percentages of undivided interest.

This argument overlooks the fact that the cluster associations reimbursed HPCA for all funds which it expended for "common area" maintenance and that the money for these reimbursements was assessed against the unit owners on a proportional basis. Thus, while the unit owners contributed equally to working surplus capital, they ultimately paid for "common area" maintenance expenses on a proportional basis. The use of the working surplus capital fund was merely a way of meeting HPCA's fluctuating cash flow needs while simplifying its bookkeeping and budgetary administration. The use of working surplus capital promoted the general welfare of the unit owners and therefore properly fell within HPCA's recognized powers. But cf. Hidden Harbour Estates v. Basso, 393 So.2d 637, 640 (Fla.App.1981).

Having rejected the plaintiffs' arguments, we further hold the appeal not to be frivolous and remand for entry of decree.

Remanded.

Page 946, read in connection with Note 5:

DUTCHER v. OWENS

Supreme Court of Texas, 1983.
647 S.W.2d 948.

RAY, Justice.

This is a case of first impression concerning the allocation of liability among condominium co-owners for tort claims arising out of the ownership, use and maintenance of "common elements." The defendant was found to be vicariously liable for the homeowners' association's negligence. The trial court ordered that the plaintiffs recover from the defendant an amount based upon the defendant's proportionate ownership in the condominium project. The court of appeals reversed in part the judgment of the trial court, holding "that each unit owner, as a tenant in common with all other unit owners in the common elements, is jointly and severally liable for damage claims arising in the common elements." 635 S.W.2d 208, 211. We reverse the judgment of the court of appeals and affirm the trial court's judgment.

J.A. Dutcher, a resident of San Diego, California, owned a condominium apartment in the Eastridge Terrace Condominiums, located in Dallas County, which he leased to Ted and Christine Owens. Ownership of the apartment includes a 1.572% *pro rata* undivided ownership in the common elements of the project. The Owenses suffered substantial property loss in a fire which began in an external light fixture in a common area.

The Owenses filed suit in Tarrant County against Dutcher, the Eastridge Terrace Condominium Association, Joe Hill Electric Company, IHS-8 Ltd. (the developer) and a class of co-owners of condominiums in Eastridge Terrace represented by the officers of the homeowners' association. All defendants with the exception of Dutcher obtained a change of venue to Dallas County. The case was tried before a jury, which found the following:

(1) The fire was proximately caused by the lack of an insulating box behind the light fixture in the exterior wall air space;

(2) The homeowners' association knew of this defect;

(3) The homeowners' association alone was negligent in failing to install an insulating box with knowledge of the defect; and

(4) The negligence of homeowners' association resulted in damage to the Owens' property in the amount of $69,150.00.

The trial court rendered judgment against Dutcher on the jury's verdict in the amount of $1,087.04. The award represents the amount of damages multiplied by Dutcher's 1.572% *pro rata* undivided ownership of the common elements of the Eastridge Terrace Condominium project.

By an agreed statement of facts filed with the court of appeals, the parties stipulated that the sole issue for determination on appeal was whether a condominium co-owner is jointly and severally liable or is liable only for a *pro rata* portion of the damages. Tex.R.Civ.P. 377(d).

In enacting the Texas Condominium Act (the Act), Tex.Rev.Civ.Stat. Ann. art. 1301a, the Texas Legislature intended to create "a new method of property ownership." 1963 Tex.Gen.Laws, Ch. 191, § 26 at 512. A condominium is an estate in real property consisting of an undivided interest in a portion of a parcel of real property together with a separate fee simple interest in another portion of the same parcel. In essence, condominium ownership is the merger of two estates in land into one: the fee simple ownership of an apartment or unit in a condominium project and a tenancy in common with other co-owners in the common elements. Scott v. Williams, 607 S.W.2d 267, 270 (Tex.Civ.App.—Texarkana 1980, writ ref'd n.r.e.); Tex.Rev.Civ.Stat. Ann. art. 1301a; see also White v. Cox, 17 Cal.App.3d 824, 95 Cal.Rptr.

259, 45 A.L.R.3d 1161 (1971); Comment, "The Condominium and the Corporation—A Proposal for Texas," 11 Hous.L.Rev. 454 (1974).

"General common elements" consist of, *inter alia,* the land upon which the building stands, the "foundations, bearing walls and columns, roofs, halls, lobbies, stairways, and entrances and exits or communication ways; * * * [a]ll other elements of the building desirable or rationally of common use or necessary to the existence, upkeep and safety of the condominium regime, and any other elements described in the declaration * * *." Tex.Rev.Civ.Stat.Ann. art. 1301a, § 2(*l*), subsections (1), (2) & (7). An individual apartment cannot be conveyed separately from the undivided interest in the common elements and *vice versa.* Id. § 9.

A condominium regime must be established according to the Act. The declaration must be filed with the county clerk, who must record the instrument in the Condominium Records. Once the declarant has complied with the provisions of the Act, each apartment in the project is treated as an interest in real property. Id. §§ 3, 4, & 7. Administration of the regime is established by the Act. Id. §§ 13, 14 & 15.

The condominium association or council is a legislatively created unincorporated association of co-owners having as their common purpose a convenient method of ownership of real property in a statutorily created method of ownership which combines both the concepts of separateness of tenure and commonality of ownership. The California Supreme Court has concluded that "the concept of separateness in the condominium project carries over to any management body or association formed to handle the common affairs of the project, and that both the condominium project and the condominium association must be considered separate legal entities from its unit owners and association members." White v. Cox, 95 Cal.Rptr. at 262.

Given the uniqueness of the type of ownership involved in condominiums, the onus of liability for injuries arising from the management of condominium projects should reflect the degree of control exercised by the defendants. We agree with the California court's conclusion that to rule that a condominium co-owner had any effective control over the operation of the common areas would be to sacrifice "reality to theoretical formalism," for in fact a co-owner has no more control over operations than he would have as a stockholder in a corporation which owned and operated the project. White v. Cox, 95 Cal.Rptr. at 263. This does not limit the plaintiff's right of action. The efficiency found in a suit directed at the homeowners' association and its board of directors representing the various individual homeowners, as well as any co-owner causally or directly responsible for the injuries sustained, benefits both sides of the docket as well as the judicial system as a whole.

Such a result is not inconsistent with the legislative intent. While the Act creates a new form of real property ownership, it does not address the issue of the allocation of tort liability among co-owners.

Nevertheless, we are guided in our decision by the other provisions in the Act which appear *in pari materia,* and which proportionately allocate various financial responsibilities. For example, the Act provides for *pro rata* contributions by co-owners toward expenses of administration and maintenance, insurance, taxes and assessments. *Pro rata* provisions also exist for the application of insurance proceeds. Tex. Rev.Civ.Stat.Ann. art 1301a, §§ 15, 18, 19, & 20.

Respondents have cited us to two bills submitted in the legislature in 1981. The bills, which did not pass, included provisions for re-apportionment of liability on a *pro rata* basis. Inasmuch as each bill involved a complete revision of the Act, we cannot draw inferences of the legislature's intent from the failure of the bills to pass. Any such inference would involve little more than conjecture. The legislative history of the Act is so scant that the most that can be said is that the Act is silent as to the matter, and hence the legislative intent is unknown. Cf. Marmon v. Mustang Aviation, Inc., 430 S.W.2d 182, 186 (Tex.1968).

The theories of vicarious and joint and several liability are judicially created vehicles for enforcing remedies for wrongs committed. Justified on public policy grounds, they represent a deliberate allocation of risk. See Newspapers, Inc. v. Love, 380 S.W.2d 582, 588–89 (Tex.1964); Landers v. East Texas Salt Water Disposal Co., 151 Tex. 251, 248 S.W.2d 731, 733 (1952); W. Prosser, Law of Torts, § 69 at 459 (4th ed. 1971).

Texas follows the rule that statutes in derogation of the common law are not to be strictly construed. Tex.Rev.Civ.Stat.Ann. art. 10, § 8. Nevertheless, it is recognized that if a statute creates a liability unknown to the common law, or deprives a person of a common law right, the statute will be strictly construed in the sense that it will not be extended beyond its plain meaning or applied to cases not clearly within its purview. Satterfield v. Satterfield, 448 S.W.2d 456, 459 (Tex.1969); see also 3 C. Sands, Sutherland Statutory Construction § 61.02 (4th ed. 1973). Since the Act is silent as to tort liability, we are dealing with rights and liabilities which are not creatures of statute but with the common law, which is our special domain, Hence, the rule we have reached is not a usurpation of the legislative prerogative. To the contrary, it is one reached in the public interest.

We hold, therefore, that because of the limited control afforded a unit owner by the statutory condominium regime, the creation of the regime effects a reallocation of tort liability. The liability of a condominium co-owner is limited to his *pro rata* interest in the regime as a whole, where such liability arises from those areas held in tenancy-in-common. The judgment of the court of appeals is reversed and the judgment of the trial court is affirmed.

F. MANAGING THE PROJECT

Page 951, insert after Note 4.

IN RE BENTLEY

United States Bankruptcy Court, Southern District of New York, 1982.
26 B.R. 69.

PRUDENCE B. ABRAM, Bankruptcy Judge:

Anthony M. Bentley ("Bentley"), the debtor herein, filed this Chapter 11 case on March 20, 1981. He owns and now occupies, and has owned since about 1975, a cooperative apartment, apartment 4M (the "Apartment"), at 75 East End Avenue, New York, New York. Bentley, a lawyer, served for a number of years as a member of the directors of the cooperative corporation. On June 29, 1981, Bentley was authorized to assume, without opposition, the unexpired proprietary lease for the Apartment as an executory contract. At the time of the assumption, Bentley was $9,163.50 in arrears in maintenance payments for the Apartment. Bentley entered into a stipulation of settlement with 75 East End Owners, Inc. (the "Lessor"), under the proprietary lease for the Apartment, which settlement was so ordered by the Court on the same day assumption was permitted. The stipulation provided that all maintenance charges were to be paid on a current basis; that the Lessor consented to the assumption; and that Bentley would reduce the arrears at the rate of $1,000 per month commencing July 15, 1981, but all arrears were to be paid before confirmation of any plan of reorganization. The arrearages have not been reduced at the agreed rate and a portion of the arrears are still outstanding.

Although a dispute exists as to Bentley's marketing efforts, there is no suggestion that the Apartment does not have a value substantially in excess of any amounts due the Lessor. In August, 1982, Bentley proposed to sell the Apartment to Dr. Russell M. Samson for $210,000 and obtain a two-year sublease for the Apartment, and thus continue in occupancy of the Apartment for the term of the sublease. The Lessor objected to the sale and sublease and refused through its Board of Directors to approve either the prospective purchaser or the sublease to Bentley. Bentley's major, if not sole, asset is his equity in the Apartment. Had the sale been approved and had a closing occurred, Bentley would apparently have been in a position to confirm the plan of reorganization he filed on April 19, 1982. At the hearing to consider the sale held on September 21, 1982, the Honorable Joel Lewittes refused to direct the Lessor or its Board to approve the proposed transaction.

Approximately 30% of the shares of Lessor continue to be owned by the sponsors of the cooperative conversion and the apartments represented by those shares are rented, subject only to approval of the tenant by the managing agent for the building.

On October 12, 1982, Bentley commenced this adversary proceeding against the Lessor and Church Management, the managing agent. The complaint alleges that the proprietary lease "is unconscionable as drawn to the extent it allows such a mechanism to prevent the sale of debtor's assets" (Complaint, ¶ 8) and seeks relief under subsection 235–c of the New York Real Property Law (McKinney Supp.1982).

On October 18, 1982, prior to answering, defendants, as permitted by Bankruptcy Rule 712, filed a motion to dismiss the complaint on the grounds that it failed as a matter of law to state a claim upon which relief may be granted. * * *

Defendants further argue that as a matter of law Bentley has no cause of action under Section 235–c of the New York Real Property Law. Various grounds are cited for the assertion including Bentley's position as a lawyer, his participation on the Board of Directors of the cooperative, his alleged acquiescence in and his detailed knowledge of the terms of the proprietary lease, and his present defaults under the proprietary lease. Section 235–c provides as follows:

"1. If the court as a matter of law finds a lease or any clause of the lease to have been unconscionable at the time it was made the court may refuse to enforce the lease, or it may enforce the remainder of the lease without the unconscionable clause, or it may so limit the application of any unconscionable clause as to avoid any unconscionable result.

"2. When it is claimed or appears to the court that a lease or any clause thereof may be unconscionable the parties shall be afforded a reasonable opportunity to present evidence as to its setting, purpose and effect to aid the court in making the determination."

The key provision in the proprietary lease relevant to this dispute is paragraph 16(c) which provides as follows:

"(c) There shall be no limitation, except as above specifically provided, on the right of Directors or lessees to grant or withhold consent, for any reason or for no reason, to an assignment."

This Court finds the provisions of paragraph 16(c) quoted above to be unconscionable as a matter of law at the time the lease was made to the extent that those provisions are applied to prevent Bentley from selling the Apartment because the result would be a forfeiture of the Apartment to the Lessor cooperative corporation. See Wilson Trading Corp. v. Ferguson Ltd., 23 N.Y.2d 398, 403–04, 297 N.Y.S.2d 108, 112, 244 N.E.2d 685, 689 (1968); Euclid Ave. Assoc. v. City of New York, 64 A.D.2d 550, 406 N.Y.S.2d 844 (1978). See also Sidnam v. Washington Sq. Realty Corp., 95 Misc.2d 825, 827, 408 N.Y.S.2d 988 (1978) (court may apply § 235–c of the Real Property Law to avoid an unconscionable result). This Court is of the view that even without the authority granted to it by Section 235–c, it would find, as a matter of contract construction, an implied covenant in the proprietary lease that the consent provision would not be utilized so as to cause a forfeiture of an apartment to the cooperative corporation and consequent benefit to other shareholders to the detriment of the apartment owner. See Halprin v. 2 Fifth Avenue Company, 75 App.Div.2d 565 at 566–67, 427 N.Y.S.2d 258 (1st Dept.1980) (dissenting opinion). Bankruptcy courts are courts of equity. Local Loan Co. v. Hunt, 292 U.S. 234, 240, 54 S.Ct. 695, 697, 78 L.Ed. 1230, 1232 (1954); 28 U.S.C. § 1481. Equity abhors a forfeiture. *In re Belize Airways Limited,* 2 CBC 2d 657, 660–661 (Bkrtcy.S.D.Fla.1980); Ringelheim v. Karsch, 112 N.Y.S.2d 130, 133 (Sup.1952). The Bankruptcy Code has, like its predecessor, many provisions indicative of a legislative mandate to prevent forfeitures of a debtor's property. See, e.g., Code § 365(e)(1).

That the provisions of the proprietary lease cannot effectuate a forfeiture is also mandated by the law of New York in the provisions of Section 270 et seq. of the New York Debtor and Creditor Law (McKinney Supp.1982) governing fraudulent conveyances. Section 544(b) of the Bankruptcy Code incorporates state law on this subject. In addition, Section 548 of the Bankruptcy Code establishes an independent basis to avoid fraudulent conveyances. A fraudulent transfer occurs when an insolvent debtor, such as Bentley, transfers or conveys property for less than fair consideration, i.e. a reasonably equivalent value. Transfer and conveyance as used in fraudulent conveyance statutes encompass every mode of disposing of or parting with property. Bentley could not voluntarily relinquish the Apartment to the Lessor in satisfaction of the arrearages unless the arrearages equaled the value of the Apartment because it would be a fraudulent transfer as to his creditors who would have been deprived without compensation of the debtor's property. It follows that the Lessor cannot do involuntarily what the debtor could not do voluntarily. See Durrett v. Washington National Ins. Co., 621 F.2d 201 (5th Cir. 1980). Cf. *In re Belize Airways Limited,* 2 CBC 2d 657 (Bkrtcy.S.D.Fla.1980) (the bankruptcy court, as a court of equity, may refuse to enforce the termination of a sublease, where, under the circumstances, termination would constitute a forfeiture).

The dispute is not one simply between Bentley and the Lessor. It is between Bentley and Bentley as trustee for his creditors in his capacity as debtor-in-possession, on the one hand, and the Lessor, on the other. It matters not that no creditors have intervened in this dispute as their interests are here through the debtor-in-possession. The Lessor has various choices on how to solve its problem with Bentley. The simplest solution would be to permit the proposed transaction to go through. Alternatively, the Lessor could find a purchaser acceptable to it for the Apartment so that Bentley and his creditors received fair consideration for Bentley's Apartment.

Perhaps at trial the Court will find that the rejection of the proposed transaction with Dr. Samson was not tantamount to forfeiture of the Apartment. But unless the Apartment is worth less than any amounts owed to the Lessor, this Court will be constrained to permit Bentley adequate time to secure a sale at a fair price to another purchaser.

Section 235–c(2) of the New York Real Property Law directs the taking of evidence when the Court finds that it should limit the application of any unconscionable clause so as to avoid an unconscionable result. This Court is of the view that oral testimony will be necessary in this case and the Court thus fixes January 20, 1983 at 10:00 a.m. as a date for trial on this complaint.

The motion to dismiss is denied.

†